The Proletarian Answer to the Modernist Question

For my children – Sara, Max and Alex – and everybody else's children, who all have to live in the World that we made in the West in the twentieth century

The Proletarian Answer to the Modernist Question

Nick Hubble

EDINBURGH
University Press

Edinburgh University Press is one of the leading university presses in the UK. We publish academic books and journals in our selected subject areas across the humanities and social sciences, combining cutting-edge scholarship with high editorial and production values to produce academic works of lasting importance. For more information visit our website: edinburghuniversitypress.com

© Nick Hubble, 2017

Edinburgh University Press Ltd
The Tun – Holyrood Road,
12(2f) Jackson's Entry,
Edinburgh EH8 8PJ

Typeset in 11/14 Adobe Sabon by
IDSUK (DataConnection) Ltd

A CIP record for this book is available from the British Library

ISBN 978 1 4744 1582 8 (hardback)
ISBN 978 1 4744 1583 5 (webready PDF)
ISBN 978 1 4744 1584 2 (epub)

The right of Nick Hubble to be identified as the author of this work has been asserted in accordance with the Copyright, Designs and Patents Act 1988, and the Copyright and Related Rights Regulations 2003 (SI No. 2498).

Contents

Acknowledgements	vi
Introduction	1
1 'Her Heritage Was that Tragic Optimism': Edwardian Pastoral	56
2 'The Common Life': Women and Men after the General Strike	87
3 'She Had Finished with Men Forever': Lewis Grassic Gibbon's *Grey Granite*	112
4 'The Raw Material of History': John Sommerfield's *May Day*	141
5 'None of That "My Good Woman" Stuff': Outsider Observations	165
Conclusion	197
Bibliography	202
Index	213

Acknowledgements

I would like to thank Jackie Jones, Adela Rauchova and Rebecca Mackenzie at Edinburgh University Press for their support and also the anonymous readers for EUP who provided me with cogent and helpful advice. I would also like to thank Eliza Wright for copyediting the manuscript.

Thanks are also due to staff at the National Library of Wales for their assistance over the last seven years.

I have benefited from the experience of teaching a number of these texts over the years at various institutions including the University of Sussex, the University of Central England, Kingston University and Brunel University London. I would like to thank the many students who have inspired me with the enthusiasm of their responses.

I am also grateful to my academic colleagues at Brunel and the other universities listed above, and to those in academic societies including the Space Between Society, the MSA, the Ford Madox Ford Society and the Literary London Society. Special thanks to Kristin Bluemel, Benjamin Kohlmann, Laura Marcus, Max Saunders, Matthew Taunton and Philip Tew. And extra special thanks to Debra Rae Cohen for telling me to stick with the title at the business lunch of the Las Vegas MSA.

Earlier versions of some of the material in Chapter 1 have appeared in *International Ford Madox Ford Studies* and *The Literary London Journal* and I thank the General Editor of the former and the Editor of the latter for their permission to reuse this material.

Last, but not least, my undying gratitude goes to Andrea Hammel for friendship, love and support – practical and intellectual – over the years.

Introduction

Proletarian literature

In *Crisis and Criticism*, first published in 1937, Alick West identified the question facing modernist writers in the interwar period: 'When I do not know any longer who are the "we" to whom I belong, I do not know any longer who "I" am either' (West 1975: 19). This book will argue that much British proletarian literature of the 1930s may be seen as a response to this 'modernist question' of the relationship between the 'I' and the 'we' and took the form, as suggested by West, of an expansion of modernist techniques and scope rather than a rejection of them. In applying his diagnosis specifically to T. S. Eliot's *The Waste Land* (1922) at the beginning of his book, West was identifying what we might now term 'high modernism' as the symptom of the crisis rather than the solution. The implication is that work such as Eliot's reflected the collapse of relatively stable nineteenth-century conceptions of the relationship between the individual and society amongst the ongoing crisis of capitalist relations that led to the First World War and the Russian Revolution without being able to free itself of those relations. West goes on to distinguish James Joyce's *Ulysses* from this critical judgement by arguing that the significance of its stylistic innovation was that it expressed a new realisation that: 'the individual's world is not within the four walls that protect money, board and bed. His world is his society' (West 1975: 117). However, from West's communist perspective, the limitation of Joyce's social world was that it ignored production, and the conflicts surrounding it, and consisted only of 'numberless acts of consuming, spending, enjoying of things that are already there' (West 1975: 120–1). The goal of the interwar years, according to this reading, was for writers to resolve the problem of how to relate 'I' to 'we' by extending the modernist trajectory established in the succession from Eliot to Joyce to represent the widest possible range of intersubjective relationships – incorporating individual, class, gender, societal, colonial, media, and mechanised production relationships – characteristic of the modern mass society which became dominant in the West following the First World War.

The understanding of 'proletarian literature' which informs this book is derived from the public usage of the term in Britain in the second half of the 1930s – what William Empson called 'the popular, vague, but somehow obvious, idea of proletarian literature' (Empson 1995: 21) – as reflected in a variety of different sources ranging from the *London Mercury*'s discussion of 'The Coming of the Proletarian Literature' in May 1936 to George Orwell's radio talk, 'The Proletarian Writer' (1940). The immediate contexts for this understanding were the experience of mass unemployment resulting from the depression and an upsurge in the publication of novels about the working class, such as Walter Greenwood's bestselling *Love on the Dole* (1933), Walter Brierley's *Means-Test Man* (1935) and Harold Heslop's *Last Cage Down* (1935); all of which received wide coverage in the general press (see Croft 1990: 71–3). However, while proletarian literature consisted of books written *about* workers, these were not necessarily always written *by* them or even (given the price of many books) published *for* them. Empson suggested that such literature worked successfully because it functioned as a form of pastoral 'based on a double attitude of the artist to the worker, of the complex man to the simple one ("I am in one way better, in another not so good")' (Empson 1995: 19). The importance of this concept of pastoral to the evolution and form of British proletarian literature is discussed below. First, however, it is useful to examine very briefly the history of the term 'proletarian' in relation to its usage in interwar Britain.

A footnote by Engels to the 1888 English edition of *The Communist Manifesto* clarifies the relationship of the bourgeoisie and the proletariat:

> By 'bourgeoisie' is meant the class of modern capitalists, owners of the means of social production and employers of wage labour. By proletariat, the class of modern wage labourers who, having no means of production of their own, are reduced to selling their labour power in order to live. (Marx and Engels 1969: 48n.)

Proletarians are wage-labourers because they own no property from which to make a living themselves. Therefore, they are also the only true revolutionary class because their material interests lie in acting collectively to overthrow bourgeois private property, 'the final and most complete expression of the system of producing and appropriating products that is based on class antagonisms, on the exploitation of the many by the few' (Marx and Engels 1969: 62). In other words, for Marx and Engels, the proletariat are the force which will overthrow the capitalist system and institute a system of holding property in common, while organising production for the public good. Paul Mason sees this relationship differently:

> Marx and Engels [. . .] found in the working class a ready-made solution to a philosophical problem. The middle-class German left had become enthusiastic communists; they wanted a classless society, based on the absence of property, religion and total freedom from work. Suddenly in the working class, Marx discovered a force that could make it happen. (Mason 2015: 182)

However, as Mason argues, the proletariat was never the completely alienated force that Marx described it as theoretically but the bearers of skill, autonomy, status and their own culture in working-class life. The proletariat never behaved as in Marxist theory because its existence was defined not by a negative content, but by a positive one. When Eric Hobsbawm surveyed the history of the British working class in 'The Forward March of Labour Halted?' (1978), he identified 'a common style of proletarian life', which was formed in the 1880s and remained dominant until the 1950s (Hobsbawm 1978: 281). As defining features of this common proletarian life, he lists not just trade unionism and steadily rising support for the Labour Party but also co-op membership, football, fish and chips, flat caps, council flats and houses, cinemas and dancehalls. It is this understanding of a whole way of British working-class life – which Hobsbawm acknowledges as benefiting from British imperialism and the world monopoly of British industrial capitalism at the beginning of the period – that conditioned the public visibility and popular understanding of 'proletarian literature' in the second half of the 1930s.

However, the narrow sense of the term has a different history dating from the Russian Revolution in 1917:

> From 1917 to the middle 1920s, Soviet literary life was dominated by various groups – the 'Proletkult', 'Smithy', 'October', 'On Guard', 'At the Post', LEF and 'Litfront' – who variously advocated the 'Proletarianisation' of culture. The claim was based on a simple application of the Marxist idea of base and superstructure, often involving a hostility to avant-garde or 'fellow-travelling' writers, and combined a preoccupation with content over form with a demand for literature to be harnessed to the political needs of the industrial working-class. (Croft 1990: 33)

Although British left-wing intellectuals were aware of the 'Proletkult', or 'Proletcult' as it became anglicised, in the 1920s, it was generally considered that a British version of such proletarian literature was only a future possibility dependent on the development of an actual proletarian culture. Then the publication of Trotsky's *Literature and Revolution* (1925) with its assertion that 'there is no proletarian culture and [. . .] there never will be' (qtd in Croft 1990: 32–3) alerted British socialists to the paradox that before a revolution the workers would always be too oppressed to create an independent culture; while afterwards the working class, itself, would no longer exist. In common with a change in Soviet policy, this realisation was reflected in the arts pages of the *Sunday Worker* between 1925 and 1929, which included a broad coverage of Soviet and Workers' Movement culture alongside coverage of contemporary literature, theatre and cinema. This period, in turn, came to an end in 1929 with the Comintern's adoption of the sectarian 'Class against Class' position, which saw the *Sunday Worker* shut and a resumption of attempts to proletarianise culture. Finally, the 1934 Soviet Writers Congress explicitly rejected all versions of the 'Proletcult' and called instead for 'socialist realism' as a genre open to both middle- and working-class writers prepared to write Balzac-style nineteenth-century realism in support of the class struggle. This position led to what was in effect the resumption of the *Sunday Worker* policy by *Left Review*, marking the beginning of what would become the Popular Front against fascism.

However, the adjective 'proletarian' had by now stuck in the national consciousness and was associated with the representations of a long-established working-class way of life, which suddenly seemed to be everywhere in the media. Therefore, while Andy Croft is generally correct in claiming that by 1935 the term 'proletarian literature' in its narrow 'proletcult' sense was considered unhelpfully sectarian and generally no longer used by communists and their allies on the British Left, the term in its wider sense remained in public circulation and this is why Empson opened his 1935 book, *Some Versions of Pastoral*, with a chapter entitled 'Proletarian Literature'. Indeed, as Croft acknowledges, Karl Radek's denunciation of the Proletcult at the Soviet Congress did not stop him continuing to refer to proletarian literature in a looser sense:

> On the one hand he used the term 'proletarian' to apply to all Soviet literature, on the other he used it specifically to denote 'socialist realist' writers. Then again he used the term synonymously with any working-class writing *and* to hail the 'beginning of a proletarian literature in England' (by which he meant the poetry of the *New Signatures* Group, writers like Auden, Spender and Day Lewis). (Croft 1990: 44)

Not only was the adjective 'proletarian' now part of common usage, it was also so central to Marxist analysis that it could not simply be abandoned and so what Radek was doing was not so much rejecting the term 'proletarian literature' as retooling it for more heterogeneous and less sectarian purposes. In this context, Empson was trying to be helpful by offering a model for how such a heterogeneous proletarian literature would function: 'Proletarian literature usually has a suggestion of pastoral, a puzzling form which looks proletarian but isn't [...] My reason for dragging this old-fashioned form into the discussion is that I think good proletarian art is usually Covert Pastoral' (Empson 1995: 13). Empson's citations of Gorki and Radek make it clear that the 'discussion' he is referring to is the one stemming from the 1934 Soviet Congress. While Empson's intervention in the debate has been seen as a joke by some critics (Hynes 1982: 170) or a rigorous refutation of a 'bogus' category by others (Haffenden 2005: 394), it is quite obviously intended as a serious piece of analysis supporting Radek's call to make proletarian literature more heterogeneous. As Empson points out, neither the narrow sense of 'the propaganda of a factory-working class which feels its interests opposed to the factory owners' nor the wider sense of 'folk literature' is that much use to a rapidly modernising socialist state such as the Soviet Union (Empson 1995: 13). Instead, he argues that the 'pastoral process of putting the complex into the simple' (Empson 1995: 25) – for example, in the manner in which Shakespeare brings lords and ladies together with simple men who unexpectedly turn out to have more sense than their betters – offers a model that such a state, with its inevitable social divide between the metropolitan intelligentsia and the workers, farmers and peasants, might usefully employ to help bring about what Gorki described at the Congress as 'an attitude of practically changing the world' (qtd in Empson 1995: 21). The significance of proletarian literature to Empson, therefore, lay in it being the latest manifestation of the pastoral tradition's tendency to generate independence of thought and performative agency from the puzzling problem of social relations.

Empson's acceptance of Gorki's account of socialist realism at the 1934 Congress – that it combined images distilling the real with a sense of the desirable and the potential into 'a revolutionary attitude towards reality, an attitude of practically changing the world' – was partly due to the fact that 'it applies to any good literature whatever' (Empson 1995: 21). On the one hand, this formula might equally be applied to modernism. On the other hand, it allows us to escape from a proletarian literature predicated on unhelpful notions of working-class authenticity, which are complicit with the potentially totalitarian 'myth' of the 'Worker' that Empson warned against (Empson 1995: 19–20). Indeed, many of the authors of proletarian literature did not have the working-class backgrounds that readers of their work might assume. Ken Worpole, Valentine Cunningham and Ian Haywood all describe John Sommerfield as working-class but, in fact, he was the son of a journalist and newspaper editor, who went to school with Stephen Spender (see Hubble 2012b: 131). Neither Naomi Mitchison, from an upper-class family of the intellectual elite, nor Lewis Grassic Gibbon, the son of a crofter, was from the working class. D. H. Lawrence was the son of a miner but he had moved a long way from his roots and even the unemployed miner, Walter Brierley, could be seen as moving out of his class by writing. However, while it was not rooted in working-class authenticity, what the category of fiction described as proletarian literature in the 1930s did do was reflect an emergent consensus that social conditions could not continue as they were and that, as Sommerfield's *May Day* (1936) proclaims, 'Everyone has agreed on the need for a big change' (Sommerfield 1936: 242).

Novels like Sommerfield's fulfilled Empson's understanding of 'literature as a social process' (Empson 1995: 22) and reflected the ongoing transition of the world. Or as Orwell was to express it in 'The Proletarian Writer' (1940): 'I believe we are passing into a classless period, and what we call proletarian literature is one of the signs of change' (Orwell 2000a: 297), anticipating his well-known argument in *The Lion and the Unicorn* about the new kind of classless culture emerging around 'the naked democracy of the swimming-pools' (Orwell 2000b: 408). Proletarian literature was able to represent this classlessness precisely because it did not focus directly on the authentic experience of the worker but on the intersubjective connections between the worker and people of other classes. Sometimes these others were the upper-middle-class men of the Auden generation who had 'gone over' to the side of the workers (see Cunningham 1988: 211–40) and the books were written from their perspective. Sometimes, as in the montages of direct reportage featured in early Mass-Observation books, multiple intersubjective encounters were reported from the perspective of every conceivable class position. Moreover, as will become clear, the key intersubjective connections were often as much between genders as classes. Lying behind these social changes was a material shift in class relations which saw working-class men and, particularly, women moving out of domestic service and into modern, mechanised factories. As the historian Selina Todd notes in *The People: The Rise and Fall of the Working Class, 1910–2010*:

> The British working class of 1939 looked very different to the working class of 1918 – or even of 1930. More workers were employed in factories and offices than in domestic service. Wage-earners were no longer servants; they increasingly worked with large numbers of other people in shops, offices, and factories, reinforcing their sense of collective interest and their bargaining power. They had fought for and achieved greater recognition for trades unions, whose leaders now played a role in regulating the working hours and wages of millions of workers. In the evenings young workers enjoyed their financial independence at cinemas and dance halls, where Hollywood glamour and raucous dance routines allowed them to explore their dreams of a better life than that of their mothers and fathers. (Todd 2014: 114–15)

Many of these gains, such as the entitlement to a week's paid holiday under the 1938 Holidays with Pay Act, were actively fought for by women workers, who sometimes had to endure the hostility of their own male-dominated union branches. While part of this resistance was about protecting existing workplace hierarchies, it also reflected a fear of being victimised by employers for any signs of militancy, which dated back to the aftermath of the General Strike of 1926. Indeed, union membership underwent significant national decline as a consequence of the Strike and the mass unemployment of the early 1930s, before starting to rise again from 1933 onwards. During this period, Britain's largest union, the Transport and General Workers Union (TGWU), targeted their recruitment drives at younger workers and women in particular with organised leisure activities and a dedicated women's page in the union magazine. The dynamics of these changes are represented clearly in works of proletarian literature such as *May Day*, in which it is a deputation from the women workers, led by the communist Ivy Cutford, that leads to all the workers at the factory featured in the novel going on strike. Ivy is not represented as an ideologue or a militant but as a young woman with hopes and desires to have more in life to go home to than 'her lonely little room' (Sommerfield 1936: 99). The material desires of working-class and other women are often the driving force within the texts analysed in this book; perhaps most forcibly articulated in the defiant refusal of Sally Hardcastle from *Love on the Dole* (1933) to tolerate the privations of traditional working-class life:

> It's sick Ah am o' codgin owld clothes t' mek'em luk summat like. An' sick Ah am o' workin' week after week an' seein' nowt for it. Ah'm sick o' never havin' nowt but what'a bin in pawnshop [...] Yaaa, who cares what folk say? [...] Ah'm not respectable. (Greenwood 1969: 246)

However, not all men are happy with the positions assigned to them by the class system either. Sally's brother Harry 'try as he would [...] could not bring himself to think himself a man' (Greenwood 1969: 75).

Thus, the British proletarian literature of the 1930s may be seen to represent what Ronald Paul describes, in relation to *May Day*, as a 'complex intersectional web of gender and class, of action and reaction' (Paul 2012: 124). Paul draws on Kimberlé Crenshaw's concept of intersectionality to read Sommerfield's novel with reference to the intricate relationships between gender and class it discloses. In the process, he reveals something missed by previous (male) critics of the novel, which is that the women characters 'form a connecting narrative throughout the story, which is characterised by their experience of having to live both under patriarchy and capitalism' (Paul 2012: 124). This kind of analysis also helps us understand why proletarian literature prompted a popular response beyond the communist cultures in which it initially developed, despite the attempt of the communist leadership and literary intellectuals to control and restrict the format.

May Day is the subject of a chapter-length case study further on in this book and so an analysis of Naomi Mitchison's *We Have Been Warned* (1935) is here used to illustrate what is at stake in taking an intersectional approach to proletarian literature. One significant point of common ground between Mitchison and Sommerfield is that both of them became very heavily involved with Mass-Observation after that organisation's foundation in 1937, which in many ways makes them jointly the key representative figures of the trajectory outlined in this book. The differences between them therefore allow us a further set of intersectional perspectives from which to examine proletarian literature. While, as Paul notes, the critical acclaim for *May Day*, both at the time of publication and since, has enabled 'it to survive the relative obscurity of its 1930s leftwing literary origins to [become] recognised today as a modern classic' (Paul 2012: 123), this has been at the cost of male critics persistently reading the book in terms of the relationships between the male protagonists. In contrast, Mitchison was always, and remains, a more prominent author but she not only had severe difficulties in getting *We Have Been Warned* published but had to endure the fact that it was 'universally despised' by critics (Bluemel 2015: 51). Despite her attempts, no one would republish it during her lifetime, and it was not until 2012 – two years after the London Books Classics edition of *May Day* appeared – that the novel was finally reissued as part of Kennedy & Boyd's 'Naomi Mitchison Library'. Even then, the back cover blurb warned potential purchasers: 'This is Naomi Mitchison's least successful novel, and new readers should not start here!' Isobel Murray's introduction notes that the book 'was a disaster for Mitchison and her literary reputation, and it is so full of faults that they cannot all be considered' (Murray 2012: v). To understand what makes this novel's reception history so overwhelmingly negative it is necessary to examine its form and content.

'Her tractors were plowing other fields': Naomi Mitchison's *We Have Been Warned*

Mitchison's early fiction was set in the classical Greek or Roman periods but incorporated socialist and feminist politics and also featured elements such as magic and characters transforming into animals. As Kristin Bluemel observes, amongst so much romantic and fantastic content, reviewers generally failed to notice that a novel such as *The Corn King and the Spring Queen* (1931) was centrally concerned with critiquing patriarchal societies and promoting female sexual and self-actualisation (Bluemel 2015: 51). *We Have Been Warned* transposes *all* of these themes to present-day England and uses a blend of free indirect discourse and realist documentary style to represent not only May Day marches, parliamentary elections, a socialist revolution and a fascist uprising – all of which is contrasted with a glowing pastoral account of the industrial and technological progress of the Soviet Union – but also free love, rape and abortion. As a result, the socialist and feminist politics were not only unmissable but present in a tightly entwined configuration including witchcraft and future speculation that alienated just about everybody, including publishers and reviewers.

The novel begins in the fictional Auchanarnish, the ancestral home of the two Fraser sisters, Dione and Phoebe, in Argyll, Scotland. While both are viewpoint characters, whose consciousnesses are reflected in long passages of free indirect discourse, it soon becomes clear that Dione is the main protagonist of the novel. Like Mitchison, herself, she has children and is married to a Labour politician. Her husband, Tom Galton, is a lecturer at Oxford, where they live, and the prospective parliamentary candidate for Sallington, a fictional West Midlands constituency. The action in the novel mainly switches between these three locations, interspersed with occasional interludes in London, but there is also a long section in the middle of the novel detailing an extended trip to the Soviet Union by Dione and Tom.

The original plan for this trip is that Dione will travel with her brother, Alex, and a party of others on an organised trip with Intourist, the Soviet state travel agency, and then meet Tom ten days later. However, the need to help the communist Donald MacLean, who has assassinated a Tory industrialist, escape the country leads to him assuming Alex's identity and travelling with Dione as her brother.

This creates an interesting dynamic because Donald, who became politicised while working in the Glasgow shipyards, is the son of Dione's mother's gardener. Therefore, a residual feudal relationship overlaps with a class relationship and the political differences between members of the Labour and Communist Parties. Dione is always aware of the difference between them, even as they sail down the Thames and she thinks of Auchanarnish, Oxford, Hampton Court and Kew while feeling 'proud of Virginia Woolf and Lawrence and Shaw and Wyndham Lewis and Aldous Huxley':

> And then she thought, what does it all mean to him? No one has ever given him Oxford or Cambridge to live in; London to him would be mean streets and dockyards [. . .] the moderns were all from the enemy class, bourgeois, traitors, even Shaw a Fabian [. . .] Her children had taken the bread from the mouths of his friends' children. (Mitchison 2012: 218–19)

This suggests that at least one of Mitchison's aims was to write something 'modern' in the manner of Woolf and Lawrence that would have meaning to proletarians.

The relationship between Dione and Donald is also complicated by a sexual tension that becomes apparent from Donald's discomfort at Dione wearing a bathing suit on the cruise ship and a subsequent discussion about Freud, which causes Dione to realise that it is not just the bourgeoisie who have hang-ups. Learning that Donald has never had sex causes Dione to wonder whether she should have a responsibility to help him overcome his repression in this respect: 'If only I can be sensible and see things steadily. If I can see what I ought to do as a socialist woman' (Mitchison 2012: 230). Deciding that socialism is about sharing and that it would be wrong to be one thing in politics and another in living, Dione promises Donald that she will sleep with him when they reach Russia. However, she soon realises that she has her own issues to overcome. When Donald kisses her on the street, she feels uncomfortable: 'she felt like a housemaid with her young man. With her out-of-work riveter' (Mitchison 2012: 252). As a socialist, she realises she needs to overcome her own class snobbery which makes her more reluctant to appear common in the street than to commit adultery in private. Before they have an opportunity to sleep together, however, Donald goes out for a walk and meets three tanned young women in short cotton dresses, who turn out to be factory engineers like him. Marfa, who can speak some English, is a Party member, on the works committee of her factory and the first divorced person that Donald has ever met. In quick succession, she helps him clear matters up concerning his status as a murderer with the Comintern, telegraphs a friend to arrange for a job for him in a factory in Kharkov, and takes him to bed. Subsequently, Donald brings Dione to meet the women and it is she who now feels out of place as neither a worker nor a communist when the others all embrace. Looking on as Marfa and one of the other women hug Donald and put jasmine flowers in his hair, she thinks that it is 'an extremely pretty scene, a pastoral: shepherd and nymphs. People ought to be able to behave like that always' (Mitchison 2012: 283).

These scenes bear out Empson's argument that '[pastoral] ideas are very well suited to a socialist society' (Empson 1995: 23) and the feeling that Dione is experiencing is precisely that one of humility which he describes as normal to pastoral: 'I now abandon my specialized feelings because I am trying to find better ones, so I must balance myself for the moment by imagining the feelings of the simple person' (Empson 1995: 22–3). The way for Dione to fulfil her desire of becoming a socialist woman is for her to balance her inbuilt class snobbery by imagining the feelings of the workers and trying to behave with the same generosity as Marfa. At the same time, it is clear that Dione – and Mitchison herself – would like to have the same freedom, rooted in the economic independence of being a worker in a socialist state, that the husband-less Marfa has to live with her child and openly contemplate having other children with other men while remaining single. Although she is unable to prove her socialism to herself by sleeping with Donald, Dione soon finds another way to display the simple generosity of Soviet working women, when she encourages her husband to have an affair with Oksana, a young radio specialist, she meets through having a letter of introduction to her father.

Oksana's father is a mathematician, her mother is a doctor and the family as a whole are intellectuals who, for example, know the work of Shakespeare and Shaw and have 'heard of Noel Coward and wished to understand his ideology' (Mitchison 2012: 291). Oksana is quick to criticise the petty bourgeois morality of England as reflected in the fact that most women do not have jobs and divorce is almost impossible to gain. Dione thinks that she will be good for Tom in terms of teaching him to treat women as equals rather than as 'something above or below to be looked up to or looked down on, in varying proportions according to [his] mood' (Mitchison 2012: 317). The final section of the Soviet-set segment of the novel describes a trip taken by Tom and Oksana together, following Dione's return to Britain. Similarly to Dione having to get over her shame at being kissed in the street, Tom has to get over his embarrassment at Oksana paying for their meals and rent. In an echo of Dione's earlier thoughts on the need to align politics and living, their discussion of Oksana's complaint that even in Soviet Russia most male comrades want women to be theirs and to belong to them for always prompts thinking about how 'it is easier to be a political Socialist than a Socialist in living' (Mitchison 2012: 331). Oksana believes that when the economic basis is right, then full gender equality will come but Tom hopes that perhaps both can be achieved simultaneously in Britain.

Overall, therefore, the Soviet Union represents a complex space in Mitchison's text. On the one hand, it is the site of utopian possibilities for new living but, at the same time, there are questions about whether it can really effect an intersectional politics and allow women such as Marfa and Oksana to live their whole lives in fulfilment of the freedom that seems to be open before them. Mitchison does register a number of reservations about Soviet society through Dione. One of these, perhaps surprisingly given Mitchison's advocacy of contraception, is during the visit to an abortion and birth control clinic when the propaganda suddenly gets too much for Dione and she sees it merely as the substitution of one type of unfreedom for another type of unfreedom. The position being advocated in the novel is that it should be a woman's right to choose whether she has babies or not: both Marfa and Oksana contemplate having babies and ultimately Dione chooses to have another baby later in the novel in spite of her sense that the correct socialist thing to do would be not to bring another baby into the world at that point. Other criticisms of Soviet society made in the novel include comments on the lack of women in high positions and Dione's reflection on schools that 'it did not seem to her particularly good or clever that a child of four could say why Capitalism is wrong and Communism right' (Mitchison 2012: 295).

One of the ways in which Mitchison represents this complexity of the Soviet Union is when Dione imagines it as 'fairyland' while trying to assuage her own fears that Tom might leave her for Oksana or even become seduced by Soviet Communism itself: 'He might go far and far into Oksana's country – which was good country, but fairyland, oh fairyland for anyone from England or Scotland [. . .] and if he ate fairy fruit there –' (Mitchison 2012: 312). The concern of course is that Tom will be enchanted and never return to her or at least not for many years. On the one hand, part of this concern amounts to a criticism of the Soviet Union as radiating a false allure or glamour through similar means to that which Empson described as the trick of the old pastoral with its apparent 'beautiful relation between rich and poor' (Empson 1995: 17). On the other hand, the reference to 'fairyland' and 'kelpies' and 'Campbell Women' ties this passage back to the opening of the novel when Dione is shifting 'in time and space' while reading about the trial of her ancestor, Green Jean MacLean, for witchcraft in the seventeenth century (Mitchison 2012: 3). A few hours later she participates in that evening's dancing with her Scottish family and their tenants as part of what she thinks of during the 'Second Eightsome Reel' as 'feudal democracy' (Mitchison 2012: 40). This phrase nicely illustrates Empson's idea of a peasant pastoral feeling in countries such as Spain in which, for example, the complex dance to tread out sherry grapes illustrates how 'some quality in their own very harsh lives made them feel at home with the rest of civilisation, not suspicious of it' (Empson 1995: 15). He suggested that one possibility for the Soviets to try in producing proletarian pastoral would be to harness similar Russian peasant feelings. In *We Have Been Warned*, Mitchison links Dione's pastoral feeling of the emotions of the workers of the Soviet Union to the pastoral feeling of Scottish 'feudal democracy' and in the process imagines the possibility of changing the world. Therefore, she is ultimately able to relax at the thought of Tom being changed by Soviet Russia because she herself is 'giving her mind to the plow tractors to furrow as they will' (Mitchison 2012: 312).

The problem with giving your mind to the 'plow tractors' of a socialist future is that sometimes you find they are 'plowing other fields' (Mitchison 2012: 359) when individually you are feeling weak. Dione's reaction to this and the sense of loss she feels on returning from the 'magic' Soviet Union to 'the ordinary world' is to re-read the accounts of witch trials to see if they had felt like this too. This sense of dislocation is a product of what Fredric Jameson identifies as the mismatch between the familiarity of current life and the alien otherness necessary for any utopian system to be genuinely radically different:

> The fundamental dynamic of any Utopian politics (or of any political Utopianism) will therefore always lie in the dialectic of Identity and Difference, to the degree to which such a politics aims at imagining, and sometimes even at realising, a system radically different from this one. (Jameson 2005: xii)

In Mitchison's work in general, the use of fantasy is an integral part of the way she explores utopian possibilities through portraying contact between identity and difference, whether this is at the level of societies or individuals (see Hubble 2013: 74–92). Her approach to alienation is never a retreat into self but always a more determined effort to engage with the next other she finds. In *We Have Been Warned*, Dione recovers from her feeling of loss after giving a lift to an unemployed man walking along the road with a bundle over his shoulder and, on learning that he is a 'Red', telling him 'I'm Red, too' (Mitchison 2012: 359). Hitherto when asked in the novel if she is a communist, she has always denied it and said that she is a socialist in the Labour Party even though this makes her increasingly sad because it leaves her an outsider. However, at this point she reaches out and despite the differences between herself and the man – she is, as he points out, driving a car – she asserts an identity with him that creates an intersubjective relationship which, although fleeting, changes *her* identity permanently. Henceforth in the novel, her actions for good or ill are always directed to the end of establishing such relationships because she has got over not just her remaining class prejudices but also a more ontological bourgeois sense of the unity of the self.

On one level, the novel suggests that being a woman gives her an advantage in overcoming her bourgeois self. In the early dance sequence, when each dance is recorded through the stream of consciousness of one of the dancers, the Foxtrot reveals the determination of Phoebe's partner, 'Pussy' Morgan, to 'keep my male unity, I will not let it be broken into by any woman' (Mitchison 2012: 29). Yet, while a feminist line of critique runs through *We Have Been Warned*, Mitchison rejects essentialist arguments. Later in the novel, after her admission to herself of being a 'Red', Dione tries to defend herself against the accusation from her sister-in-law that her time in the Soviet Union has changed her by objecting that she 'didn't accept it – whole':

> 'I should hope not, indeed! Don't you still believe in a certain modicum of liberty?'
> 'But I don't think liberty and *laisser-faire* are really compatible. At any rate till people begin to have an automatic sense of decency – loving one's neighbour as oneself – Communism, I suppose. When we're all Communists we can all be free.'
> 'You mean when men begin to be brought up in the feminine tradition of self-sacrifice?'
> 'But even women aren't supposed to be self-sacrificing all round.'
> (Mitchison 2012: 343)

She rejects this essentialist criticism of men because, even if they do often behave as though they possess a 'male unity', if that were really the case then women would really be defined mainly by their capacity for self-sacrifice. In other words, 'the feminine tradition of self-sacrifice' is a product of women being effectively excluded from the patriarchal order in which men have symbolic 'selfhood'. Instead, Mitchison insists on an intersubjective selfhood in which the self can only be expressed through mutual interaction with the other; meaning that such selfhood would be equally open to men and women. Such a position depends, in broadly Lacanian terms, on rejecting the allotted place in the symbolic order that follows from saying 'I am' and thereby refusing to give up 'the claim to imaginary identity with all other possible positions[,] with the mother and with the world' (Moi 1985: 99).

To this end, Mitchison employs fantasy and magic, with their implicit claims that all things are connected, to generate imaginary spaces in her texts where both identity and difference and consciousness and unconsciousness become intermingled in an intersubjective mix. In parts of *We Have Been Warned*, such as the opening pages, this can be read as similar to the *écriture féminine* associated with Hélène Cixous, rejecting binary oppositions and taking pleasure in a continuous open-ended blend of free indirect discourse and dialogue between the sisters (see Cixous 1981; Moi 1985: 102–26). In other parts of the text, though, she depends instead on fantasy devices, such as having the witch, Jean MacLean, appear to Dione, or the pastoral devices described above. In this latter respect, Empson's comments on Bottom not being afraid of the fairies in *A Midsummer Night's Dream* and 'the clown [having] the wit of the Unconscious' (Empson 1995: 18) indicate that pastoral, itself, offers a means of bypassing the symbolic order to enable imaginary identifications. Furthermore, all of these devices have the effect of allowing Mitchison to express attitudes that she could not openly admit to holding or even allow Dione, who is obviously her fictional alter ego in the novel, to hold. Hence, the division of Mitchison's identity into the sisters and the use of the Soviet women workers to express desires and judgements of Britain's petty bourgeois morality.

Nevertheless, as one of Mitchison's biographers, Jenni Calder, notes, on one level perhaps there was still not enough 'translation from "fact" to "fiction"' in the novel, which was obviously self-reflective (Calder 1997: 123). Sixty years later, Mitchison complained that 'the book seems to have a lot of photos about myself' (qtd in Calder 1997: 124). Indeed, friends of hers, such as Zita Baker and G. D. H. Cole, appear in the text as friends of Dione's. Ironically, the need in the text for certain things to be done to protect Tom's public standing as a Labour politician was replayed in real life when Mitchison finally accepted cuts in the text introduced by the publisher at proof stage for the sake of her husband's political career. If these factors are combined with the negative effects of the overtly hostile critical reception – her first biographer, Jill Benton, states baldly that 'Naomi never recovered her literary reputation in England' (Benton 1992: 106) – then it is easy to see why Mitchison might have wanted to move on at the time and towards the end of her life found the book not entirely satisfactorily; although she clearly did not find it so unsatisfactory back in 1984 when she was hoping that Virago would republish it alongside *The Corn King and the Spring Queen*, *The Bull Calves* and *Travel Light*. Judging from Murray's introduction to the Kennedy & Boyd edition, the problem that people had with the novel was with the inclusion of the magic – the witch and the kelpies – alongside the more realist passages. However, in 2016, with science fiction and fantasy now considered fully acceptable as part of literary culture and discussed prominently in leading journals such as the *Los Angeles Review of Books*, and given also the tendency of literary books to blend and evaporate genres, *We Have Been Warned* looks a significant, trailblazing work that was very much ahead of its time. If Mitchison had lived to see the work received in this context, then she may well have revised her opinion of it again.

New critical paradigms have also emerged that provide a framework within which to read works of this kind. Max Saunders's revival and rethinking of the little-known Edwardian concept of 'autobiografiction' as a category that exceeds autobiographical fiction by allowing writers to transform themselves performatively and represent a different understanding of selfhood, seems ready made for *We Have Been Warned*:

> Autobiografiction can include material that writers may prefer not to own in their own person; but rather than suggesting that their fiction gives them away, either consciously or unconsciously, they are claiming that the fictional permits a *fuller* autobiography. This is partly a matter of its being able to include the shameful as well as the honourable, and thus assemble a more complete, more human, picture. (Saunders 2010: 205)

Rather than seeing *We Have Been Warned* as giving Mitchison away, it makes more sense to consider it as a successful expression of a more complete autobiography by her; it enabled her to express herself in a way that was not otherwise possible at that time for a woman of her social class. Instead of having to project herself as a male point-of-view character in classical antiquity, as she did in her first novel *The Conquered* (1923) and obviously felt obliged to do so again in the first novel she wrote after *We Have Been Warned*, *The Blood of the Martyrs* (1939), she was able to project herself as she was: a married woman with four children, who not only had progressive views but yearned for a classless, gender-equal society and understood that to achieve that society it was necessary to overcome contemporary conceptions of morality and good taste. It is difficult to see the negative response by reviewers and the continued critical reaction to the novel as anything but an example-setting punishment for so flagrantly transgressing the norms of the day. However, the facts that Mitchison was so insistent on the importance of the book in her fight with publishers to get it into print, and remained passionate about it in the relevant volume of her memoirs, *You May Well Ask* (1979), suggest that it did represent a significant milestone in her own personal development. It does appear as though the process of writing it enabled her to move beyond having sympathy for progressive causes to the point of becoming actively committed to the struggle for political change. Like Dione, she did not swallow communism as a whole but she did become a 'Red' in the sense of being committed to the revolutionary future rather than the liberal norms of bourgeois society.

A crucial aspect of Mitchison's self-transformation was being able to include the shame that she/Dione feels in certain situations, which Saunders identifies as a feature specifically enabled through autobiografiction. As Helen Merrell Lynd notes:

> It is no accident that experiences of shame are called *self*-consciousness. Such experiences are characteristically painful [. . .] But it is possible that experiences of shame if confronted full in the face may throw an unexpected light on who one is and point the way toward who one may become. Fully faced, shame may become not primarily something to be covered but a positive experience of revelation. (Lynd 1958: 19–20)

Lynd's *On Shame and the Search for Identity* (1958) is written to address a perceived uncertainty about identity in an era of rapid postwar social change but her analysis that it is a social as much as an individual problem echoes West's framing of the modernist question: 'The kind of answer one gives to the question Who am I? depends in part upon how one answers the question What is this society – and this world – in which I live?' (Lynd 1958: 14–15). Lynd hypothesises that the role of shame in answering this question is due to the fact that it can only be understood with reference to transcultural values – values beyond the society that the individual is in. This is because shame is not a simple but a double feeling involving first 'feeling shame for things that one believes one should feel ashamed of and feeling shame that one is ashamed of feeling because one does not actually accept the standards on which it is based' (Lynd 1958: 37). Dione experiences this sequence when first she experiences shame at being kissed by Donald in the street and then she feels shame as a socialist for feeling ashamed because of bourgeois standards of behaviour. It is possible to speculate that Mitchison, herself, felt shame at the treatment of her novel by publishers and reviewers and then shame at being ashamed because she had not met those standards, which she did not actually believe in. As Lynd explains, 'Shame sets one apart [. . .] one has opened oneself and the openness has been misunderstood or rejected' (Lynd 1958: 65–6).

The two general types of response to shame are either to retreat from the position of exposed selfhood back into a life lived according to societal conventions or to face up to it and treat it as a revelation of oneself, society and the wider possibilities which existing social conventions prohibit. Lynd was keen to move away from the Freudian notions (still reflected in postwar Ego Psychology, which privileged successful adaptation to societal norms above all other considerations) of an economics of scarcity, with respect to psychic energy, and reward–punishment theories – which she dismissed along with other unhelpful binaries such as active/passive and masculine/feminine in an anticipation of Cixous's rejection of such oppositions as the product of patriarchal binary thought – and advance instead a psychology of potential abundance. Such a psychology would, for example, see love and sexual desire as inexhaustible and finding their fulfilment not in the discharge of tension but in the sustainment of themselves through ever renewed acts. This is the type of emotional economy that operates in Mitchison's work in general and explicitly in *We Have Been Warned*. In such a post-scarcity economy, there is no inherent conflict between individual self-realisation and group welfare if the type of society is one which is capable of giving expression to, and support for, a diverse range of identities and relationships. The self in such a society would expand 'beyond its own limitations in depth of feeling, understanding, and insight' by entering 'into relations of intimacy and mutuality' (Lynd 1958: 159). By representing Dione facing up to her shame and consequently experiencing the self-realisation that what was really important to her was not contemporary social norms but the transcultural values of a future utopian society, the autobiografiction of *We Have Been Warned* enabled Mitchison to undergo this same self-realisation herself.

Retrospectively, the ambivalence displayed in the novel about the Soviet Union means that its value did not disappear with the discredit and fall of Communism; although this might have been the source of Mitchison's eventual capitulation to dissatisfaction with the novel in the mid-1990s. The links made between the pastoral relations of the Soviet women workers and Scottish 'feudal democracy' indicate another potential location for Mitchison's utopia to be realised. As Anna McFarlane notes, *We Have Been Warned* 'is a compelling read in contemporary Scotland in the aftermath of the 2014 Independence referendum and the ongoing discussion about the nature of nationalism' (McFarlane 2016: 2). Tellingly, Tom's first impression of the Soviet Union is that it is 'like Scotland without John Knox' (Mitchison 2012: 298) and Dione later tells a communist friend that the clansmen are the equivalent of the proletariat and that they want the land back: 'it's on the cards that there might be a green revolution up here' (Mitchison 2012: 521). In the final pages, Jean MacLean appears again to Dione and shows a vision of the future in which there is first a socialist revolution in England and then a fascist uprising in which the revolution is quashed and Tom shot. It is this that leads to Dione's closing statement 'we have been warned' even as she feels the baby within her move for the first time. Discussing the double-edged nature of nationalism – which can involve either regressive nostalgia or the progressive desire to build a new society – McFarlane argues that Mitchison equates it with history, which is not just the past but also a map for the future: 'Jean's warning of things that may come to pass coincides with the quickening of Dione's baby in a move that shows the inevitability of the future and the power of the past in shaping that future' (McFarlane 2016: 3). If, as Orwell argued, the existence of proletarian literature in general heralded the change to a more classless society, the fiercely intersectional *We Have Been Warned* also heralded changes to women's position in society and to Scotland that only very recently become potentially realisable. In order to understand the delay between the end of the 1930s and the twenty-first-century re-emergence of the politics expressed in the proletarian literature of that decade, it is necessary to understand how that literature was regarded across the intervening years.

The reception history of proletarian literature

Whether the age of social democracy ushered in by the landslide election of the Labour Party in 1945 was as classless as the future desired and anticipated at the end of the 1930s is open to question but it certainly marked a difference of kind rather than degree from the interwar period. However, what it did not do was meet the desires of emancipated women like Mitchison's Dione Galton or Sommerfield's Ivy Cutford. It also saw a rapid diminution in the cultural value of proletarian literature because from the perspective of the welfare state, the experiences of the 1930s appeared, as stated in the closing frame of the wartime film version of *Love on the Dole* (1941), to be a state of affairs that must never be returned to: 'Our working men and women have responded magnificently to any and every call made upon them. Their reward must be a new Britain. Never again must the unemployed become forgotten men of the peace.' Never mind Sally Hardcastle's revolt against respectability, family allowances and full employment would meet all the permissible desires of women.

The advent of the Cold War led to an ideological assault on the kind of politically explicit writing that had characterised the 1930s. Not only did writers, editors and publishers such as Stephen Spender, John Lehmann and Victor Gollancz publicly recant and take up positions critical of their earlier work but, as Croft notes, they also highlighted the idea of proletarian literature as summing up exactly where they had gone wrong, as though the very idea of anyone from the working class writing a worthwhile book was self-evidently absurd. Lehmann apologised for the 'proletarian realism' which had appeared in *New Writing* and Spender asserted that 'the workers do not care for the "Proletarian novel"' (qtd in Croft 1990: 339). Cyril Connolly questioned in *Horizon* whether there *was* any literature representing the working class. As Croft summarises:

> By the time *Horizon* closed down in 1950 it was all over. A *cordon sanitaire* had been thrown around the 1930s, literature and politics had been separated, political commitment turned into a psychological problem and working-class writing – *working-class experience* – banished from 'English Literature'. (Croft 1990: 340)

While *Love on the Dole*, which continued to sell in the postwar decades, was included in the Penguin Modern Classics series in 1969 and then went through subsequent numerous reissues, other well-known working-class novels from the 1930s, such as Walter Brierley's *Means-Test Man* (1935), went out of print. The period did generate its own working-class fiction by writers such as Stan Barstow and Alan Sillitoe, but, in an age of full employment, these reflected a different type of class consciousness to the 1930s. Arthur Seaton of Sillitoe's *Saturday Night and Sunday Morning* (1958) is dissatisfied and rebellious but he does not want to take over the means of production, he wants to be liberated from work. In this respect, he is not so different from the working-class white-collar protagonists of 'angry young men' novels such as Keith Waterhouse's *Billy Liar* (1959) and John Braine's *Room at the Top* (1957). Also, as Ken Worpole describes, the influence of American writers such as Hemingway, Chandler and Hammett, who combined vernacular narrative, adjective-less prose and terse sentences into a 'masculine' style, distinguishes male working-class fiction of the 1950s, such as the work of Sillitoe or Bill Naughton, from the socialist writing of the interwar years (Worpole 1983: 29–48). This trend continued into the 1970s as demonstrated by William McIlvanney's *Docherty* (1975) and *Laidlaw* (1977). As Worpole notes, the denial of reciprocity in sexual relationships common to such work represents a continuation of its hard-boiled American antecedents that borders on misogyny and has its 'material basis [. . .] in the relative autonomy which men possess within the culture of work and social relationships compared with women' (Worpole 1983: 47). Unsurprisingly, therefore, many women of all classes felt excluded by this style of writing and this had a bearing on the reception of all working-class writing.

In his 1972 study of literature and politics in England in the 1930s, *The Auden Generation*, Samuel Hynes simply stated that 'virtually no writing of literary importance came out of the working class during the decade' (Hynes 1982: 11). However, following the breakdown of the postwar political consensus and the return of mass unemployment for the first time since the 1930s, the 1970s were to see a resumption of interest in working-class and proletarian writing of the 1930s. In 1975, the Literature Group of the Communist Party launched *Red Letters*, which was initially subtitled 'Communist Party Literature Journal' before evolving to consider all forms of cultural production. Early articles by Roy Johnson and Carole Snee focused on the question of the distinction between working-class and proletarian fiction with special reference to *Means-Test Man*. Snee subsequently crystallised the arguments in her essay 'Working-Class Literature or Proletarian Writing?' for the 1979 essay collection *Culture and Crisis in Britain in the Thirties* which she co-edited with other critics involved in *Red Letters*. Snee points out that despite the then current flowering of Marxist literary criticism in British universities and polytechnics, only certain working-class texts, such as Robert Tressell's *The Ragged Trousered Philanthropists* or Lewis Grassic Gibbon's *A Scots Quair* had been 'appropriated as "Literature" whilst working-class writing in general is ignored' (Snee 1979: 165). She puts forward the argument that class-conscious proletarian writing, as opposed to work simply written by a member of the working class about the working class, has the power to challenge 'Literature' as an ideological construct and she supports this position with readings of the work of Greenwood, Brierley and Lewis Jones. She finds *Love on the Dole* to be characterised by an intense personal and individualistic approach married to pessimism concerning the prospect of change. While *Means-Test Man* is praised for its unromantic realistic depiction of life of unemployed miner, Jack Cook, and his wife, Snee is much more critical of Brierley's second novel, *Sandwichman* (1937), which she sees as a self-consciously literary account of one man's attempt to educate himself out of the working class. In conclusion, she finds Greenwood to be totally trapped by liberal ideology – both in terms of world view and concept of the novel as a literary form – and hence the success of his novel as literature, whereas Brierley simply lacks the sufficient ideological stance to oppose liberal ideology effectively and therefore ultimately it is implied that his work has no currency. In contrast, Jones is shown as writing from a conscious political stance and thereby moving towards a proletarian writing because 'although it is a realist novel [. . .] *We Live* (1939) breaks with the liberalism of the form by not producing an individualistic philosophy' (Snee 1979: 187). Snee's approach has been criticised by Andy Croft as a form of policing what is 'allowed into the rather empty Hall of Fame occupied only by such rare examples of "proletarian writing" as can be found' (Croft 2011: xiii). Nonetheless, Snee raises pertinent questions concerning the nature of the literary canon and in response to Hynes – whose denial of the existence of 1930s working-class writing of literary importance is taken as one of the epigraphs for her essay – makes a critical case for the ongoing importance of working-class and proletarian writing as reconfigurations of literature and sources of ideological demystification. In particular, she is acute in her analysis of how Brierley reveals marriage to be an institutionalised form of capitalist social relations and of how Jones foregrounds the role of women in political struggle by extending his focus beyond the traditional structures of the labour movement. In this respect, Snee's work anticipates an intersectional approach to proletarian literature.

Snee consciously chose to focus on examples of working-class writing employing the realist novel form because it offered the most direct access both to readers and to writers not coming from a particular literary background. She does not directly refer to socialist realism but its presence can be implicitly felt in her contention that realism can incorporate 'a *conscious* ideological or class perspective' (Snee 1979: 169). Another essay published in 1979, H. Gustav Klaus's 'Socialist Novels of 1936' shifts the terms of debate from questioning the difference between working-class or proletarian realism by using 'socialist' as the adjective connoting that the author was writing from a class-conscious perspective. As Klaus notes, while this definition excludes working-class fiction lacking a class-conscious approach, it extends the category of interest in other ways: 'it will include the fiction of writers who do not come from the working class' (Klaus 1979: 144). In this manner, Klaus gets closer than Snee to the parameters of the works which were publicly perceived as proletarian literature in the second half of the 1930s. Moreover, amongst the texts he focuses on are two works that depart from the realist template through their 'openness to formal experimentation' (Klaus 1979: 149): Sommerfield's *May Day* and James Barke's *Major Operation* (1936). Both of these novels display the influence of John Dos Passos in blending stream-of-consciousness with documentary description in a form of montage; although these latter elements are much more overt in Sommerfield. While Klaus finds *May Day* to be more successful – not least in its anticipation of the actual London Busmen's strike which took place on May Day 1937 – his criticism of *Major Operation* for the static nature of its hero – 'devoid of any inner struggle or contradiction' (Klaus 1979: 155) – is intended to raise the more general issue of how substituting a positive socialist hero for the problematic hero of the bourgeois liberal novel does not really solve the problem of negotiating the relationship of the individual to the collective within the traditionally individualistic form of the novel. Therefore, Klaus ends his essay by concluding that the central problem facing the socialist novel is 'how to relate the central fact of the class struggle to the lives of the individuals' (Klaus 1979: 158). In particular, the problem is the need for a satisfactory treatment of the inner lives of individuals that leads the reader into the class struggle rather than away from it. This might be seen as reversing the modernist question identified by West into a proletarian question: when I do not know any longer who 'I' am, I do not know any longer the 'we' I belong to. Klaus does not go any further by way of conclusion but in his analysis of *May Day* he had already noted that the novel absorbs the influence of *Mrs Dalloway* better than that of the documentary movement. Through showing how the 'invisible spiderwebs' linking individual destinies originate in the production process, Sommerfield gives the intersubjective links in *May Day* a more real foundation than the rather mystical bonds uniting the characters in *Mrs Dalloway*. Thus also the march which, at the end of *May Day*, unites so many different people beneath the same banners has a deeper, more active meaning than the party which concludes *Mrs Dalloway* and brings together people who have little in common apart from being members of the upper class. (Klaus 1979: 152)

Furthermore, as discussed in Chapter 4 of this book, through the use of these Woolfian techniques, Sommerfield was much more successful than Barke or many other male proletarian writers in incorporating modern female consciousness alongside class consciousness rather than in opposition to it. One might argue that in drawing on such techniques, Sommerfield was creating a modernist answer to the proletarian question and this issue is examined as part of the close analysis of the novel.

Klaus's essay appeared in a volume of the published proceedings of one of the now rather neglected series of Essex conferences on the Sociology of Literature. Significantly, the papers given at the July 1978 conference '1936: The Sociology of Literature' were divided into two volumes: *The Politics of Modernism* and *Practices of Literature and Politics* (both 1979), with Klaus's essay appearing in the second of these alongside essays about Grassic Gibbon, Orwell, Edward Upward and the Popular Front. The apparent (ideological) naturalness of this division obscures the links between the two and also accentuates a gendered division. The only substantial reading of a woman writer in *Practices of Literature and Politics* is the analysis of Stella Gibbons's *Cold Comfort Farm* (1932) in the very first essay, 'Thinking the Thirties', by the English Studies Group from the Centre for Contemporary Cultural Studies (CCCS). As they note, and as is borne out by the rest of the collection, 'the thirties, in literature and history, is a masculine decade. The politics, narrowly defined class politics from which issues of gender and sexual politics are excluded, are a male preserve' (ESG 1979: 3). In discussing the shift in status of literature across the decade, they note that with the partial exceptions of Lawrence and Woolf, there was 'no indigenously English modernism' (ESG 1979: 5) and that many texts display 'a widespread crisis of masculine identity' (ESG 1979: 6). Hence, the focus on Gibbons, and mention of writers in a similar position such as Dorothy Sayers and Winifred Holtby, as exposing 'the contradictory situation of the female reader-writer, unable to read-write either highbrow, lowbrow or middlebrow fiction, because no kind can carry the assertion of her distinctive and in many ways opposite femaleness' (ESG 1979: 19). In retrospect, it is possible to see how connections could be made between this analysis and a more intersectional reading of *May Day* than the one Klaus provides. A further connection could be made to Michèle Barrett and Jean Radford's essay in *The Politics of Modernism*, 'Modernism in the 1930s: Dorothy Richardson and Virginia Woolf', which reads the two writers in the light of the opposing theories of modernism of Georg Lukács and Julia Kristeva. They show Woolf, in particular, to use subjective consciousness as a medium for exploring social relations, especially but not exclusively those between men and women, without her work collapsing into either subjectivism or a feminine essentialism.

In summary, elements were emerging at the end of the 1970s which might potentially have enabled new kinds of collective readings of texts that were conventionally regarded as belonging to the distinct categories of modernism, middlebrow writing and proletarian literature. Moreover, the opportunity begins to appear, as discussed further below, to situate this new textual grouping in the space left by the lack of an indigenous English modernism. But, then again, another cultural production of the time, David Smith's *Socialist Propaganda in the Twentieth-Century British Novel* (1978), reminds us that the Cold War context for these works was very much alive. The focus of the book is the incompatibility of aesthetics and propaganda, which is remorselessly demonstrated by a sequential analysis that finds, to stick with the examples discussed by Klaus, Barke's writing to be 'slipshod', his characterisation 'improbable' and the ideology to be too 'aggressively obtrusive' (Smith 1978: 64), and Sommerfield's people to be 'ideological chessmen' (Smith 1978: 66). Because Smith excludes novels, such as *Love on the Dole* and Lionel Britton's *Hunger and Love* (1931), which he considers do not actively advocate socialism, the net effect of his study is to argue that all socialist novels are unbalanced by their propaganda in one way or another with the exceptions of *A Scots Quair* (1932–4) and Robert Tressell's *The Ragged Trousered Philanthropists* (1914).[1] Smith's admiration for these two works is undoubtedly genuine but overall his book, whose inside jacket cover confidently asserts that 'predictably, many of these works . . . turn out to be literary ephemera', is in tune with the re-emergence of reactionary politics at the end of the decade that culminated in the election of the right-wing Thatcher Government.

However the rise in political conflict across the 1970s and the return of mass unemployment in the early 1980s created a context – alongside the steady increase in critical interest – for the republication of *Means-Test Man*, *May Day*, *Last Cage Down*, *We Live* and other working-class novels in new editions with critical introductions, often by Andy Croft. Ken Worpole's *Dockers and Detectives* (1983) mapped out several directions for study in a lively and concise manner. Aside from analysing the influence of American hard-boiled fiction on the new urban male style which began to appear at the end of the 1930s, he specifically discusses the work of Jewish working-class writers such as Simon Blumenfeld and Willy Goldman, and also investigates 'A Different "Proletarian" Fiction', which he defines as 'expressionist' in contrast to the 'documentary realism' he associates with Brierley and Greenwood (Worpole 1983: 77–9). His examples of this expressionist proletarian literature – focusing not on community but on the characteristically fragmentary modernist experiences of dislocation, rootlessness and psychological isolation – are the Liverpool-Irish seamen writers, James Hanley, George Garrett and Jim Phelan. Worpole links these three writers with Sommerfield, in order to argue that their work is the equivalent of city symphony films such as Walter Ruttman's *Berlin: Symphony of a Great City* (1927). However, this brief sketch of different types of proletarian-modernist work was outweighed by the ongoing formalisation of 'working-class writing' as an institutional subject of study in its own right.

In the introduction to his 1984 edited collection, *The British Working-Class Novel in the Twentieth Century*, Jeremy Hawthorn challenges the perception that the concept of a 'working-class novel' is a contradiction in terms given that the novel is the definitive expression of bourgeois individualism:

> An interest in a character's individuality or subjectivity is not incompatible with an interest in the character as representative of the class. Middle-class critics have been rather too fond in recent years of explaining to working-class people how many of their values, aspirations and ideals are 'bourgeois'. As Roger Webster shows in his essay on *Love on the Dole*, a novel repeatedly criticised in these terms can be read in a far more productive way and seen as a much more complex text than such attacks presume. (Hawthorn 1984: ix)

While Webster attempts to defend *Love on the Dole* from critics such as Snee by showing how it questions its own realism and reveals the contradictions of the liberal form of the novel, part of the way he does this is at the expense of the main women characters in the novel: 'It is in fact appropriate that the identity Sally acquires towards the end of the novel is only "real" in conventional realist terms, thus emphasizing the falseness of the values she eventually accepts' (Webster 1984: 54–5). Aside from the violence this does to the sense of female agency which is one of the central features of the novel, it actually serves to place a limit on the complexity of Greenwood's position because it diminishes the extent to which Sally's choice to become the mistress of Sam Grundy is not just an indictment of 1930s capitalism but also of the internal values of working-class communities. The net effect of this analysis is to prescribe the limits of what working-class fiction can be in a manner that is probably more limiting than the position taken by Snee.

Hawthorn notes that the aim of the collection was to change 'our view of the past of our literature' in order to start to 'alter our conception of its present' and not to establish a rival canon (Hawthorn 1984: ix–x). However, the emphasis on the collective possessive pronoun while clearly laying a claim to literature also potentially functions to exclude those who do not identify as either or both British and working class in the prescribed manner. Not all the contributions are as prescriptive in terms of gender as Webster's – the collection also includes Deirdre Burton's 'A Feminist Reading of Lewis Grassic Gibbon's *A Scots Quair*' – but its tendency towards exclusivity looks politically problematic from the perspective of 2017. Rather than challenge the dominant conception of literature, *The British Working-Class Novel in the Twentieth Century* does what it claims not to, by mainly serving to generate a rival canon of working-class writers: Walter Greenwood, Lewis Grassic Gibbon, Walter Brierley, Lewis Jones, and Jack Common. Ironically, the one canonical literary writer included, D. H. Lawrence, has been steadily receding in status ever since the 1970s. Such a canon may be extended, by adding writers such as Harold Heslop, James Hanley and James Barke amongst others, and diversified by adding Simon Blumenfeld, Ellen Wilkinson and Ethel Carnie Holdsworth – as convincingly done by Ian Haywood's *Working-Class Fiction: From Chartism to Trainspotting* (1997) – but in and of itself it can appear as little more than a sub-canon.

Still, sub-canons are nonetheless part of literature and therefore require to be covered by authoritative surveys. The not insignificant result of over a decade's critical work on working-class fiction was that it was established as a field that could not be simply ignored. A work on the 1930s could no longer plausibly take the line that Hynes did in 1972. Accordingly, Valentine Cunningham included an extensive discussion of working-class writing in *British Writers of the Thirties* (1988). While this enables him to discuss proletarian fiction as the heterogeneous category it was popularly understood to be in the second half of the 1930s and thereby capture the inclusive diversity of the period, he nonetheless concludes that such writing was not a success because 'the desired new literary forms simply kept failing to materialize in the desired fashion' (Cunningham 1988: 318). Moreover, despite being amusing about 'not all big proletarians' actually being called Jim, as there are also Joes and Jocks, Cunningham fails to point out that writers such as Heslop, Barke and Gibbon employ such representations to self-consciously reflect and metafictionally comment on, or even (in the case of Gibbon) satirise, the role of the worker hero in proletarian literature. The impression is given that much of this work is humourless and straightforwardly bad; although apparently not as bad as the trite, sentimental melodrama of 'bourgeois authors trying hard to sympathise with the working-classes' as typified by Mitchison in *We Have Been Warned* (Cunningham 1988: 309). Mitchison's 'excitement' about casual sex and birth control is a problem, apparently, because 'rubber goods have no particular politics and spicing up your sex-life didn't at all depend on being a Socialist' (Cunningham 1988: 247). While it might perhaps be taken as a positive facet of the National Health Service, that birth control is not such a markedly political issue in the UK (with the exception of Northern Ireland) as it is elsewhere in much of the world, this statement is still startlingly unaware for the time. From today's perspective, Mitchison's sex-positivity would also be seen as a key political concern. Apart from anything else, Cunningham's account demonstrates how the development of intersectional approaches has transformed our capacity as critics to understand the complexity of 1930s writing which does not fit into what were originally a very small number of narrowly defined categories. In any case, even when Cunningham is on firmer ground, such as his point that, in terms of production, 1930s proletarian writing remained the same time-honoured solitary occupation as that followed by the bourgeois novelists of the nineteenth century, this does not alter such work's capacity to have the practical consequences and significations of social change that Empson and Orwell had discussed at the time.

Another significant context for the revaluation of proletarian literature was the collapse of Eastern European Communism in 1989, which relieved some of the ideological constraints inhibiting unbiased criticism. While Croft had been working on *Red Letter Days: British Fiction in the 1930s* through much of the 1980s, its publication in 1990 benefited from the end of the Cold War and the recent illustration across Eastern Europe that political change driven by mass movements was not merely the topic of wishful fiction. In Britain, the Conservative Party had won three consecutive General Elections since 1979 and Croft was keen to reassert the importance of imaginative literature for the pursuit of ideological and political struggle. As he points out, in the 1930s 'the Left took its concerns, its enthusiasms and its literature into the mainstream of British life, and was welcomed as a valuable, necessary and natural part of that life' (Croft 1990: 11). Therefore, there was something to be learnt from the cultural practice of the period:

> For a few years, the Left seems to have genuinely understood how culture works, how impossible it is to legislate for the imagination, how different books can come to life in such different people's heads, how the unlikeliest of texts can make the heart beat faster in the unlikeliest of readers, how most of us win our ideas about ourselves, others, our society, about the possibilities of being human in our time, from the culture we inhabit. It was a generous moment, a critical and creative intervention that sought to be instructive, to build a broad and popular imaginative and intellectual alliance against fascism, against unemployment, poverty, bad housing, dangerous working conditions, educational waste – to isolate the intellectual forces of the enemy. (Cunningham 1988: 9)

Croft's own generosity and refusal to be sectarian means that the range of work covered in his book makes it indispensable as a scholarly guide to the decade. Not only has it continued to be read long after publication but also its importance is actually increasing as the tenor of our times makes comparison with the 1930s ever more apposite. More pragmatically, his avowed intention 'to lengthen the reading lists, widen the syllabuses, open the book-boxes of the canon' (Croft 1990: 10) has directly contributed to the twenty-first-century resurgence of interest in working-class and proletarian writing. Where previous accounts of working-class fiction had functioned, directly or indirectly, to emphasise its exceptional status, *Red Letter Days* shifted the debate from focusing on what made it different from mainstream culture in general to a consideration of what had made it central to the mainstream culture of the 1930s.

On the one hand, Pamela Fox's *Class Fictions: Shame and Resistance in the British Working-Class Novel, 1890–1945* (1994) builds on the work done in the 1980s (she does not consider Croft's book) to establish the existence of working-class literature, which she takes as a given: 'I focus on fictional narratives produced during a particularly charged period of working-class culture – 1890 to 1945 – which constitute a recognized, if long neglected, working-class literary canon' (Fox 1994: 2). On the other hand, she is critical of the tendency of much of this work – such as the Webster essay on *Love on the Dole* discussed above – to 'isolate estrangement devices' and uncover 'encoded oppositional manoeuvres' in what are generally very conventional realist narratives (Fox 1994: 21). The problem with such 'deconstructive guerrilla tactics', she suggests, is that it assumes that cultural production occupies 'a certain middle-class terrain': 'Preserving avant-gardism as the privileged term and conceiving of resistance as a primarily discursive activity, post-structuralist theory can misidentify the cultural resources available to working-class writers and misread the very issues in question' (Fox 1994: 22). This is not to say that by the 1930s there were no sophisticated working-class writers aware of the capacity of literary discourse but, rather, that recording everyday working-class experience was at least as important to any project of contesting dominant culture. Moreover, Fox continues, critical work on working-class writing to date 'has thus far shown little commitment to exploring the impact of gender difference within this class cultural context' (Fox 1994: 22). Instead, drawing on the work of Lynd and the inspiration of Carolyn Steedman's *Landscape for a Good Woman* (1987), Fox proposes a theory of resistance rooted in material desires – particularly women's desires – and shame. This latter experience, so prevalent in many working-class texts, is for Fox a route to self-knowledge and, ultimately, a means of acquiring 'a self of one's "own" that conflates individualist and collective consciousness' and which affords the agency to act, and to desire, freely (Fox 1994: 203). As a result of this focus, *Class Fictions* opened up a whole new set of approaches which liberated a text such as *Means-Test Man* from the now sterile debate of whether it was working-class writing or proletarian literature, individualist or class conscious, and placed it within a new continuum of texts about working-class desires alongside *Love on the Dole*, *A Scots Quair*, *Cwmardy*, *We Live*, Wilkinson's *Clash* (1929) and various works by Carnie Holdsworth.

These approaches were followed by Haywood in *Working-Class Fiction* (1997), which skilfully surveys the interwar years as part of its wider coverage of British working-class fiction across over 150 years. Haywood's analysis exposes 'the faultline of gender roles and their internal contradictions' (Haywood 1997: 59) in the novels he selects so that, for example, in contrast to Webster he finds 'the moment [in *Love on the Dole*] when Sally harangues her parents for haranguing her [to be] one of the novel's most, original, moving and ironic scenes' rather than a subtle exposure of the falsity of her position (Haywood 1997: 55). In the quarter of a century that separated Haywood's book from Hynes's *The Auden Generation*, the proletarian literature of the 1930s had not only become a major area of study but also been demonstrated to exceed the workplace-set masculine concerns that had become associated with working-class writing in the postwar period by prefiguring very contemporary feminist concerns.

Meanwhile, a range of work began to appear exploring, in the words of the title of both the first volume of conference proceedings from the 1978 Essex conference discussed above and Raymond Williams's last book as posthumously compiled by Tony Pinkney in 1989, *The Politics of Modernism*. Williams related modernism to bourgeois individualism not to damn it by association but to work out the full implications of such a position and in the process he raised a range of questions that would resonate increasingly across the next quarter century. He identified modernism as the product of the middle of three main phases in the rapid development of artistic movements during the late nineteenth century:

> Initially, there were innovative groups which sought to protect their practices within the growing dominance of the art market and against the indifference of the formal academies. These developed into alternative, more radically innovative groupings, seeking to provide their own facilities of production, distribution and publicity; and finally into fully oppositional formations, determined not only to promote

their own work but to attack its enemies in the cultural establishments and beyond these, the whole social order [...] (R. Williams 1996: 50–1)

In his introduction to *The Politics of Modernism*, Pinkney suggests that Williams oscillated between the position that modernists could only relate to the working class through a form of 'negative identification' and that there was a potential dialectical synthesis of reform and revolution hinted at by placing the avant-garde in juxtaposition with Leninism (Pinkney 1996: 25–6). The difficulty in working through these positions – and obviously Williams did not live to complete the book – lies in the fact that for Williams the modernists were clearly a product of the bourgeoisie they were trying to define themselves against.

As he pointed out, the most likely eventual position of these artists, however avant-garde they might be in their youth, was to become successful bourgeois proprietors of their own artistic work and image, which was not surprising given that controlling their own production and property was a fundamental part of their modernist practice. On the other hand, Williams suggests that because these artists had to take their criticism of the bourgeoisie from outside bourgeois culture, they had a choice of emulating older aristocratic forms of dissent or newer forms rooted in socialism or working-class experience; a choice that would ultimately lead some modernists into explicitly supporting either fascism or communism. While the identification between the artists and the workers would probably be negative – based on each group feeling oppressed and therefore acting out of a temporary alliance of interests – Williams did also think that 'positive identification' was possible 'in which artists would commit themselves, in their art and out of it, to the larger causes of the people or of the workers' (R. Williams 1996: 55). It is not clear, but the way Williams phrases it suggests that the subset of artists who joined the workers through positive identification is not necessarily the same subset who became communists; although there is no suggestion the groups were mutually exclusive either.

Rather than definitively conclude on the existence of a connection between socialist politics and modernism, Williams regards all of the above possible political positions as a synchronic range of anti-bourgeois bourgeois revolt. The tendency of such revolt to produce what he considers to be increasingly bourgeois positions – a continual desire for ever more individual freedom – leads him to analyse a range of diachronic positions. Specifically, he identifies critique of the constraints of the bourgeois family as 'a critique and rejection of all forms of social reproduction' (R. Williams 1996: 57). What he is worried about is a kind of desire for liberation that can never 'be achieved in a settled relationship or in a society' (R. Williams 1996: 57) and this can be related to his longstanding concerns about the spread of the 'mobile privatisation' of individuals effectively enabling the erosion of society and opening the way to an individualist politics as happened with Thatcherism (see Williams 1990: 26, 1985: 187–90). However, his own analysis also highlights a gendered element to this rejection of the family by modernist figures, such as Nietzsche or Strindberg, which he claims is not really a rejection of property and control but of 'domesticity' in general and women and children in particular. Williams, with his desire for some form of return to social community, finds it ironic that women – across all diachronic phases of modernist revolt – also wish to be liberated from the property and economic controls of family. Yet, the motivations of those men like Nietzsche or Strindberg might not simply be reducible to the desire for an unrealisable liberation of the self that Williams sees it as. He describes their 'resentment and hatred of women' as the logical outcome of this desire given that there is 'little option for celibacy, and only a limited option [. . .] for homosexuality' (R. Williams 1996: 57). Yet the extension of social possibilities generated by metropolitan perception – the mode of experience that he argues developed in the major urban centres – can be shown historically to have created a wide variety of options for sexuality and gender expression. This is no doubt more obvious in 2016 than it was in the 1980s, but historiography over the intervening years has also demonstrated that the extension of these possibilities was a process already happening in exactly that late nineteenth-century period when the phases of modernist identity formation identified by Williams began. Viewed from a twenty-first-century perspective, men like Nietzsche and Strindberg look like Men's Rights Activists and their hatred for women does not appear solely as a logical by-product of their desire for self-liberation but as a more direct product of a desire for a more overtly male-dominated form of patriarchal society. In this context, the desire of women (and others uncomfortable with such male dominance) for liberation from the social forms of property and control is an understandable and rational desire for liberation from the patriarchal order and not part of some general bourgeois desire for an unrealisable liberation of the self. Once, this distinction is in place, then the politics of modernism comes into a very different focus and it arguably becomes less difficult to work through the various positions. In the same way that the reception history of proletarian and working-class writing of the 1930s has come to value its capacity to simultaneously address class and gender oppression, a similarly intersectional approach to modernism has the capacity to identify those artists and texts which do demonstrate a 'positive identification' with moving beyond a patriarchal bourgeois society.

However, even if the question of 'positive identification' can be more readily assessed than Williams allows, his main point that the status of modernism must not be allowed to occlude material analysis of the modernist's class-based role in the production process is still entirely valid. In fact, if anything, it is even more important than Williams considered. If modernism is genuinely an artistic function of the individual liberation afforded by metropolitan perception then it should be expected to be widespread and diverse in its representation of the entire range of possible modes of living enabled by modernity. For modernism as a field of study to encompass this diversity it would need to overcome the specific problems that Williams identifies. Namely, it has to move beyond a grouping of specific authors – Eliot, Joyce, Pound, Woolf, etc. – that, in fact, offer 'a highly selected version of the modern which then offers to appropriate the whole of modernity' (R. Williams 1996: 33). The difficulty of doing this, especially from within academic institutions, is that the canonisation of modernism was a product of the Cold War and the 'postwar settlement and its accompanying, complicit academic endorsements' (R. Williams 1996: 34). More specifically, as Pinkney notes, the literary theory which held sway in English departments in the 1980s and 1990s did not have the tools to grasp modernism in the contexts Williams was discussing because it was itself a product of the procedures and strategies of canonical modernism. The answer to the central question of 'when was modernism?' was that its once innovatory futures had become the fixed-forms of a timeless present so that everything coming afterwards was discounted: 'stuck in the post', as Williams put it acidly (R. Williams 1996: 35). At the time, the only way he could see of escaping from 'the non-historical fixity of *post*-modernism' was to return to the earlier decades of the century and search for neglected works from which to counterpose an alternative tradition to modernism (R. Williams 1996: 35). In fact, the escape from postmodernism, which now looks increasingly like an anomalous historical artefact of the 1990s, was not gained through providing a diverse alternative to modernism but by finding neglected works and adding them to a revised modernist tradition, identified under the rubric of the 'New Modernist Studies', which gradually began to reflect the diversity of the full spectrum of liberation afforded by metropolitan perception. Of course, had Williams lived to witness it, he might have regarded this timely development as extending the life of modernism and, therefore, a less desirable outcome than an alternative tradition; because it would still preserve something of the old canonical modernism, and the possibility that a selective form of modernism might return once more to cultural dominance.

Certainly, the New Modernist Studies can be seen as saving modernism. By the early 1990s, as Sean Latham and Gayle Rogers note in *Modernism: Evolution of an Idea* (2015), academic modernist studies had 'arrived at a complicated, even precarious juncture' as 'the rise of gender, ethnic, and cultural studies, postmodernism, Theory, new Marxisms, media history, and New Historicism had unwound the cables that had bound together the high modernist canon' (Latham and Rogers 2015: 149). From many of these perspectives, the monumental canonical edifice of modernism appeared elitist and reactionary. Awareness of the fragmentary way in which it had historically developed was leading to the widespread acceptance that rather than one modernism, there were modernisms; not just the range of movements – Futurism, Expressionism, Cubism, Dada and Surrealism – covered in Peter Nicholls's *Modernisms* (1995) but multiple forms of cultural expression from across the world. It was at this point, over the period of years that included the launch of the journal *Modernism/modernity* in 1994 and the first conference of the Modernist Studies Association (MSA) in 1999, that the New Modernist Studies came into existence, characterised by an approach, that has continued until today, in which

> Once foundational concepts like autonomy and difficulty, for instance, are now no longer essential to the branching definitions of modernism, but instead are treated as one of many complex, multifaceted responses to a bewildering variety of historical, literary, cultural,

and other forces that created a global twentieth century modernity. (Latham and Rogers 2015: 150)

The range of primary material covered under the rubric of the New Modernist Studies, as might be the subject of papers at the MSA conference or the topics of articles in *Modernism/modernity* or the journal *Modernist Cultures* (founded in 2005), includes everything from advertising to pulp fiction, from radio and film productions to fashion; even difficult poetry sometimes. Through this revisionist approach, modernism has even become, in a way that was unimaginable only twenty years ago, a plausible framework within which to discuss proletarian literature – a distinct cultural response to the onset of modernity – and consider writers such as Sommerfield, Mitchison and Gibbon, who were simultaneously confident across a different range of media, able to blend realistic description and formal complexity in their writing, and, above all, open to the rhythms of everyday working-class life.

While the New Modernist Studies became established during the 1990s following the fall of communism, another political shift as significant as that change has since occurred with the 2008 world financial crash. In Britain this was experienced as a series of events impacting on the high street, such as the closure of the general store Woolworths which was so central to mass modernity in the 1930s that the production of Penguin paperbacks only went ahead after being okayed by the Woolworths buyer. As time has passed the consequences of the changed state of the global economic order have gradually become more obvious. Austerity government has cut public spending in Western countries in order to pay for the money used to bail out the banks. Various populist political movements have appeared to challenge the mainstream political parties and there is a sense of social uncertainty of an unprecedented scale since the 1930s. As Paul Mason notes:

> The civil war in Ukraine, which brought Russian special forces to the banks of the Dniestr; the triumph of ISIS in Syria and Iraq; the rise of fascist parties in Europe; the paralysis of NATO as its populations withhold consent for military intervention – these are not problems separate from the economic crisis. They are signs that the neoliberal order has failed. (Mason 2015: xii)

To which signs, we can add the July 2016 referendum vote for the UK to leave the European Union and the November 2016 victory of Donald Trump in the US presidential election. It might be expected that such events would lead to a resurgence of Marxism and renewed interest in social class and, more indirectly, working-class and proletarian writing. It may well be the case that the anti-capitalist movements that arose after the 2008 crash have already played a role in increasing interest in the oppositional cultural practices of the 1930s. However, as Mason points out, Marx's nineteenth-century theory of cyclical crisis is not sufficient to offer salvation in the face of 'survival level changes' on a global scale (Mason 2015: 54). While there still was an industrial working class sufficiently organised to resist wage cuts and the imposition of worse working conditions, capitalist businesses were forced to maintain dynamism through technological innovation and the development of new business models. From 1979 onwards, though, organised labour collapsed steadily and the pressure to innovate was lifted as profit margins could be maintained by changing working conditions, reducing workforces and allowing a large reservoir of the unemployed to accumulate in the West. Over the same period, Mason notes, 'the global workforce has doubled in size':

> Offshoring, globalization and the entry of former communist countries into the world market have boosted the number of waged workers to above 3 billion. In the process, what it means to be a worker has changed. For about 150 years, the word 'proletariat' meant a predominantly white, male, manual labour force located in the developed world. Over the past thirty years it has become a multicoloured, majority-female work-force, centred in the global south. (Mason 2015: 177)

In order to confront or even understand the challenges of the current situation, it is necessary to have a concept of a possible future because the criteria of neither the past nor the present are sufficient to cope with the current situation. For Mason this future is a postcapitalist, post-work, post-gender-gap world, achievable by supporting certain trends in society and resisting others. The solution is not that of 1945, combining a welfare state with full male employment, because there is no trend leading to that, only away from that.

Therefore, the huge social shift caused by globalisation (soon to be accentuated by automation) – and the resultant political crisis which is currently gripping the West – might seem to render the literature of the 'predominantly white, male, manual labour force' of 1930s Britain as a nostalgic irrelevance. Yet what that proletarian literature embodied – as Croft captures so well – was a vibrant working-class culture within capitalism similar to the one that we have seen Mason describe in relation to the English labour movement before 1848 (Mason 2015: 184). Such a culture – because it includes everyday resistance, subjectivity and intersubjectivity, material desires and a challenge to traditional gender relations, and links them to an understanding of capitalist social relations – provides resources from which to build social relations for the radically changed conditions now emerging in the twenty-first century. We know this because, as the trajectory of the reception of proletarian literature shows – a tendency that this book is designed to contribute to – the British proletarian literature of the first half of the twentieth century was not in fact simply the expression of a 'predominantly white, male, manual labour force', nor was it fundamentally concerned with taking over the means of production, but rather it was the output of a much more intersectional set of cultural values which subsequently underpinned social change outside the patriarchal hierarchy. It is for such reasons that the renewed twenty-first-century interest in working-class and proletarian writings has focused on texts with intersectional values. For example, following the initial wave of reprints in the 1970s and 1980s, new editions of *Clash* and *Means-Test Man* appeared in 2004 and 2011 respectively, while Carnie Holdsworth's novels from the early twentieth century, *This Slavery*, *Helen of the Four Gates* and *Miss Nobody*, were republished in 2011, 2012 and 2013. A new edition of *May Day* was released by London Books Classics in 2010 as one of a set of London-based working-class texts, which also included Blumenfeld's *Jew Boy* (2011). Interest in these works and others like them, including comparable works from other countries and cultures, is likely to rise in the years ahead.

The argument of this book

The Proletarian Answer to the Modernist Question is neither a book about modernism *and* proletarian literature nor a comprehensive survey of books written by proletarians *containing* modernist features; but the complex cultural mapping of a relationship explored by the detailed analysis of a small selection of texts. The four longer case studies focus on well-known, or at least relatively well-known, novels ranging from *Lady Chatterley's Lover* and *A Scots Quair* at one end of that scale to *We Have Been Warned* and *May Day* at the other end. While the first two of these are established classics (despite the devaluation of Lawrence's literary status) and continuously available in mass market editions, the second two are also currently (at the time of writing) in print. The significance of this fact, apart from demonstrating that there is still a readership for the type of fiction discussed in this book, is that they may all be included on syllabi and, indeed, would make an excellent core set of texts for a course on 'The Proletarian Answer to the Modernist Question'. The wider question of identity on which West's explicit formulation of the modernist question hinges is every bit as relevant today as when it was posed in 1937, in what can be seen in retrospect as the run-up to global war.

The proletarian answer to that question was not as simple as including first-hand knowledge of the class relations of the capitalist production process within the social world depicted by Joyce. On the one hand, it also depended on drawing on all the everyday knowledge embodied in what Hobsbawm described as the 'common proletarian life'. On the other hand, it further required a formal solution to the problem identified by Empson in respect of the narrow ('proletcult') type of proletarian literature: 'To produce pure proletarian art the artist must be at one with the worker; this is impossible, not for political reasons, but because the artist never is at one with any public' (Empson 1995: 19). As we have seen, Empson suggested that the way to get round this problem was to adapt the pastoral trick of representing the double attitude 'of the complex man to the simple one ("I am in one way better, in another not so good")' so that it demonstrated instead the double attitude of the bourgeois to the proletarian. The effectiveness of such an approach is demonstrated in Mitchison's *We Have Been Warned*, in which the relationship of Mitchison's alter ego Dione with the proletarian riveter, Donald MacLean, and the Soviet women workers they meet, allows her to reassess her sense of self by learning both who she is and the collective group to which she belongs. The question of identity is solved by overcoming the limits – and, indeed, as Lynd would argue, the emotional economy of scarcity – of the bourgeois self, which Dione achieves by facing up to her shame and entering into intersubjective relations of intimacy and mutuality, which would be the hallmarks of a new society of the future.

Significantly, the writers that Lynd discusses in *On Shame* as providing clues to solving the search for identity are the modernist writers, Lawrence, Joyce and Woolf. These three, she argues, broke free of the restricted 'signals' of narrowly restricted meaning to develop 'symbols' of the richness and multiplicity of language and experience (Lynd 1958: 245). She suggests that only such language of symbol, paradox and abundant meaning – in other words, modernist language – can 'communicate the deeper and more elusive ranges of human experience' (Lynd 1958: 250). However, as discussed further below with respect to Joyce, these writers access these wider ranges of experience through employing a 'double attitude' similar to that identified by Empson; whether that is the double attitude of Stephen Dedalus to Leopold Bloom, or Clarissa Dalloway's attitude to Septimus Warren Smith, or Connie Chatterley's to Oliver Mellors. In all of these cases the class difference in the relationship enables the pastoral features described by Empson to operate and the process of self-realisation undergone by the viewpoint character turns on the mechanism of shame identified by Lynd. Indeed, Woolf's own shame at various matters, including her writing and the opinions of reviewers and of her father, forms a minor thread running through Lynd's book. Moreover, Lynd also acknowledges Empson directly as the most important contemporary critic because of his 'specific attention to ambiguity and manifold meaning in words, as well as to the part that rhythm and sound play in determining structure of language' (Lynd 1958: 245). Considering Empson's 'Proletarian Literature' chapter alongside *On Shame*, suggests the existence of an intersubjective framework, dependent in part on the expressions of such feelings as humility and shame, which are common to both certain modernist and certain proletarian texts. The parallels between the thinking of Empson and Lynd are clear, and nowhere clearer than in the final paragraph of *On Shame*:

> Pride in the sense of self-respect transcends shame, but is fully consonant with humility. Only the man with true pride in his capacities as a human being can have a significant humility; only the truly humble

in apprehending the immensity of the universe and the world beyond himself can have a significant pride – a sense of his own identity. (Lynd 1958: 258)

Similar questions of identity also lie behind Saunders's understanding and analysis of 'autobiografiction' in *Self Impression: Life-Writing, Autobiografiction, and the Forms of Modern Literature* (2010). In reconsidering 'what "autobiography" and "autobiographical" mean [across] the long turn of the century, from the 1870s to the 1930s', Saunders draws on the study of life-writing 'to redefine modernism' as 'precipitated' by the generic fusion between autobiography and fiction: autobiografiction (Saunders 2010: 5, 13, 164). His book includes a wealth of complex and wide-ranging analysis but the main argument is that a dialectical modernist engagement with the forms of life-writing – including the employment of 'mock-autobiography' (Saunders 2010: 9), which is reminiscent of Empson's concept of 'mock pastoral' (Empson 1995: 18) – is central to modern self-representation. Saunders's approach is illustrated by the way he reads George Eliot's last book, *The Impressions of Theophrastus Such* (1879), to set up a discussion of Joyce's *A Portrait of the Artist as a Young Man* (1916). He describes Eliot's motivation in writing the book, which consists of a series of impressionist portraits of various characters from the limited point of view of a fictional narrator, as stemming from a moral and political position:

> she isn't content to remain inside the world of her own imagination, but worries about the imaginative worlds of other subjectivities, and their views of her subjectivity [. . .] The portrait collection is important for Eliot because it enacts a reciprocity, a social mutuality, that offers the release from the prison house of solipsism. Portraying others may be legible as autobiography. But, conversely, autobiography is legible as biography. The habit of self/portraiture represents a mode of intersubjectivity, avoiding the traps of a delusory objectivity and a delusory subjectivity. If this is a requirement of moral health for Eliot, it is also a requirement of mental health, certainly for Theophrastus, who remarks on the complementary spectres of 'self-flattering lunatic', or the 'lunacy of fancying oneself everybody else and being unable to play one's own part decently.' (Saunders 2010: 245–6)

One might see this as the answer to the pre-modernist question of how to relate the self to the collective through generating an intersubjective space. However, the fact that subjectivity and objectivity are seen as delusory suggests that the nineteenth-century symbolic order was already undergoing destabilisation. Williams suggests that this process was at its most acute in the big cities, where 'the new relationships of the metropolis, and the inescapable new uses in newspapers and advertising attuned to it, forced certain productive kinds of strangeness and distance' (R. Williams 1996: 46). Because nobody knew their exact place within these new relationships, a new consciousness of social conventions developed and with it a consciousness of the malleability and potential openness of these conventions. The modernist quest for identity was a response to both the collapse of the old social order and the possibilities of a new form of social being beyond restrictive conventions. In this context, Joyce's *Portrait* may be read as 'a modernist version of the "imaginary portrait"' (Saunders 2010: 297–8). There is nothing straightforward about this approach as the text might be variously an imaginary self-portrait, a portrait of an imaginary artist, an imaginary self-portrait by that imaginary artist or, because we cannot tell between these possibilities, all of them at once. While the element of parody in the work suggests that 'the self being portrayed is itself an imaginary work: a conscious performance of an already parodic nature' (Saunders 2010: 302), it is also possible to see that what is driving this is not so much Joyce's seemingly perverse desire to always stay at least a move ahead of his critics, but precisely the moral or political obligation to avoid being constrained within a false subjectivity or false social conventions.

Saunders identifies seven distinct levels of narrative construction in the novel. The first is childish experience, the second is the adult reliving childish memories and so on up to the sixth in which Stephen is seen as the narrator of the novel as well as the focalised and the focaliser, which results in the double stream of consciousness of 'adult Stephen being conscious of younger Stephen's consciousness':

> What proves Stephen an artist is not only this hyper-self-consciousness, but the way he can be seen at every stage to fix his experiences in language. Such a reading usually stops short of the *seventh*, and final, level, in which Stephen doesn't only think the book but writes it; in which he is not only its intradiegetic narrator, but its imaginary author. (Saunders 2010: 323)

This seventh level is – similarly to Lynd's accounts of such intersubjective processes operating beyond the notional unity of the self – reminiscent of Empson. His seventh type of ambiguity describes the process by which a simultaneous awareness of all the opposed tendencies operating at one particular moment enables the possibility of escaping from the restriction of the unified subject by satisfying apparently opposed sets of desires, in a similar manner to the 'condensation' of the Freudian dream-work (see Empson 1961: 193). The ambiguity Joyce achieves through the narrative structure of *Portrait* generates a liberated subjectivity, which is modernist but also itself ambiguous in that it might be part of a desire for ever more liberation that can never be achieved – as Williams worried – or it might be the necessary first step towards new forms of social living rooted in a less constricted form of subjectivity than bourgeois selfhood. Either way, the reader is invited to share in this liberated subjectivity by actively participating in the different narrative levels of *Portrait*. As Empson notes:

> the way in which a person lives by these vaguely-conceived opposites is the most important thing about his make-up; the way in which opposites can be stated so as to satisfy a wide variety of people, for a great number of degrees of interpretation, is the most important thing about the communication of the arts. (Empson 1961: 221)

Because *Portrait* works by superimposing an older consciousness over a younger one, it does not relate the sense of identity it generates to a wider social world beyond the context of Stephen's childhood, which is to say that it does not show anything which Williams might accept as 'positive identification' with a new form of social living. However, *Ulysses*, which finds Stephen back in Dublin and still trying to find his way as an artist in the world, does relate liberated subjectivity to a wider social world. Here, the interaction between Stephen and Leopold Bloom enables the depiction of intersubjectivity in a manner similar to Eliot's portraiture. As West comments, the relationship between them is 'conceived in terms of relation, not of distinct, demarcated consciousness. What they stand in relation to is part of their being. Bloom is not himself without Stephen, nor Stephen without Bloom' (West 1975: 119). West locates the technique of *Ulysses*, which we would now describe as modernist, precisely in Joyce's metropolitan perception of the new possibilities arising from the openness of conventions: 'a new vision of society growing out of its new social basis' (West 1975: 118). Moreover, Joyce understands the implications of the old conventions and meanings becoming redundant and shows that:

> Reality is not what is perceived as such by members of the bourgeois class because of its direct effect on their financial and emotional affairs. Reality, as expressed through [Joyce's] technique [. . .] is the sum of all social relations, whether directly connected or not. (West 1975: 118)

However, West's criticism of *Ulysses* is that the things missing from this representation of the sum of social relations are industrial workers and any acknowledgement of the role of the production process in shaping social relations: '[Joyce's] selection of the social relations to be described is that of the consumer' (West 1975: 121). Rather as in Williams's critique of modernist revolt as a desire for a liberation that can never actually be achieved, West diagnoses Joyce/Stephen's problem as being that, given his refusal to register the class basis of society, his individualism is the only thing he has and therefore he cannot give it up. The introduction of Bloom, therefore, is a kind of contrivance – what Empson might call a 'trick' – by which Joyce rescues Stephen from his intellectual impasse. Unlike Stephen, Bloom is prepared for self-sacrifice in the interests of others and so he connects Stephen to the social reality that his individualistic idealism otherwise separates him from. Yet, for West, the fact that, ultimately, 'Joyce prefers to live through Bloom rather than Stephen' (West 1975: 124) is actually a retreat from the proper task of intellectually engaging with the material basis of social reality. In effect, Joyce is choosing a passive but pleasant lower-middle-class existence of the flesh that is reinforced by the ending of the book with Molly Bloom's final stream of consciousness. Framed in Williams's terms, therefore, West's analysis situates *Ulysses* as an example of negative identification between the modernist artist and the workers.

A different way of reading the consequences of the autobiograficational relationship between Joyce, Stephen and Bloom that West's analysis accurately identifies, is as a version of pastoral in which Stephen/Joyce experiences a humility similar to Dione/Mitchison's in *We Have Been Warned* through the encounter with Bloom. West even identifies the moment of Stephen's shame in the description in

Portrait of Stephen blushing and turning aside, when confronted by McCann as a reactionary: 'The colouring of his cheeks was the recognition that McCann was right. Bloom is the positive recognition that Stephen had become a mummer, as well as an escape from him' (West 1975: 117). West's implication is that the shame and then the identification with the pleasantly passive life of Bloom, confirms Joyce's refusal of political commitment with the Irish National movement and subsequent retreat even from the empty idealist position represented by Stephen. However, the sequence may be more convincingly read in terms of Stephen experiencing the double feeling of shame, which Lynd describes as first feeling shame for not acting in accordance with the convention and then feeling shame for feeling ashamed. His identification with Bloom is a positive moment of self-realisation and alignment of himself with the post-scarcity economy of emotion that Bloom (and Molly) represents. In this respect, *Ulysses* does function as proletarian literature in the wider sense and not in the narrower 'proletcult' sense, which is essentially its fault in West's eyes. The difference, as Empson jokes, is that the wider (pastoral) proletarian literature 'brings in the absolute less prematurely' (Empson 1995: 25) and this seems fittingly appropriate to Bloom's practice of deferral and self-sacrifice. As Lynd approvingly quotes Ernest Schachtel, the potentially inexhaustible love and desire of a post-scarcity emotional economy lies 'not in a discharge of tension but, rather, in a maintenance of it, in sustained and ever renewed acts of relating to the beloved person' (qtd in Lynd 1958: 155–6).

Plenty of working-class proletarian literature similarly turns on a combination of shame and autobiografiction; for example, Brierley and Heslop (who both draw on the example of Lawrence's autobiografiction), Gibbon (who draws on Lawrence and Joyce), Carnie Holdsworth and Wilkinson all self-consciously, sometimes playfully – even to the point of self-parody – portray their selves as imaginary fictions dependent on an intersubjective relationship with other imaginary portraits drawn from their experience. In the same manner, writers such as Mitchison and Sommerfield, who were not born in the working class, wrote autobiografiction (compulsively in Mitchison's case) that can be read as inclusive, intersubjective proletarian literature. Orwell is a more complex case because his fictionalisations of himself are often outsiders in the social contexts he writes about, who undergo a process of shameful self-realisation but then fail to commit themselves fully to the new social possibilities that have opened up to them and end up by retreating into the safety of societal conventions. However, 'George Orwell' is in many respects an autobiografiction written by Eric Blair; having the name Orwell on the cover of books like *Down and Out in Paris and London* (1933) and *The Road to Wigan Pier* (1937) is the structural equivalent of presenting *Portrait* and *Ulysses* as though they were written by Stephen Dedalus. Therefore, while there is a case for arguing that Blair/Orwell is employing all seven levels of narrative construction and thereby generating a similar liberated subjectivity to that produced by Joyce in *Portrait*, this is not immediately clear to his readers. The relationship of Joyce to Stephen is one of identity and difference; but the relationship of Orwell to Orwell just appears to be straightforward identity. Consequently, more Joyce readers will be aware that they are reading a complexly constructed narrative than is the case with Orwell readers. Nevertheless, the apparent exceptionalism of Orwell aside, the point here – and the implicit argument of this book – is that all of these writers share a broadly compatible structural approach which demands that they be treated in similar ways rather than as belonging to radically different categories. In other words, the proletarian literature writers and Joyce, and Woolf for that matter, were all engaged in what Helga Geyer-Ryan explains as the project of how to reconstruct human subjectivity 'in such a way that would meet the demands of cultural modernism without at the same time dissolving the capacity for political action' (qtd in K. Williams 1991: 177). Indeed, the presence of this finely balanced combination might be the best means of identifying otherwise elusive examples of positive identification between modernist artists and workers.

The existence of this positive identification and what might be termed a proletarian-modernist outlook rooted in a politicised aesthetics of self-realisation and commitment to a post-scarcity society has consequences for how we think about both modernism and proletarian literature because it posits a desired destination. In *We Have Been Warned*, Dione thinks to herself: 'In a thousand years men and women will be so different from us, so changed, to us now so terrible and shocking, that we dare not assess them or imagine the future' (Mitchison 2012: 66). These writers did not generally anticipate that such a society was immediately realisable or shortly imminent; they are not those artists that Williams describes whose criticism of the bourgeoisie led them into explicit support of fascism or communism.

This is not to say that none of these writers ever had any involvement with such positions; indeed, the encounter with fascism and/or communism is often a component of the self-realisation process. However, both of those political movements were ultimately concerned with the establishment of closed totalitarian systems that operated on a scarcity model of both the emotional economy and the production economy – albeit that a strand of Soviet thinking was concerned with post-scarcity economics (see Spufford 2010). Embracing these closed systems was the equivalent of retreating from the shaming experience of self-realisation into the comfort of rigid social conventions; proletarian modernists took the other option and faced up to the shame by opening themselves to new social possibilities. Even Sommerfield, who was in the Communist Party for over twenty years up until 1956, was always a popular-front type communist, interested in intersubjective heterogeneous formations such as those uncovered by Mass-Observation, rather than a doctrinaire follower of the party line committed to uniformity with convention. His 'Author's Note for the 1984 Edition' of *May Day* might have been expected to criticise Thatcherism and the roll back of the welfare state but instead marvels at the positive transformation of the 'material circumstances and social climate of everyday life' in Britain and the fact that genuine idealism was 'still alive and hopeful' (Sommerfield 1984a: xix). His attitude remained focused on long-term trends rather than distracting arguments about the past. Similarly, the autobiografictional narrator of his 1978 novel, *The Imprinted*, burns his collection of notebooks, cuttings and Spanish Civil War mementoes in an affirmation of the future (see Sommerfield 1977: 173–5; Hubble 2015: 69–70). This future was imagined neither as the result of steady progress nor revolutionary renewal but as the consequence of an intersubjective shift in social relations by which the oppositional encounters between unified selves dissolved into the more intimate and mutual interactions of a post-scarcity emotional economy. The way to achieve it was through aesthetic practice that remained open both to others and to social change, as demonstrated variously by work such as *Ulysses* and *We Have Been Warned*. The maintenance of this open stance throughout the postwar decades and into the post-1979 period of neoliberalism by those proletarian modernists still alive at that point, such as Sommerfield and Mitchison, suggests an alternative history of modernism and proletarian literature to the accounts which record their decline and disappearance after the end of the 1930s.

Here, the present book follows the arguments advanced by Kristin Bluemel in the introduction to her edited collection, *Intermodernism: Literary Culture in Mid-Twentieth-Century Britain* (2009). The term 'intermodernism' is designed to address a problem similar to that raised by Williams of the distortions caused by 'modernism' gathering a 'highly-selected' group of authors and then claiming to speak for 'the whole of modernity' (R. Williams 1996: 33). The point of the term is, first, to delegitimise the implicit binary oppositions that structure modernism in opposition to both other artistic production of its period, which becomes modernism's other, and artistic production after its period, which becomes postmodernism; and, second, to draw attention to precisely that artistic production which overlaps these boundaries. The writers that Bluemel specifically mentions at the beginning of her introduction include Orwell, Heslop, Empson, Storm Jameson and Stella Gibbons. The inclusion of the latter serves to relate *Intermodernism* to the concerns raised by the CCCS English Studies Group at the 1978 Essex Sociology of Literature Conference. Then, as discussed earlier, a rigid division of the conference proceedings into volumes on modernism and (other) practices of literature and politics reinforced both modernism's status and a gender divide. Thirty years later, intermodernism now potentially provided a framework in which to read Gibbons and the other women writers mentioned by the CCCS English Studies Group, Sayers and Holtby, outside hierarchical literary categories and therefore in conjunction with writers such as Woolf, who were also experimenting with intersubjective consciousness as a means of exploring the social relations between classes and genders.

What distinguishes intermodernism from the New Modernist Studies generally is Bluemel's understanding that the key features of this work lie in a concern with, and a belief and a hope in people – in the masses – which points towards the promise of a more liberated society in the future. Intermodernism therefore extends forward across the Second World War and up to an unresolved present, contesting other limiting categories such as postwar British social realism and postmodernism. While, in practice, the New Modernist Studies has also expanded across the same terrain, it tends to retain canonical modernists as the benchmarks for its comparisons. The primary focus remains on art and language rather than people and, as a consequence, the dominant narrative becomes one of decline. Referring, for example, to Tyrus Miller's *Late Modernism:*

Politics, Fiction, and the Arts Between the World Wars (1999), Bluemel comments:

> Miller's exemplary late modernists, Wyndham Lewis, Djuna Barnes, Samuel Beckett and Mina Loy, support his characterisation of late modernist writing as 'not particularly successful in either critical or commercial terms', with each work tending towards 'formal singularity, as if the author had hit a dead end and had to begin again. In content, too, these works reflected a closure of the horizon of the future' ([Miller] 1999: 13). Intermodernism, in contrast, describes works that struggle with different problems: the problem of popularity (not unpopularity), of perceptions of reproducibility (not singularity), of engagements with a future felt to be dynamically manifest in the present (not doomed to closure, to 'decline and fall'). (Bluemel 2009: 15n.)

As Bluemel implies, the future-oriented readings of intermodernism offer ways of rethinking and, therefore, building on the concept of late modernism.

However, other readings of decline from modernism are more potentially hegemonic. Jed Esty's *A Shrinking Island: Modernism and National Culture in England* (2004) takes the steady decline of English literature across the twentieth century as so self-evidential that it can simply be asserted without any supporting case. From this starting position, he argues by implication that the issue of which collective 'we' modernists belonged to was intensified by the break-up of the British Empire; a problem that modernists such as Eliot and Woolf resolved by actively 'assisting the rise of an Anglocentric cultural paradigm' (Esty 2004: 2). He suggests that the works of these English modernists in the 1930s and 1940s de-emphasised the 'redemptive agency of *art*' and promoted instead, by means of an anthropological turn, 'the redemptive agency of *culture*', which is restricted to national borders (Esty 2004: 2–3). This places a lot of weight on the distinction between art and culture as opposed to the model of 'communication of the arts' described in the Empson quote above and which might alternatively be seen as having operated across the entire period. By Esty's logic, though, this anthropological turn closed down the presentation of opposites to the reading public and thereby created a successful solution to the problem of belonging by switching off the modernist desire for self-liberation. The net effect of this short-term success was a more profound decline: 'This small but central constellation of modernists in England actively manages the cultural transition between empire and welfare state. Their works reveal the inner contours of a major literary culture caught in the act of becoming minor' (Esty 2004: 3).

Proletarian literature, itself, is absent from Esty's book but we can imagine how, if it was set alongside Orwell's documentary and Mass-Observation in a similar manner to that in which Cunningham grouped all of these together in *British Writers of the Thirties*, it would fit into the following statement:

> At the same time, English writing – ranging from Orwell's urban fiction to the 'home anthropology' of the Mass Observation movement – increasingly made the nation into an object of documentary observation, a knowable unit of cultural and social relations rather than a fractured metropole. (Esty 2004: 16–17)

In contrast, this book argues that the effect of much proletarian literature, Mass-Observation, and even Orwell's 'urban fiction', was to focus on the subjectivity and collective intersubjectivity of the nation. Rather than restrict the 'fractured metropole' into a knowable cultural unit, their effect was the opposite – literally so in the case of Mass-Observation who collected far more material than could be analysed or classified or reduced to a workable functional anthropology of Britain and whose publications actively promoted heterogeneity. Indeed, the net effect of Mass-Observation, proletarian literature and parts of the documentary movement was to spread what Esty follows Raymond Williams in calling 'metropolitan perception' around the country. From the point of view of the desires underpinning proletarian literature, the welfare state was just as much a restrictive settlement enforcing cultural homogeneity as Esty shows it to be.

Furthermore, as Marina MacKay argues, 'there is a case for saying that Woolf and Forster, as well as Lawrence, West, Ford and others had been much preoccupied by domestic questions from the 1910s onwards' (MacKay 2007: 17). Any 'anthropological turn' had happened at least before 1910 in response to the impact of modernity and its class- and gender-conscious everyday culture; the same forces which generated modernism in the first place. There was never any retreat or diminution from an aesthetic to a cultural focus because the modernism of Ford, Lawrence, Joyce and Woolf draws on that everyday culture to politicise aesthetics. This is not to deny that there was a decisive cultural shift in Britain during the Second World War that led to a configuration that was in some (but by no means all) respects restrictive and insular, but rather to ascribe this to the containment of the combined modernist and proletarian impulse within a mythologised wartime deep Englishness. A more radical impulse to cultural transformation, found across much modernism and proletarian literature alike, was thwarted; resulting in a curious anomaly identified by Angus Wilson in the 1950s: 'Without in any way departing from my adherence to the post-war social novel, I fear that the central characters are inferior in reality and depth to Virginia Woolf's' (Wilson 1983a: 133). While this was, on one level, a relative decline in English literature, Wilson's response was to advocate a renegotiation of the aesthetic terms of the postwar settlement by 'the liberation of fancy, the liberation of imagination, the liberation from the real world around us' (Wilson 1983b: 243). As examples of how this could be done, he suggested his own *The Old Men at the Zoo* (1961) and Anthony Burgess's *A Clockwork Orange* (1962); works he consciously identified as science fiction. Wilson went on to support the British New Wave of science fiction by authors such as Michael Moorcock, J. G. Ballard and Brian Aldiss. Paul March-Russell argues that the cultural moment of the New Wave traces 'the many deaths of [. . .] modernism' and the process by which the male gaze of high modernism gives way to 'the [hitherto] absent female perspective' (March-Russell 2015: 10, 152). Another way of thinking about this cultural moment would be to see it as the return of the proletarian-modernist desire for a liberated future, represented also by works such as Mitchison's *Memoirs of a Spacewoman* (1962) and those of her one-time protégé, Doris Lessing, in the 1970s and 1980s. Even Sommerfield uses his protagonist's love of science fiction in *North West Five* (1960) as a means of projecting this desire for a radically changed future into a social-realist novel about the postwar housing shortage (see Sommerfield 1960: 33–4; Hubble 2016b: 203–4).

Therefore, while this book focuses on a proletarian-modernist outlook that achieved a brief cultural prominence in the 1930s, it sees the influence of this interaction extending long afterwards. Indeed, the proletarian answer to the modernist question of identity will remain relevant as long as that liberated society of the future has not come into being. Furthermore, this book identifies the origin of the relationship between proletarian literature and modernism in their shared origins in Edwardian literature. In 'The Proletarian Writer', Orwell suggests that proletarian literature 'started just before the last war, when Ford Madox Ford, the editor of the *English Review*, met D. H. Lawrence and saw in him the portent of a new class finding expression in literature' (Orwell 2000a: 295). Chapter 1 of this book explores the extent to which Ford was already anticipating the ideas of Empson in his Edwardian pastoral, which is seen as neither the insular nor colonial force that Esty describes, but as a mode of discourse concerned with rethinking social relations, and a key progenitor of both modernism and proletarian literature. The chapter also discusses Ford and Wells as uneasy collaborators in 'music-hall' modernism and the urban explorations of both Katherine Mansfield and Virginia Woolf. Chapter 2 analyses the after-effects of the General Strike and the consequences this had on gender relationships in books including Lawrence's *Lady Chatterley's Lover*, Wilkinson's *Clash* and Brierley's *Means-Test Man*. Chapters 3 and 4 are long case studies of respectively Gibbon's *A Scots Quair* and Sommerfield's *May Day*. Finally, Chapter 5 analyses work by Woolf, Orwell, Sommerfield and Mitchison, in an investigation of the destinations of the proletarian-modernist trajectory in the postwar welfare state.

Sommerfield and Mitchison were both significantly involved in Mass-Observation, which sometimes described itself as collecting material for future historians and therefore can be presented as a source of 'social context' for the literary aspects of the 1930s, rather than as an aesthetic practice in its own right. Proletarian literature has also been treated in this way and therefore the two are sometimes linked as, for example, demonstrated by Cunningham's inclusion in *British Writers of the Thirties* of both Mass-Observation and proletarian literature in the same chapter titled 'Mass Observations'. However, they can be linked in another way. As Ben Highmore has noted of the reports written by ordinary people for MO, awareness that these might be read by future historians generates a 'temporal atmosphere' of awareness of the future, which 'places the intimate politics of living within the realm of the day-to-day imagining of narrative cohesion, continuity and change' (Highmore 2011: 92). In such a context, according to Adam Smyth, living and writing about living become blurred, autobiographical forms feed back into the lived life and 'conventions of representation (like, for example, a modernist self-reflexivity) tumble out of the text and into the world' (Smyth 2016: 4). As Hinton shows in *Nine Wartime Lives* (2010), wartime Mass-Observation women diarists gained self-realisation and agency; contributing to the slow process of a democratisation of British society that would not become publicly visible until the 1960s and 1970s. Similar processes can be seen with respect to the complex temporality of proletarian literature. The authors were aware of the historicity of their texts. Sommerfield used Marx's maxim, '[people] make history – but not as they please', as the epigraph for *May Day* and expressed the hope in his 'Author's Note for 1984 Edition', that people would read it as a historical novel 'in relation to our own times' (Sommerfield 1984a: xix). In her foreword to the 1935 edition of *We Have Been Warned*, Mitchison described it as a 'historical novel about my own times' (Mitchison 2012: xxi). Such texts were both the product of, and the contributors to, an ongoing process of social change, which is why perceptive critics such as Orwell saw them as the sign of an emergent classless society.

Note

1. *The Ragged Trousered Philanthropists* is not discussed in this book on the grounds that it is more of a product of the late nineteenth-century labour movement than the proletarian-modernist trajectory which emerged in the early twentieth century.

Chapter 1

'Her Heritage Was that Tragic Optimism': Edwardian Pastoral

Ford Madox Ford and the origins of proletarian literature

In 'The Proletarian Writer', Orwell argues that proletarian literature 'started just before the last war, when Ford Madox Ford, the editor of the *English Review*, met D. H. Lawrence and saw in him the portent of a new class finding expression in literature' (Orwell 2000a: 295).[1] Ford's own account in *Portraits from Life* (1937), states that he first came across Lawrence through reading the manuscript of 'Odour of Chrysanthemums' and realising after the first paragraph that he had a genius who could write about the lives of the other half (see Ford 1987). Max Saunders suggests, following the argument of Lawrence's biographer John Worthen, that in reality they met before this occasion and that it was Ford who suggested to Lawrence that he should write from his knowledge of the mining community when writing 'Odour of Chrysanthemums' and his first play, *A Collier's Friday Night*: 'Their subject-matter and use of dialect are almost unprecedented in his *oeuvre*, but characterize his major subsequent work' (Saunders 1996: 325). Much could be said about this – not least that Lawrence, like those successful working-class writers who followed him, captured the reality of that experience not by recourse to his own authenticity but by recognising and then fully mapping out the extent of his own differences from working-class life. However, it can also be argued that the origins of what Orwell meant by proletarian literature lie in Ford's writing, itself, independently of Lawrence and it was precisely this already existing tendency which allowed him to 'discover' Lawrence.

There is an extraordinary passage in the first chapter of *The Soul of London* (1905) in which Ford describes how the successful internalisation of the city's ceaseless routine completes the process by which a typical young provincial is transformed into a Londoner: 'Daily details will have merged as it were into his bodily functions, and will have ceased to distract his attention' (Ford 2003: 10). London, Ford argues, is experienced unconsciously by its inhabitants: 'a matter so much more of masses than of individuals' that 'it can only be treated as a ground bass, a drone, on top of which one pipes one's own small individual melody' (Ford 2003: 11). Here, he repeats a metaphor from the book's 'Introductory', in which historic London is described as 'like a constant ground bass beneath the higher notes of the Present' (Ford 2003: 4). These two themes are linked throughout Ford's trilogy, *England and the English*, as a fragile individualism, forever threatened with complete submersion in a dehumanised mass society, struggles to realise the promise of the 'Future'. It is for this reason that Ford equates the Londoner with the modern and describes that embodiment of mass society, the suburbanite, in terms hitherto reserved for the romantic artist: 'in each of these houses dwells a strongly individualised human being with romantic hopes, romantic fears, and at the end, an always tragic death' (Ford 2003: 5).

Ford relates an anecdote of how he offered to find a job on a farm for a recently unemployed man, who had come to London from the country as a boy, only to be rebuffed:

> 'London's the place,' he repeated. I objected that he could not see much of London inside a soap factory. He considered for a moment and said: 'No, but it's the Saturday afternoons and the Sundays.' He paused. 'It's when ye hahve your leisure.' (Ford 2003: 67)

Ford concludes: 'Thus what London attracts with the mirage of its work shining across the counties and the countries, London holds with the glamour of its leisure' (Ford 2003: 67). In no other observable phenomenon was this as self-evident as in the groups of shop girls and clerks parading up and down before the reflections of their fantasy-selves in shop windows; offering a vision of the future, Ford somewhat playfully observes, to warm the heart of all good democrats. In an earlier passage he has already suggested that it is precisely this weekend emulation of the leisured class which keeps London working and, therefore, which paradoxically enables the very existence of the leisured class – all are one part of a unified social system in which the function of 'the leisured class remains as a lure, as a sort of Islands of the Blest, glamorous in the haze above Park Lane and Mayfair, an incentive to health because wealth means leisure, wealth means work, and work health' (Ford 2003: 73). As Ford suggests, over a decade before the extension of suffrage in 1918, the masses have already voted decisively against classical individualism.

The fundamental changes which Ford describes are similar to those Jürgen Habermas later diagnosed in *The Structural Transformation of the Public Sphere* (1962) as stemming from the reversal of the separation between state and civil society and the consequent rise in state intervention; and marking the depoliticisation and 'downfall' of the public sphere 'from the time of the great depression that began in 1873' (Habermas 1989: 141–3). According to Habermas, the bourgeois public sphere had first come into being with the amalgamation between 'court' and 'town', which brought together a public display of authority descended from feudal society with a civil society separated from the state because based on the economics of private property. Thus, the term 'public' no longer simply designated all those who were subject to public authority as in the early Middle Ages but came to indicate an increasingly autonomous sphere. The development of print culture facilitated the exchange of ideas and enabled the existence and enlargement of this public sphere composed of 'private people engaged in rational-critical debate' (Habermas 1989: 106–7, 117). In particular, the widespread expression and discussion of private opinions was collectively manifested in the new historical phenomenon of public opinion: the high point of classical individualism and liberalism. However, the public sphere began to break down under the pressures of industrial expansion in the second half of the nineteenth century, as its political function declined from that of a critically debating public into that of a mass electorate. Increasingly, public authority came to be inextricably linked with emergent state institutions and legislation (health, education, employment, etc.), creating a universal social sphere in which the formerly distinct concepts of 'public' and 'private' were merged. A new form of social experience came into being that was shared between those who would formerly have been described as workers and those who could formerly be said to have exercised control over the means of production. That is to say that a management process, largely separate from the exercise of property rights, emerged as commercial success became increasingly dependent on the internal functioning of the social sphere and correspondingly independent of the capital market.

This change in society is very clearly described by Ford in his account of the origin and rise of the 'Modern Type': the entrepreneur who like Napoleon combines an aim to replicate others' past successes with the cultivation of popularity by attempting to fulfil social and functional needs he knows to exist from his own experience, such as the provision of a cheap reliable collar stud (see Ford 2003: 49–50). Mass success becomes dependent precisely on the extent to which social experience is shared across classes and the emulation characteristic of leisure activities is extended into the world of business, where clerks imitate millionaires 'gesture for gesture' (Ford 2003: 51). This imitative tendency of mass democracy had been, and would be, identified by commentators from John Stuart Mill to Wyndham Lewis as a force for the suppression of differences (Trotter 2001: 8). In *Paranoid Modernism* (2001), David Trotter argues that the desire to resist this 'social mimesis' eventually drove writers such as Ford, Lewis and Lawrence to a paranoid imposition of distinct values and meanings by which 'they deluded themselves into modernity' (Trotter 2001: 5). However, he concedes that *England and the English* precedes this cultural shift and is a democratic and perhaps liberal book. Indeed, in *The English Novel in History 1895–1920* (1993), Trotter praises the trilogy precisely for the reason that at the height of Edwardian patriotism, when Englishness was being reasserted as a defence against the rise of modern mass society, Ford calmly avoids apocalyptic prophecy by insisting that the English way has always been to rub along together. Instead, Ford's disinclination towards modern society is expressed through an 'ironic measuring of "personal deterioration" [which] establishes a critical attitude impervious both to sentimentality and to paranoia' (Trotter 1993: 166).

This ironic distance of Ford's to the spiritual homelessness or alienation inherent to modern mass society was bolstered by identification with a fantasy – almost parodic – vision of the 'Country': 'For if each man have (and each of us has) his own Heart of the Country, to each assuredly that typical nook, that green mirage that now and then shines between him and his workaday world, will be his particular Island of the Blest' (Ford 2003: 113). For Ford, it is precisely the pursuit of such utopia which complements the metropolitan pursuit of leisure and by maintaining individualism in mass society holds alive the possibility of the 'Future'. This is an example of what Empson describes as 'the pastoral process of putting the complex into the simple' (Empson 1995: 25).

Indirectly anticipating Alick West's argument that the modernist question of identity can only be answered by understanding its relationship to the social collective, Ford seems always to have been aware that a modernist identity could not be constructed in opposition to modern mass society, but only in conjunction with it. Ford's personal desire was not to oppose the social mimesis of the masses but to go beyond it: an outcome he achieved in *The Good Soldier* (1915). The whole point of this book is that Edward Ashburnham, the good soldier of the title, is not in the least exceptional. Not only does the narrator, John Dowell, explicitly label him as a 'normal man' (Ford 1988: 214), but on the last page of the book he delivers the punch line that Ashburnham's 'mind was compounded of indifferent poems and novels' (Ford 1988: 229). It is Dowell, himself, who is the exceptional person because he develops self-awareness and an implicit critique of society:

> Mind, I am not preaching anything contrary to accepted morality. I am not advocating free love in this or any other case. Society must go on, I suppose, and society can only exist if the normal, if the virtuous, and the slightly deceitful flourish, and if the passionate, the headstrong, and the too-truthful are condemned to suicide and madness. But I guess that I myself, in my fainter way, come into the category of the passionate, of the headstrong, and the too-truthful. For I can't conceal from myself the fact that I loved Edward Ashburnham – and that I love him because he was just myself. (Ford 1988: 227)

This astonishing declaration is deeply and knowingly ironic because the Ashburnham that Dowell loves is his own invention: it is not the empty-headed 'good' soldier who occasionally shows through, but a courageous, virile figure whose agency both leads to, and derives from, Dowell's own agency as narrator. Dowell achieves this narrative trick by adopting what Empson subsequently termed 'ironical humility' (see Empson 1995: 171).

Dowell's apparently passive imitation may be linked to the apparently passive social mimesis characteristic of mass democracy through the existence of an early, brief version of the story of *The Good*

Soldier told as an anecdote in *The Spirit of the People* (1907), the final volume of Ford's English trilogy. Here, a gentleman takes indefinite leave of his young ward, with whom he has fallen in love, without a word being spoken between them. Ford views this incident from two radically different but linked perspectives: as an appalling manifestation of English repression and as an example of the evolution of English manners. He describes this productive ambiguity as arising from the puritan divorce of principle from poetry which originated with the Reformation. Viewed from this context, the governing project of *England and the English* is to suggest that the emergence of mass society offers the possibility for some form of reconciliation between principle and poetry and, therefore, the renewed possibility of human agency, because the passive imitation of the leisured aristocratic class by the masses creates a utopian fantasy relationship with the residual individualism and poetic common sense of the idea of the 'Countryside' still embodied by that aristocratic class. In more practical terms, such reconciliation also promised an end to the cruel disjunction between sexuality and manners, featured in *The Good Soldier*, which Ford kept falling so spectacularly foul of in his personal relationships. While *The Good Soldier* does not resolve this issue, it clearly highlights it and, in the negative form of Dowell's plaintive remark that 'society can only exist if the normal, if the virtuous, and the slightly deceitful flourish' (Ford 1988: 227), expresses the utopian desire that things be otherwise. Therefore, it is not fanciful to suggest that Ford was pursuing a project similar to proletarian literature in that if the end point was not exactly classless society as commonly understood, it would at least involve everyone getting on together in the absence of sexual hypocrisy. *The Good Soldier* was an important stage on the road to fulfilling this project, which can be traced in sequence through several of his novels.

In *A Call* (1910), the two main male characters, Robert Grimshaw and Dudley Leicester, are also doubled in a manner similar to Dowell and Ashburnham in *The Good Soldier*. The model for these relationships was the real-life friendship of Ford and his paternalist Tory friend, Arthur Marwood. Saunders notes that 'Many of his descriptions hover between a sympathetic identification on the one hand, and on the other seeing himself and Marwood as being at opposite ends of human creation' (Saunders 1996: 210). The meaning of this relationship to Ford can perhaps be seen as the key expression of his sense of duality, which extends beyond the uncanniness of the doubles which infect *fin-de-siècle* literature, to an understanding of intersubjectivity as the precondition for conscious existence. For this reason, Saunders takes Ford's duality as the focus of his biography: particularly the relationship between Ford's own dual perspective – 'seeing himself from outside while describing his deepest interiority' – and the dual effect he produces in the reader 'of a felt discrepancy between what we read and what we know (or suspect)' (Saunders 1996: 22, 9). The relationship with Marwood offered Ford a similar opportunity at the individual level to the one he recognised as being created by the rise of mass society at a collective level: it enabled poetry and principle to be brought into a productive ambiguity. The 'multiplicity of political personalities' inhabited by Ford in the 1890s were resolved by the mutual encounter with Marwood into the ambiguously poised position of 'Tory anarchist' (Saunders 1996: 28, 63–4, 251). It is worth noting that in 1930, on Orwell's full emergence into the world of politics and letters following his formative experiences in the Imperial Burma Police and as a tramp, he also styled himself to the staff of the socialist journal, the *Adelphi*, as a Tory anarchist (see Crick 1982: 174).

Like Ashburnham, Leicester, the Marwood character in *A Call*, is an empty vessel; only we know this from early in the book and the plot partly revolves around Grimshaw's attempt to provoke him into an active subjectivity. Grimshaw loves two women, Pauline and the temporarily unavailable Katya, but opts to marry Pauline to Leicester and wait for Katya. Subsequently, Leicester gets led astray by his ex-fiancée and inveigled into her house at night but there he answers the phone and because the caller recognises his voice, is plunged into a catatonic state of guilt. We eventually learn that the caller is, of course, Grimshaw, who had seen them in the street, and hopes in some way to trigger Leicester into a more active partner for Pauline. However, the practical consequence is that Grimshaw is thrown more into Pauline's company leading to the eventual realisation that it is she with whom he longs to live permanently and not Katya. This melodramatic reversal is completed when Grimshaw agrees to Katya's demand that they should live together unmarried, whereupon she says that in that case they can marry after all, prompting his disconsolate reply: 'So that you get me both ways' (Ford 1984: 158).

In discussing the sadness and waste of passion in *The Good Soldier*, Saunders cites Michael Ignatieff's description of the horror 'rooted in the primal insatiability of all human desiring, in the inability of any actual objects to satisfy our initial desire to regain a oneness with the world' (qtd in Saunders 1996: 413). However, we know this 'oneness' to be illusory: the self can only be perceived as a unity from an external position which means that it is always non-identical with the interiority it is referring to. Perhaps this recognition is the true source of the desolate horror experienced by Grimshaw at the end of the novel; the acknowledgement that Katya can get him both ways making it no longer possible for him to avoid his own essential duality, which he has hidden from himself by transposing it into the apparently simultaneous love for two women. Therefore, his attempt to escape this duality through the altruistic renunciation of Pauline to Leicester was always doomed to failure. This does not mean, though, that his marriage to Katya is necessarily as appalling as Saunders implies (see Saunders 1996: 302). The very fact the book – not including the epistolary epilogue – ends with Katya's claim to have him 'every way and altogether' (Ford 1984: 158) at least holds out the promise for both of them of getting beyond duality to an intersubjective existence.

The reason why *The Good Soldier* works so much better than *A Call* is that Dowell is able to renew and transform his imitative fantasy in the same movement by which he radically breaks from it. His awareness of being simultaneously a copy of, and yet not the same as, Ashburnham, becomes the generator of his agency because it shows him that he can act differently. Of course, this latter novel benefited not only from the experience of writing the earlier one, but also from the reflection enabled by the passage of time. The various versions of *A Call* were written over the period during which both Ford's marriage and friendship with Marwood were ending and his relationship with Violet Hunt was beginning, and so the recognitions and understandings it fictionalises are no doubt those Ford felt most strongly at the time. In particular, the relationship with Marwood must have seemed a product of self-delusion after hearing that Marwood had made improper advances to his wife. Yet, ultimately, the fictional reworkings of this relationship were a productive source for his books because through repetition he was able to map out a composite Marwood–Ford identity – most notably Tietjens in *Parade's End* (1924–8) – which enabled him to continue to attempt to fulfil the utopian fantasy, embodied in the actual relationship with Marwood, of bringing poetry and principle into productive ambiguity.

One utopian element in *A Call* concerns, as we have seen, the possibility of a new intersubjective relationship between the sexes but another exists at a deeper, unconscious level. There is a moment when Ellida, Katya's sister, suddenly realises that Grimshaw has 'given' Pauline to Leicester even though he loves her:

> She stopped, and then she uttered suddenly: 'Oh, Robert, you oughtn't to have done it; no good can come of it.'
>
> He turned upon her sharply. 'Upon my word,' he said, 'you talk like an old-fashioned shopkeeper's wife. Nothing but harm can come of it! What have we arrived at in our day and our class if we haven't learnt to do what we want, to do what seems proper and expedient – and to take what we get for it?'
>
> . . .
>
> 'Oh, our day and our class,' Ellida said slowly. 'It would be better for Pauline to be the old-fashioned wife of a small shopkeeper than what she is . . .' (Ford 1984: 21–2)

The repressed insight of *A Call* is that one way out of the bourgeois horror of trying to reconcile the unified self with the fragmenting impact of desire is to become like a shopkeeper.

This repressed content emerges with spectacular consequences in *The New Humpty-Dumpty* (1912), published by Ford under the pseudonym of Daniel Chaucer and written at a time when his marriage had finally come to its messy end, the friendship with Marwood was over and his editorship of the *English Review* had been lost. In it, Ford represents himself as the persecuted but altruistic Count Macdonald, encumbered with an estranged spouse described as a typical 'English shopkeeper's wife' (Ford 1912: 40) and a best friend, Mr Pett – a thinly veiled caricature of that son of a shopkeeper, H. G. Wells – a 'product of [the] Education Act of 1870' (Ford 1912: 27), who 'had commenced his career of public usefulness as booking-office clerk at a suburban station' (Ford 1912: 314) before rising through the ranks of the Fabians. Early in the book, Pett outlines his programme:

> 'The whole world's just engaged in manufacturing middle-class Englishmen . . .'
>
> Lady Aldington said: 'That's very interesting, now.'
>
> 'It means,' Mrs Pett said, 'that we're gradually approaching to a unity of mankind. We're bringing the whole word to one standard. Then the brotherhood of man will begin.'

'When we're all English middle-class?' Lady Aldington asked.
'Your ladyship means lower middle-class,' Mr Pett said. (Ford 1912: 17–18)

In the first half of the novel, Ford succeeds in opening up the higher ethical field of intersubjectivity in a great pantomime of class, which, rather than rendering everyone lower-middle class in the sense implied by Pett, registers the full pastoral interaction between the aristocracy and the lower-middle class to create something like a classless society in which Macdonald's servant-less wife can send the Duke of Nottingham 'into her kitchen to fetch the kettle for tea' (Ford 1912: 46). However, the second half of the novel loses sight of this utopia, as Macdonald's adherence to a convoluted moral code marks a regression into a fantasy of persecution and undoes the intersubjectivity of the first half as he gradually breaks relationships with Pett and the others (thus replaying the end days of the *English Review*) before eventually dying for high culture: shot for insulting the author of *The Count of Monte Cristo*.

As in all Ford's books, the real-life influences for these characters and relationships are overdetermined so that the relationship of Pett to Macdonald is not just that of Wells to Ford but also that of Ford to Marwood. In other words, Pett symbolically represents the reformist lower-middle-classness linking Wells and Ford; Macdonald represents the Tory anarcho-paternalism linking Marwood and Ford. While by dying for his altruism, the latter appears to be privileged by the text, we can also interpret his death as the necessary elimination of ethical substance in order to free the intersubjective writer to go on to write *The Good Soldier*. Here, the comparable relationship is obviously that between Dowell and Ashburnham but Ford's advance, as we have seen, was to allow Dowell to liberate himself by narrating Ashburnham. This development, in turn, enables *Parade's End* to be centred on a single figure rather than a doubled pairing. Of course, this is not to say that Tietjens does not have relationships with figures such as Macmaster and McKechnie but these are not necessary to represent his non-identity and duality to the reader, who like the suffragette Valentine Wannop, is almost immediately affected by him 'queerly as being both in and out of place' (Ford 1982: 86). The novels turn on Tietjens first becoming conscious of his own duality and then on his struggle to realise the potential agency entailed by that. Therefore, the central relationship is not between two doubled characters as is the case of much of Ford's earlier fiction but between a younger and an older Tietjens.

There is no causal progression from the past to the future but a gap which has to be repeatedly opened in the present to allow an alternative order to emerge through an uneven process of superimposition. One analogy for bridging these sundered states of being is provided, as in *A Call*, by the idea of telephony as Tietjens suddenly hears himself speaking ten years earlier: 'His voice – his own voice – came to him as if from the other end of a long-distance telephone. A damn long-distance one!' (Ford 1982: 281). The words he hears himself saying – 'I stand for monogamy and chastity. And for no talking about it' (Ford 1982: 281, 18) – are the echo of his previous dogmatic assertion of a unitary oneness that has been subsequently undermined by his desire for Valentine, who represents the hope of escaping the patriarchal order into the possibility of an intersubjective existence. Significantly, Tietjens originally declares his monogamy in the context of a discussion of the lower classes, or more specifically the lower-middle classes:

> 'The lower classes,' Tietjens continued equably, 'such of them as go through the secondary schools, want irregular and very transitory unions. During holidays they go together on personally conducted tours to Switzerland and such places. Wet afternoons they pass in their tiled bathrooms, slapping each other hilariously on the backs and splashing white enamel paint about.
> . . .
> 'Yes, a war is inevitable . . . there's the multitude who mean to have bathrooms and white enamel. Millions of them; all over the world. Not merely here. And there aren't enough bathrooms and white enamel in the world to go round.' (Ford 1982: 19–21)

Yet, despite appearances, this is not negative comment; Tietjens describes such desires as healthy and observes: 'All the same when the war comes it will be those little snobs who will save England, because they've the courage to know what they want and say so' (Ford 1982: 20). This sounds paradoxical: how can this mass desire of the Wellsian shopkeepers and clerks for bathrooms be both the cause of war and salvation? The answer, of course, is by the same ethical movement we have seen in Ford's earlier fiction; in which imitative fantasy is renewed and transformed even as it is broken, thus enabling the possibility of the future. In the central passages of *Parade's End*, Ford extends his description of such a radical transition from the individual level to that of the 'whole front' with its millions of men: 'Everyone of them is desperately afraid. But they go on. An immense blind will forces them in an effort to consummate the one decent action that humanity has to its credit of recorded history' (Ford 1982: 453–4).

Ford's depiction of Tietjen's participation in the First World War, replaying his own participation, records the ultimate ethical triumph of intersubjectivity. In being stripped down to this sole activity of 'going on', Tietjens and Ford themselves were released from their former constraints and enabled to find a future. The essence of this transformation is conveyed in, and by the title of, the third volume of *Parade's End*: *A Man Could Stand Up –* (1926):

> The sergeant beside him said:
> 'Then a man could stand hup on an 'ill. . . . You really mean to say, sir, that you think a man will be able to stand up on a bleedin' 'ill . . .'
> [. . .]
> 'You're a Lincolnshire man, aren't you? You come from a Fen country. What do you want to stand up on a hill for?'
> The man said:
> 'Ah, but you *do*, sir!'
> He added:
> 'You want to stand up! Take a look around . . .' He struggled for expression: 'Like as if you wanted to breathe deep after bein' in a stoopin' posture for a long time!'
> Tietjens said:
> 'Well, you can do that here. With discretion. I did it just now . . .'
> The man said:
> 'You sir . . . You're a law hunto yourself!' (Ford 1982: 570)

Ford is right to register this pastoral exchange as the most considerable reward of Tietjens's military career because it represents a mutual exchange of ironical humility by which, in Empson's terms, the 'important' is classed with the 'lowest' in order to raise everyone's standards. Tietjens has discovered freedom while in a 'stoopin' posture' and so the act of standing necessarily expands his sphere of actions and makes him truly a law unto himself. Not only has the old patriarchal order been destroyed but meaning has also been discovered outside it:

> Feudalism was finished; its last vestiges were gone. It held no place in it for him. He was going – he was damn well going! – to make a place in it for . . . A man could now stand up on a hill, so he and she could surely get into some hole together. (Ford 1982: 668)

The transition from Ford–Marwood to Ford–Marwood–Wells is complete and Tietjens escapes the last post and the parades and is finally seen in the guise of the Wellsian (antiques) shopkeeper hero, bicycling off into the sunset to support his new family.

Music-hall modernism

The Ford–Wells relationship can also be viewed from a different perspective; that of Wells. Saunders argues that Ford's *English Review*, launched in 1908, 'signalled the presence of English modernism' by publishing Lawrence, Lewis, Pound, Conrad, James and Ford, himself (Saunders 1996: 248–9). However, it also published Wells, Bennett and Galsworthy. One might argue that the first place to look for the modernism of the *English Review* is in *Tono-Bungay*; often considered Wells's best book. Indeed, Saunders points out that 'Wells's bravura performance' in the first-person mode was a possible influence on Ford's *The Good Soldier* (Saunders 1996: 454). The reason why the serialisation of *Tono-Bungay* from the eighty-first page of the first number of the *English Review* is absolutely fitting and integral to that journal's modernist project is because it is simply the best fictional account – probably the best sociological account as well – of what happened to England in the closing decades of the nineteenth century:

> The great house, the church, the village, and the labourers and the servants in their stations and degrees, seemed to me, I say, to be a closed and complete social system. About us were other villages and great estates, and from house to house, interlacing, correlated, the Gentry, the fine Olympians, came and went. The country towns seemed mere collections of shops, marketing places for the tenantry, centres for such education as they needed, as entirely dependent on the gentry as the village and scarcely less directly so. I thought this was the order of

the whole world. I thought London was only a greater country town where the gentlefolk kept town-houses and did their greater shopping under the magnificent shadow of the greatest of all fine gentlewomen, the Queen. It seemed to be in the divine order. That all this fine appearance was already sapped, that there were forces at work that might presently carry all this elaborate social system in which my mother instructed me so carefully that I might understand my 'place,' to Limbo, had scarcely dawned upon me even by the time that Tono-Bungay was fairly launched upon the world. (Wells 1972: 8)

Tono-Bungay describes the unprecedented social change that resulted in the emergence of twentieth-century mass society: the historical condition from and against which all versions of modernism arose. More than anyone else, Wells, the son of a shopkeeper and a domestic servant, embodied that social change by becoming one of the major writers of the age. Wells sometimes comes across as conceited but it needs to be remembered that he was exceptional: very few people ever underwent a comparable career path because of the difficulty not only of overcoming the external barriers but also of the internal mindsets. Much of the thrust of *Tono-Bungay* stems from Wells's attempt to analyse how he himself broke free from those mental frameworks and yet still maintained sanity. Ultimately, the narrator, George Ponderevo, defines himself as an escaper from a decaying society – defined by his mental purpose and symbolically represented in the closing passages of the novel as he cuts through the Thames and out into open waters in a destroyer of his own design. It is actually a very high modernist moment, as Jason Harding points out:

> The novel closes with a journey down the Thames in which the ancient river is contrasted with the ugliness and vulgarity of modern London. Wells's lyrical description of this oily, polluted river-front anticipates the 'sandwich papers' and 'cigarette ends' drifting towards Greenwich in T. S. Eliot's *The Waste Land* (1922), as well as evoking Conradian allusions. (Harding 2006: 143)

Indeed fog pervades *Tono-Bungay*, as it does Conrad's *The Secret Agent* (1907), and Ponderevo's departure at the close of the novel might be interpreted as Wells's rejection of the muddled moral and political uncertainty that characterised Edwardian England.

But, of course, that is not the whole story of the novel. Much of the enjoyment and interest is generated from the middle sections in which the fog is penetrated by the amazing powers of Tono-Bungay, as depicted in one of the sketches for advertising posters Wells inserts into the body of the text. Tono-Bungay is the dream child of George's uncle Edward, who is presented as a caricature of Ford, or at least Wells's impression of Ford as someone out of touch with moral and factual reality, shamelessly drawing other people into their unsound financial schemes:

> 'I want to get you into this' – puff – 'George,' said my uncle round the end of his cigar. 'For many reasons.'
>   His voice grew louder and more cunning. He made explanations that to my inexperience did not completely explain. I retain an impression of a long credit and a share with a firm of wholesale chemists, of a credit and a prospective share with some pirate printers, of a third share for a leading magazine and newspaper proprietor.
>   'I played 'em off one against the other,' said my uncle. I took his point in an instant. He had gone to each of them in turn and said the others had come in.
>   'I put up four hundred pounds,' said my uncle, 'myself and my all. And you know—'
>   He assumed a brisk confidence. 'I hadn't five hundred pence. At least—'. (Wells 1972: 107)

This is clearly a fictional version of the profit-sharing scheme Ford employed to secure friends as contributors for the *English Review*. Certain writers including Wells waived their normal fees and contributed work to the journal on the basis that they would share in the profits. The irony in this case is that Wells was satirising the arrangement in the piece of work he was contributing under its conditions. However, the potential negativity of this caricaturing of Ford is leavened by Wells, at the outset of the novel, describing Edward Ponderevo as the 'Napoleon of domestic conveniences' and thus invoking Ford's own description of the 'Napoleons' of business in *The Soul of London*: 'It would be fanciful to make Buonaparte too responsible for the Modern Type; but he, upon the whole, was the discoverer of the principle: apply yourself to gain the affection of the immense crowd' (Ford 2003: 50). Edward Ponderevo is a character to whom the novel's readers, and presumably its author, feel affection. The personal satire is therefore less important than Wells's understanding of Ford's idea that the attempt to meet mass desires is potentially utopian. This potentially utopian outcome is the dream behind a high-concept product, whether that is Tono-Bungay or the *English Review*, or as George Ponderevo's bohemian artist friend, Ewart, puts it, the 'poetry' of such an undertaking:

> 'And it's not your poetry only. It's the poetry of the customer, too. Poet answering to poet – soul to soul. Health, strength, beauty in a bottle – the magic philtre like a fairy tale . . .'
> [. . .]
> 'Think of the little clerks and jaded workers and overworked people. People overstrained with wanting to do, people overstrained with wanting to be . . . People, in fact, overstrained . . . The real trouble of life, Ponderevo, isn't that we exist – that's a vulgar error; the real trouble is that we *don't* really exist and we want to. That's what this – in the highest sense – much stands for! The hunger to be – for once – really alive – to the fingertips!' (Wells 1972: 130)

The narrative struggle in *Tono-Bungay* is between what Wells takes to be a higher mode of active existence, symbolised by the destroyer leaving the Thames, and a more fluid subjectivity which generates the possibility of a 'Future' through ironic accommodation with modern society, symbolised by the quack medicine pushed by the Fordian Edward Ponderevo. Wells's choice of symbolism and the way he ends the novel appear to indicate a conscious decision to reject the Fordian position, but the whole feel of the book – the actual pace and wit and enjoyment of it – actually tends in the other direction. One explanation for this inconsistency is that Wells is drawn to side with Ford, but cannot because it would contradict his public persona as a man of science and reason. A similar dynamic underpins Wells's late novel, *The Bulpington of Blup* (1932), as he implicitly acknowledges in his autobiography:

> Throughout my life, a main strand of interest has been the endeavour to anchor *personas* to a common conception of reality [. . .] But this theme of the floating *persona*, the dramatized self, returns at various levels of complexity and self-deception, in Mr. Hoopdriver in *The Wheels of Chance*, in the dreams of Mr. Parham, in *Christina Alberta's Father*, and most elaborately of all, in *The Bulpington of Blup*. This last is a very direct caricature study of the irresponsible disconnected aesthetic mentality. It is friendship's offering to the world of letters from the scientific side. (Wells 1934: 624)

The ostensible reason, therefore, that Theodore Bulpington is a floating persona is, of course, that he is modelled on Ford and, in particular, Wells's conception of Ford's departure from his more rational Edwardian persona; a transition which became conspicuous after the war: 'his extraordinary drift towards self-dramatization – when he even changed his name to Captain Ford' (Wells 1934: 622). The novel culminates in a postwar evening during which Bulpington, now referred to by the text as 'the Captain', tells ever greater lies about the war – including single-handedly capturing the Kaiser – before launching into a theatrical soliloquy:

> I am a liar in a world of lies. Lies? Dreams! World of dreams. Hidden world [. . .] World of self-delusion. But most of us never find out it is self-delusion. I happen to know. And because I know it, I shape my life as I like, past and future, just as I please. What wasn't true is true now. See? I *make* it true. I enlisted by a trick when the doctors had rejected me. Yes, I did, I tell you. I led that rally before Amiens. I – your humble servant. I took the Kaiser prisoner. I talked to him for hours. And so forth and so on. If I wish it, it has to be so. From now henceforth. Lie for lie. Who believes my lie is my friend. It's a fair trade, and plenty doing. I shall find plenty of friends. Was friendship ever anything but a lie-exchange? Corroboration. Love me, love my lie. And who will object? (Wells 1932: 403)

But is this self-dramatisation simply a bravura act of ventriloquism on Wells's behalf or a more complex self-reflexive passage of displaced reflection on his own construction of a scientific persona?

Wells seemingly accounts for Ford's duality – fictionally represented by Theodore Bulpington and his fantasy alter ego the Bulpington of Blup – as an act of self-deception that enables him to love two women, Margaret and Rachel, simultaneously. Of course, real-life examples of Ford loving two women simultaneously are too numerous to list and nor was Wells entirely immune to the same phenomenon. Ford simultaneously wanting two women, as with Grimshaw in *A Call*, was a way of hiding his duality from himself and actually affecting a notional unity of purpose. However, it never became a way of life for him in the way that maintaining unity at all costs was for Wells. Wells transfers his own fault onto the Ford character in this novel and that is what gives the book both its intensity – which is that of unconscious autobiography and, of course, it really becomes all lies then because Wells was certainly not in the war let alone at the front – and its poignancy. Because in the end the book is a lament for a lost time and place – the radical milieu of London circa 1909, just before the world changed according to Virginia Woolf – when the main protagonists Theodore, Teddy and Margaret seem on the cusp of a shared transformative vision. It is this overwhelming sense of loss that dominates the novel but in the process of retelling the story once again, Wells comes his closest to recapturing the poetic sociology of *Tono-Bungay* which characterised the modernism of the *English Review*.

That modernism was not the pre-lapserian utopian wholeness that Wells mourned. It is better conceptualised, drawing an analogy deriving from Ford's tendency to edit the manuscripts for the *English Review* while 'sitting in a box or the stalls of the local music-hall' (Saunders 1996: 247), as music-hall modernism. This form of modernism operates as a series of theatrical turns in which the complex performative interactions, both with mass audiences and fellow modernists, are integral elements of the overall experience. In other words, the works of these writers endlessly dramatise their relationship with other writers in what would be completely ridiculous manners if it were not for the fact that they are also performances intended to satisfy the demand of mass audiences for entertainment. This can be seen clearly in the case of Wells and Ford, as they took turns to tell the story of their interaction over the *English Review* in increasingly bizarre ways: whether as the mass marketing of a quack medicine in *Tono-Bungay* or as the struggles of a group of conspirators plotting a counter-revolution in a small foreign country as in *The New Humpty-Dumpty* (1912). Arguably, these frenzied and melodramatic reworkings actually express something about modernism that the more traditional accounts of impersonality miss out; self-liberation was never actually achieved by the self but only through the intersubjective relationships which selves formed with each other in complex chaotic performances. In the end, it remains the case that Ford almost always comes across in Wells's fiction as an object of affection whatever Wells's intentions might have been. The use of the friendly nickname 'Bulpy' for the hero, or perhaps anti-hero, of *The Bulpington of Blup*, makes him impossible to dislike and undermines the attempted sustained satire. The fact that Wells linked the novel with *Kipps* (1905) and *The History of Mr Polly* (1910) as creations of which he was not ashamed suggests that it was, after all, more labour of love than hatchet job. Through his compulsive caricaturing of Ford, Wells kept himself in touch with the everyday dreamer in himself that he otherwise consciously sought to transcend. It was friendship's offering to the scientific side from the world of letters.

The freedom of the city

Ford noted that 'the fascination of life in London is essentially its freedom' (Ford 2003: 69). On 24 June 1917, Katherine Mansfield wrote to Virginia Woolf offering her that freedom: 'But pray consider how rare is it to find some one with the same passion for writing that you have, who desires to be scrupulously truthful with you – and to give you the freedom of the city without any reserves at all' (qtd in Lee 1997: 388). As Hermione Lee argues, Mansfield was a significant influence on the way that Woolf 'developed her writing in the early 1920s' (Lee 1997: 385) – a development which resulted in the series of modernist classics for which she is celebrated today, particularly *Mrs Dalloway* (1925). However, Mansfield's offer of the freedom of the city was a double-edged gift as Mansfield's own stories repeatedly show. For example, in 'A Cup of Tea' (1922), Rosemary Fell undergoes a transformation equivalent to gaining such a freedom. In a London antiques shop, she is shown an 'exquisite little enamel box' but on finding the price to be twenty-eight guineas asks the shop assistant to keep it for her. Outside on the street, she is accosted by a young woman for the price of a cup of tea. Rather than hurry away or simply ignore the injunction, Rosemary is moved to treat the encounter as an 'adventure':

> It was like something out of a novel by Dostoyevsky, this meeting in the dusk. Supposing she took the girl home? Supposing she did do one of those things she was always reading about or seeing on the stage, what would happen? It would be thrilling. And she heard herself saying afterwards to the amazement of her friends: 'I simply took her home with me,' as she stepped forward and said to that dim person beside her: 'Come home to tea with me.' (Mansfield 1981: 401)

However, of course, things do not work out entirely as anticipated. Far from proving that 'rich people had hearts, and that women *were* sisters' (Mansfield 1981: 402), Rosemary ends up symbolically reducing the young woman – who is apparently, judging from Rosemary's husband's throwaway remark about *The Milliner's Gazette*, an out-of-work shop girl – to the level of a prostitute: amusing herself with her in her bedroom before paying her and sending her on her way. As in other Mansfield stories such as 'Bliss' (1918), the upper-middle-class protagonist is made simultaneously aware of her own desire and how it functions as part of a wider economy of desire which precludes its ever being met – a point brought home as the story closes with Rosemary's husband pulling her onto his knee and promising to buy her the enamel box for twenty-eight guineas even as she realises that this is not in fact what she wants.

While it is generally accepted that Rosemary is a fictionalised version of Mansfield's cousin, Elizabeth von Arnim, it is nonetheless tempting to read 'A Cup of Tea' as Mansfield's comment on the relationship between herself and Woolf. By representing herself as a shop girl, one of the representative figures of the modern mass society that had sprung up in London over the preceding decades, she could show how shabbily she felt she was treated by Woolf even as she revealed to her the inability of Edwardian conformity to satisfy her desires. In reviewing Woolf's *Night and Day* in 1919, Mansfield had written:

> We had thought this world had vanished for ever [. . .] Yet here is *Night and Day*, fresh, new and exquisite, a novel in the tradition of the English novel. In the midst of our admiration it makes us feel old and chill. We had never thought to look upon its like again! (Mansfield, qtd in Lee 1997: 386)

The review reflects a personal anger at perceived injustices; possibly stemming in part from a realisation that illness was effectively preventing her from remaining an equal to Woolf. However, never again would a work like *Night and Day* see the light of day after Mansfield's influence.

It is also instructive to follow Trotter's reading of the story as a case study of how modernist writers link linguistic norms with symbolic ones, before disrupting the linguistic norms in order to explode the symbolic ones. Trotter's analysis focuses on the sentence, 'The discreet door shut with a click' (Trotter 1993: 71; Mansfield 1981: 400). This is the door of the antiques shop closing behind Rosemary as she walks into the street just prior to her encounter with the young woman. By the end of the story, we will know this to have been a symbolic threshold – the door closing on the old Edwardian and

Victorian respectability, as the freedom of the city opens up before the protagonist – but, as Trotter argues, if the sentence simply read, 'The door shut with a discreet click', it would not register with the reader as such a threshold on first reading. As it is, the reader is forced to pause momentarily after reading about 'the discreet door' to process all the ways in which a door might be discreet:

> the sentence draws attention to itself. Its semantic ordering flouts the conventions of normal discourse, conventions which the story has hitherto adhered to. In Relevance Theory terms, it guarantees an increase in contextual effect, but only at the cost of an increase in the effort required to process it. In my terms, it constitutes a threshold. By withholding the kind of relevance we might have expected – a straightforward cumulative 'filling in' of a not unfamiliar fictional world – it invites us to exercise our powers of inference: to access more remote contexts in search of other kinds of relevance. Modernism is another name for that invitation. (Trotter 1993: 74)

But what does it mean if this invitation is being made from Katherine Mansfield to Virginia Woolf, from the symbolic shop girl to the symbolic Edwardian lady? If these 'other kinds of relevance' are to be found in the streets – if they are, in fact, a necessary consequence of the freedom of the city – what does it tell us about modernism? One way to think about this question is to look back to Mansfield's first short story, 'The Tiredness of Rosabel', written in 1908 but only published posthumously in 1924. In this story, another shop girl, Rosabel, spends an evening kneeling before the window in her lodging-house room recalling the day in the milliner's shop where she works. In particular, she remembers a young well-dressed upper-class couple who came in:

> 'What is it exactly that I want, Harry?' she had said, as Rosabel took the pins out of her hat, untied her veil, and gave her a hand-mirror.
> 'You must have a black hat,' he had answered, 'a black hat with a feather that goes right round it and then round your neck and ties in a bow under your chin, and the ends tuck into your belt – a decent-sized feather.'
> The girl glanced at Rosabel laughingly. 'Have you any hats like that?' (Mansfield 1981: 515)

The change in tense obviously signals a temporal shift, but this appears not to be a direct flashback so much as the entry into a daydream in which Rosabel is simultaneously inside and outside of the day's events. It rapidly transpires that none of the shop's hats will satisfy the couple until Rosabel remembers 'the big, untouched box upstairs' (Mansfield 1981: 515). Similarly to the enamel box in 'A Cup of Tea', the hat box is symbolically connected with desire. Indeed, in this case, it functions analogously to Pandora's Box of legend; once opened, desire is unleashed. Of course, the couple are instantly captivated but, then, the girl, unexpectedly, hands the hat to Rosabel and asks to see it on her:

> Rosabel turned to the mirror and placed it on her brown head, then faced them.
> 'Oh, Harry, isn't it adorable,' the girl cried, 'I must have that!' She smiled again at Rosabel. 'It suits you beautifully.'
> A sudden, ridiculous feeling of anger had seized Rosabel. She longed to throw the lovely perishable thing in the girl's face, and bent over the hat, flushing. (Mansfield 1981: 516)

The anger at the time had been at being brought into an economy of desire in which the only possible role for her was the one made clear by the man when he leaned over her and asked 'Ever been painted?' (Mansfield 1981: 516). But in her daydream world, Rosabel ignores this insolent familiarity and concentrates on the implicit promise of the exchange of hats: 'Suppose they changed places' (Mansfield 1981: 516). She becomes the one who drives off with Harry, stopping only to have her maid fasten her new hat, before moving on to lunch. This trip through London extends itself through Gerard's, the Carlton, an afternoon matinee, tea at the 'Cottage', the ball that night and right on up until:

> Harry came across the room and caught her in his arms – 'Rosabel, Rosabel, Rosabel . . .' Oh, the haven of those arms, and she was very tired.
> (The real Rosabel, the girl crouched on the floor in the dark, laughed aloud, and put her hand up to her hot mouth.) (Mansfield 1981: 518)

The fact that this reference to the 'real Rosabel' is parenthetical is significant. It confirms the earlier impression that her 'real' self is somehow inside the daydream. However, it can also be read as further implying that her 'real' self can only exist in such a daydream.

To reference Slavoj Žižek, the lesson of Rosabel's daydreaming is not the apparent error of confusing fiction for reality but the exact opposite: *'we should not mistake reality for fiction* – we should be able to discern, in what we experience as fiction, the hard kernel of the Real which we are able to sustain only if we fictionalise it' (Žižek 2002: 19; original emphasis). Rosabel is 'real' at precisely this moment because she is aware of her essential non-identity: the difference between her conscious and unconscious identities. However, even when not actively maintaining this awareness by fictionalising her experience in this manner, her non-identity is never far from the surface as a consequence of her historical class position. The sudden emergence in the late nineteenth century of mass modernity as the cumulative product of unprecedented urban immigration represented an intense psychological liberation from rural stasis to the freedom of the city. The anxiety inherent to this uprooted position, combined with the uncertain social positions of the new forms of employment in shop and clerical work, militated against the easy formation of any fixed identity.

It is not just that Rosabel's lack of fixed identity makes her acceptable to the upper-class girl as a model for her hat – which, is to say, makes her acceptable to the upper-class girl as a stand-in for herself – in a way that a domestic servant would not be acceptable, but also that it makes Rosabel attractive because she represents a freedom which the upper-class girl does not have. The freedom of the city does not lie in the upper-class condition of being physically present at all the society spots of London, but in simultaneously being and not being in those places. This facility of being able to fade in and fade out at the right moments coincides with Rosabel's 'tiredness'. When her reverie resumes, jumping straight to riding in the park next morning and a sequence involving engagement and wedding, it fades out at the point of her wedding night as she becomes 'tired' once more. At one level, her 'tiredness' clearly functions to evade the overtly sexual moments but this is not from reticence or timidity so much as from the unconscious knowledge that any such moment would actually break the magic of the daydream world. But, more fundamentally, what Rosabel is tired of is her own desire being caught up in a wider economy of desire that will never permit it to be satisfied, when it can be satisfied much more intimately by sustaining herself as 'real' in the manner described above.

In this respect, one of Mansfield's achievements in this story, writing only a few years after the original publication of Freud's *The Interpretation of Dreams*, is to anticipate the key Lacanian concept of 'traversing the phantasy'. As Richard Boothby notes:

> 'Traversing the phantasy' [. . .] does not mean that the subject somehow abandons its involvement with fanciful caprices and accommodates itself to a pragmatic 'reality,' but precisely the opposite: the subject is submitted to that effect of the symbolic lack that reveals the limit of everyday reality. To traverse the phantasy in the Lacanian sense is to be more profoundly claimed by the phantasy than ever, in the sense of being brought into an ever more intimate relation with that real core of the phantasy that transcends imaging. (Boothby, qtd in Žižek 2002: 18)

By fully identifying with her fantasy daydream world, Rosabel is continually exposed to the lack of meaning in her everyday life and, therefore, made increasingly aware of the mismatch between her conscious and unconscious identities – an awareness that is the nearest human subjectivity can get to an apprehension of what Žižek would call the Real, which 'is not the hardcore which persists as the Same, but the hard bone of contention which pulverises the sameness into the multitude of appearances' (Žižek 2006: 26). The story demonstrates perfectly how a circle is established in which the more Rosabel apprehends the 'Real', the further she is drawn into her fantasy. However, even this 'real Rosabel' eventually has to get into her coarse, calico nightdress and go to sleep:

> And the night passed. Presently the cold fingers of dawn closed over her uncovered hand; grey light flooded the dull room. Rosabel shivered, drew a little grasping breath, sat up. And because her heritage was that tragic optimism, which is all too often the only inheritance of youth, still half asleep, she smiled, with a little nervous tremor round her mouth. (Mansfield 1981: 519)

This 'tragic optimism' is not a value judgement by Mansfield, but an attempt to portray faithfully Rosabel's kernel of the Real, her essential non-identity, which can be compared with the approach that Ford advocated to himself only three years earlier in his attempt to portray faithfully the London of that time:

> [The author] must not only sniff at the 'suburbs' as a place of small houses and dreary lives; he must remember that in each of these houses dwells a strongly individualised human being with romantic hopes, romantic fears, and at the end, an always tragic death. (Ford 2003: 5)

Ford opens up the wider context of this paradox of 'tragic optimism'. What might always turn out to be tragic at an individual level – as she gets older, Rosabel may not always be able to identify with her fantasy and, thus, sustain the 'real Rosabel' – may also be viewed from his perspective that the possibility of a 'Future' is dependent on the relationship between the fantasy lives of clerks and shop girls, like Rosabel, and the upper-class leisure society: 'whilst there is emulation there is hope' (Ford 2003: 73). Arguably, Ford shows the Londoner like Rosabel, with her fantasy daydream world and related freedom of the city, to be the archetypal figure of modernity. As with the writing of Ford and Wells discussed above, this reinforces why modernist identity should not be understood as some form of active presence in distinction to the passive imitative tendencies of the masses. Not only does 'The Tiredness of Rosabel' anticipate later intermodernist texts by simultaneously celebrating 'the imaginative lives of readers and the interests of the workers themselves' (Bluemel 2004: 133), it achieves this by functioning as a version of pastoral in which Mansfield is able to use the apparently simple life of Rosabel to represent complex consciousness. In this respect, the story can be seen as anticipating the proletarian literature of the 1930s. Furthermore, it also illustrates that the reason why proletarian literature is the answer to the modernist question is because it creates a space outside the bourgeois patriarchal order, in which desires do not necessarily conflict with identity.

These aspects of the story are evident in the opening paragraphs, as Rosabel travels home from work on the bus. It is raining, her feet and the bottom of her skirt are wet and muddy, and she is aware of her individuality merging into the undifferentiated mass of her fellow workers: 'There was a sickening smell of warm humanity—it seemed to be oozing out of everybody in the bus—and everybody had the same expression, sitting so still, staring in front of them' (Mansfield 1981: 513). Yet this is not simply a vision of commuting hell because the merging of smells, bodies and identities is also exciting and sexually charged. Rosabel is drawn inexorably into the mass-produced fantasy being consumed by the girl sitting next to her:

She glanced at the book which the girl read so earnestly, mouthing the words in a way that Rosabel detested, licking her first finger and thumb each time that she turned the page. She could not see very clearly; it was something about a hot, voluptuous night, a band playing, and a girl with lovely, white shoulders. Oh, Heavens! Rosabel stirred suddenly and unfastened the two top buttons of her coat [. . .] (Mansfield 1981: 513–14)

This moment is the precursor of the fantasy which she later traverses, but we are clearly shown that it is a shared moment, generated by the shared culture of mass modernity, and that Rosabel is ultimately allowed to become aware of her real self precisely because she identifies with the masses rather than defining herself against them. Although arguably Mansfield's use of the term 'voluptuous night' is as much a disruption of linguistic norms as 'the discreet door' in 'A Cup of Tea', it is clear here that a normative style is not simply established to enable a modernist eruption: the sudden moment of being, which will become one of the key signifiers of modernist writing, is here inextricably linked with the mundane details of everyday life established through realist description. This is not to imply that the relationship is somehow organic but that it is inextricable in the asymmetric manner ascribed by Žižek to parallax shifts: 'One of the two levels appears to be able to stand on its own, while the other stands for the shift as such [. . .] In other words, [. . .] Two stands for the very move/shift from One to Two' (Žižek 2006: 42).

Modernism and social realism are asymmetrically linked in the same way: modernism is not in fact a separate entity to social realism but the very move/shift from social realism to modernism. Despite this readily recoverable relationship, however, modernism has come to be privileged over social realism as a separate entity and it is for this reason that the term 'intermodernism' is useful. This intermodern shift is rendered visible when Rosabel gets off the bus in Westbourne Grove – a location which is specifically identified by Ford as one of the key London sites of emulation of the upper-class leisure society by the new society of clerks and shop girls: 'In Westbourne Grove the young shop assistant raises his bowler, drawls "How are you, Miss?" for all the world as they do in Rotten Row' (Ford 2003: 85). The whole shift from realism to modernism is represented in Mansfield's transformation of Westbourne Grove into the locus of all possibilities – cultural, sexual and magical:

> Westbourne Grove looked as she had always imagined Venice to look at night, mysterious, dark, even the hansoms were like gondolas dodging up and down, and the lights trailing luridly—tongues of flame licking the wet street—magic fish swimming in the Grand Canal. (Mansfield 1981: 514)

Returning to Trotter's argument that 'modernism' is another name for that invitation to access more remote contexts than the straightforwardly familiar; and to the subsequent question, raised above, of what does it mean if this invitation is being made from Katherine Mansfield to Virginia Woolf: the answer is that 'intermodernism' is yet another, perhaps better, name for that invitation. As suggested at the beginning of this section, the place to look in order to see how this invitation was received is *Mrs Dalloway*. Lee notes how Woolf's thoughts in October 1924, as recorded in her diary, switch immediately from the writing of the last words of the novel – 'For there she was' (Woolf 2000a: 165) – to Mansfield, who had died the previous year: 'Yes, if she'd lived, she'd have written on, & people would have seen that I was the more gifted – that wd. only have become more & more apparent' (qtd in Lee 1997: 400). Placed in context, this is a more gracious statement than it sounds because what it really acknowledges is both Woolf's acceptance of Mansfield's gift of the freedom of the city and her use of it to generate a sustained work of fiction big enough to deal with London as a whole.

This change of scale allows for possibilities of the freedom of the city to be investigated in a much wider context encompassing a much fuller investigation of the social, cultural and political consequences than ever appears in Mansfield. For example, in a passage quoted by Rachel Bowlby in which Mrs Dalloway's daughter, Elizabeth, rides through the centre of London on top of a bus, Rosabel's daydreamy passive freedom is transformed into a fantasy of agency:

> Oh she would like to go a little further. Another penny, was it, to the Strand? Here was another penny, then. She would go up the Strand.
>
> She liked people who were ill. And every profession is open to the women of your generation, said Miss Kilman. So she might be a doctor. She might be a farmer. . . . It was quite different here from Westminster, she thought, getting off at Chancery Lane. It was so serious; it was so busy. In short, she would like to have a profession. She would become a doctor, a farmer, possibly go into Parliament if she found it necessary, all because of the Strand. (Woolf 2000a: 115–16)

Bowlby argues that while 'Elizabeth's imaginative venture could be taken as a positive sign of a woman's progress', the novel as a whole still seems to leave her a sharp choice between participating in masculine power structures 'and what appears as an ignominious succumbing to a "trivial" femininity as the object of male admiration' (Bowlby 1988: 83, 87). However, she goes on to imply that Elizabeth's only route out of her unquestioning internalisation of the binary gender associations of masculine seriousness and feminine triviality, is precisely this bus journey down the Strand, with its opportunity for full identification with the fantasy of becoming professional and, therefore, the possibility of sustaining a real Elizabeth on a permanent basis (see Bowlby 1988: 97–8). This reading, with its promise of arrival at a feminist destination through the combination of fantasy and professional career, is derived only by contrasting Elizabeth's experiences with those of her mother, Clarissa, whose own youthful bus ride is described further on in the novel:

> But she said, sitting on the bus going up Shaftesbury Avenue, she felt herself everywhere; not 'here, here, here'; and she tapped the back of the seat; but everywhere. She waved her hand, going up Shaftesbury Avenue. She was all that. So that to know her, or any one, one must seek out the people who completed them; even the places. Odd affinities she had with people she had never spoken to, some women in the street, some man behind a counter – even trees, or barns. It ended in a transcendental theory which, with her horror of death, allowed her to believe, or say that she believed (for all her scepticism), that since our apparitions, the part of us which appears, are so momentary compared with the other, the unseen part of us, which spreads wide, the unseen might survive, be recovered somehow attached to this person or that, or even haunting certain places, after death. (Woolf 2000a: 129–30)

The idea of the freedom of the city presented here is clearly related to that found in Mansfield but the expression is clearly that of Woolf; indeed, the first part of this passage summarises the essential structure and ideas of the novel as a whole. While the last part resonates with aspects of Woolf's experience, the transcendental aspects suggest Mansfield's interest in the teachings of Gurdjieff. Whichever way this passage is unpacked, it demonstrates how Clarissa embodies both Woolf and Mansfield. As Lee argues, while Woolf clearly shows pity for Mansfield in her October 1924 diary entry, 'she also acknowledges what Katherine has meant to her, as, in the novel she has just finished, the living make sense of their life through their thoughts of the dead' (Lee 1997: 400–1).

In *Mrs Dalloway*, it is Clarissa who makes sense of her life through the death of Septimus Warren Smith: 'She felt somehow very like him – the young man who had killed himself. She felt glad that he had done it; thrown it away while they went on living' (Woolf 2000a: 158). Empson analyses this passage in his essay '*Mrs Dalloway* as a Political Satire' (1932):

> At the end, at the triumph of her party, her assertion of the same order of her tribe, she hears of the suicide of the man who thought of himself as Christ and scapegoat and feels that her sense that she might have done the same is a sort of proof that she is genuine; she feels outside her snobbery because she can understand him; he becomes indeed to her for a moment what it was his madness to think he was to everybody; he is the sacrificial hero and his tragedy reconciles her to the world. (Empson 1988: 451)

Empson wrote this essay during the period when he was writing *Some Versions of Pastoral* and it is clear that he is also analysing *Mrs Dalloway* as pastoral. However, he is not treating it as a version of the 'mock pastoral' he valorises, in which the scapegoat figure effectively serves to satirise the Christian tradition, but as its mirror opposite, the empty allegorical form of pastoral which 'describes the lives of "simple" low people to an audience of refined wealthy people, so as to make them think first "this is true about everyone" and then "this is specially true about us"' (Empson 1995: 159). For Empson, the real irony of the passage in which Peter Walsh mentally celebrates the triumph of civilisation on hearing the bell of an ambulance, which is in fact bearing away the dead body of Septimus, is not a critical irony intended to make us see that Peter is wrong, but actually an ironic accommodation on the part of Woolf and her readership with that civilisation despite their awareness of its faults. Therefore, he concludes sharply that *Mrs Dalloway* is a 'blank statement of conflict' in which Woolf 'shows she can feel on both sides [. . .] and takes that for an achievement, which indeed it is, but not a fertile one' (Empson 1988: 452). What he does not take into account in this otherwise perceptive reading, is the double irony of the novel arising from the fact that both Septimus and Clarissa demonstrate correspondences with Mansfield. Clarissa's gladness at the suicide of Septimus is really a form of identification with, and therefore traversal of, her own fantasy of suicide, which frees her from the tyranny of fixed identity. In this manner, Clarissa is actually functioning in accordance with Empson's own account of how a character fully aware of the arguments of both sides is 'forced into isolation by sheer strength of mind, and so into a philosophy of Independence' (Empson 1995: 171).

In a different essay, 'Virginia Woolf' (1931), Empson criticises Woolf's early stories such as 'Kew Gardens' for using the 'vase of flowers' method:

> things seen in the same mood are described together, and there they are; two lovers and a slug; so you stop [. . .] the range of interest (identifying oneself with all the characters and so forth) in the crudest melodramatic story is much greater than the range of interest (mainly contrast and correspondence) in a vase of flowers. (Empson 1988: 448)

However, as we have seen, Mansfield's stories – there is no shortage of scope for identification in 'A Cup of Tea' or 'The Tiredness of Rosabel' – demonstrate how a vase of flowers can be melodramatic. Likewise, Woolf blends identification with contrast to create an imaginary correspondence between clerks and shop girls on the one hand and her upper-middle-class protagonists on the other. It is this correspondence which enables Peter to sit in front of his hotel and share in a mass moment of being – 'joy of a kind, cheap, tinselly, if you like, but all the same rapture' (Woolf 2000a: 137) – with the crowds of young people passing in the street, released from their shops and offices, and on their way out to enjoy themselves on a summer evening in London. It is also this correspondence which underwrites the possibility of a bus ride down the Strand becoming a transformative experience for Elizabeth, in particular, and for women in general. The novel, as a whole, registers how the emergence of a modern mass society had transformed Britain utterly by the 1920s: a 'shift in the whole pyramidal accumulation which in [Peter's and Clarissa's] youth had seemed immovable' (Woolf 2000a: 137). Therefore, it can be seen that Woolf's achievement is actually fertile by Empson's standards and that *Mrs Dalloway* should be considered a version of pastoral that might fittingly have been discussed in his chapter on proletarian literature. Peter's questions at the end of the novel can be asked on behalf of all its readers: 'What is this terror? what is this ecstasy? he thought to himself. What is it that fills me with extraordinary excitement?' (Woolf 2000a: 165). It is the freedom of the city.

Note

1. 'The Proletarian Writer' is the transcript of a radio discussion between Orwell and Desmond Hawkins, who was the actual speaker of the lines quoted; but as Davison observes in an editorial footnote: 'For broadcasting convenience, parts of the discussion were spoken by a participant whether or not he had generated the ideas initially.' The script would most likely have been adapted from a treatment written by Orwell and therefore the words have here been attributed to him.

Chapter 2

'The Common Life': Women and Men after the General Strike

> Some day men will cultivate their happiness in gardens

> Ours is essentially a tragic age, so we refuse to take it tragically. The cataclysm has happened, we are among the ruins, we start to build up new little habitats, to have new little hopes. It is rather hard work: there is now no smooth road into the future: but we go round, or scramble over the obstacles. We've got to live, no matter how many skies have fallen. (Lawrence 1994: 5)

The opening of *Lady Chatterley's Lover* (1928) encapsulates something of the magnitude of the change to consciousness that happened over the early part of the twentieth century even though many tried to carry on as before. Paul Mason cites this passage in connection to the English aristocracy retreating shattered into its stately homes after 1918 as a comparison for the behaviour of the global financial elite after the catastrophe of 2008, equally determined to carry on as before and ignore the fact that the whole global economic system was now on borrowed time (Mason 2015: 258). The defining feature of such tragic/catastrophic situations is that they cannot be negotiated with respect to the past because the problem is precisely that the past order has collapsed beyond salvage. There needs to be a sense of the future to provide a perspective and this is present in *Lady Chatterley's Lover* in the reconfigured gender and class relations that Lawrence imagines at the end of the novel:

> If the men wore scarlet trousers, as I said, they wouldn't think so much of money: if they could dance or hop and skip, and sing and swagger

and be handsome, they could do with very little cash. And amuse the women themselves, and be amused by the women. (Lawrence 1994: 299)

Both this passage and *Lady Chatterley's Lover* itself have been the subject of a fair amount of amusement over the years, which has tended to undermine the radical nature of Lawrence's utopian imagination and the logic of his argument. It is the possibility of this implicitly classless and not-sexually-repressed future that opens up the prospect at the end of the novel of Lady Constance Chatterley being able to live happily in a mutually consensual relationship with 'her husband's gamekeeper' Oliver Mellors on a small farm. The past is rejected and the novel is orientated to a future, which was subsequently brought several steps nearer following its publication as a paperback at the beginning of the 1960s and Penguin's subsequent successful defence of it from state prosecution under the Obscene Publications Act. The outcome of the trial, in which the prosecuting barrister asked the all-male jury, 'Is it a book that you would even wish your wife or your servants to read?', is rightly seen as a landmark event in British social history; symbolically relegating a constricting British combination of class deference, sexual repression and gender-segregated public life to the past. In terms of public significance and real-world consequence, *Lady Chatterley's Lover* should be considered the most important British novel of the twentieth century.

The context for Lawrence's writing of *Lady Chatterley's Lover* was the General Strike and its continuation in the mining districts such as Eastwood, where Lawrence was born and grew up, and which he visited during this period in September 1926. His account of the visit, 'Return to Bestwood', written before he began writing the first version of *Lady Chatterley* at the end of October, begins with memories and the statement that he remembers his family's Co-op number better than his date of birth, but quickly turns into an account of what has changed. On the one hand, the striking men are doing things as unmanly as picking blackberries to sell and carrying them home in little baskets while respectable women are being taken to court for insulting and obstructing the police: 'They were two women from decent homes. In the past they would have died of shame, at having to go to court. But now, not at all' (Lawrence 1971: 148). Seeing these working-class women, including girls he had played with at school, waving red flags leads Lawrence to reflect on his mother's enthusiasm for progress – in 'getting on' – which was coupled with an absolute belief in 'the ultimate benevolence of all the masters': 'You can have your cake and eat it, while the cake lasts. When the cake comes to an end, you can hand on your indigestion' (Lawrence 1971: 149). His point is that the hypocrisy of late Victorian and Edwardian respectable working-class culture in wanting to have it both ways has broken down into class antagonism and the imminent possibility of a class war. If working-class aspirations had been different – not orientated to property but to freedom – then 'we could, if we would, establish little by little a true democracy in England; we could nationalize the land and industries and means of transport, and make the whole thing work infinitely better than at present' (Lawrence 1971: 156).

At the time, with the miners still on strike and an air of overt class antagonism, it would have been difficult for Lawrence, or most other people, to envisage that less than twenty years later a new political settlement – in the shape of the Labour General Election victory of 1945 and the establishment of the welfare state – would nationalise industries and place collectivist working-class values and culture at the heart of British society. Viewed in retrospect, however, the capitulation of the Strike after nine days did not so much mark the failure of the organised working class in Britain to achieve a Soviet-style revolution as the swan song of British syndicalism and a masculine trade union based politics dating from the 1880s. The miners were the emotional core of the British Labour Movement; they represented an ideal of working manhood and had been the last major union to come round to supporting women's suffrage. The purpose of the Strike had been to prevent a mine owners' lockout designed to lower wage rates, and, after the other unions returned to work, the miners stayed out alone in an ultimately doomed attempt to prevent this outcome. At the time, this looked like the last stand of a culture and this is reflected by Lawrence's comments on how the miners who once seemed so full of the zest of life have become silent. These men, that had gone to the board school with him and with whom he still felt a shared destiny despite the very different conditions of their lives, were now full of despair. It was the 'madness' (Lawrence 1971: 155) of this inner surrender to doom when other possible ways of life still lay open to them that prompted Lawrence to reverse his previous decision to abandon the novel form and write *Lady Chatterley's Lover* as a means of representing a different kind of future destiny for the working class based on freedom.

However, what this prolonged strike did achieve was not only to help respectable working-class women transcend their shame and wave red flags in the street, as Lawrence recorded, but also to make clear the full emergence of women as political players in the British socialist movement; a theme foregrounded in the Labour MP, Ellen Wilkinson's novel about the General Strike and its aftermath, *Clash* (1929):

> As Joan talked to influential women among the miners – the wives of the county councillors, the officials of the Women's Co-operative Guild, women guardians, the committee of the Labour Women's Sections, she was struck by the power these women wielded in the area. The domination of the whole district by the one union had given important positions to simple working women to an extent that she had not met with in other parts. (Wilkinson 2004: 148)

In their excellent recent study, *Writing the 1926 General Strike* (2015), Charles Ferrall and Dougal McNeill argue that the message of the defeat of the Strike, captured in both *Lady Chatterley's Lover* and *Clash*, was the need to fuse political and sexual desire into 'a new politicised and gendered imagination for struggles to come' (Ferrall and McNeill 2015: 145). As discussed further below in this chapter, the response to this need can be traced across the working-class fiction of this period despite the fact that much of this work has been traditionally seen as dealing mainly with masculine concerns. In this respect, Lawrence can be seen as fully contributing to the politics of proletarian literature, which would develop in the 1930s, and the intense debates concerning it. Even if his novel could not be read because of its suppression by the state, it could be read about in, for example, the pages of the *Sunday Worker*. As Croft details, the paper's arts page was run by Ralph Fox and T. A. Jackson and provided broad cultural coverage: 'readers of the *Sunday Worker* reported that they cut out the arts page to keep, "an education in itself", "because it helped me and my mates to understand good books which otherwise would have remained closed to me"' (Croft 1990: 37). On 3 March 1929, an article by 'Leveller' complained about the banning of *Lady Chatterley's Lover* and argued for its importance as a

> declaration of faith by one English novelist who has not completely sold himself to the commercialism of British capitalism . . . we can admire the honesty of his creative effort, and the frankness of his

personal confession, neither of which could come from a middle-class writer. ('Leveller', qtd in Croft 1990: 59)

It is true that the article did draw criticism but this was part of a long-running sectarian attack on the arts page from adherents of the narrow conception of proletarian literature. However, even though the *Sunday Worker* closed before the end of the year following the adoption of the 'Class Against Class' policy by the Comintern and the return of Proletcult-style dominance until 1934, Lawrence still remained the main influence on young working-class writers from the mining areas: 'there was no readily available, familiar, *native, national* working-class literary tradition to which they could see themselves belonging. All they had was D. H. Lawrence' (Croft 1990: 67; original emphasis). Indeed, in Walter Brierley's *Sandwichman* (1937), Arthur Gardner can identify the countryside his bus passes through by the Lawrence novels it features in and he almost seems to be in one of them himself:

> He glanced down the street where Lawrence was born; a shabby street with flat-face houses and a grimy chapel. All the adult students in his group at Trentingham were crazy over Lawrence. Nancy [Gardner's girlfriend] was like some of the women in his books – well, she had been lately – sex-driven out of all balance. (Brierley 1990: 48–9)

Lawrence's own work still drew on the traditions of Edwardian pastoral; indeed, *Lady Chatterley's Lover* with its woodland scenes is quite explicitly pastoral.

Before analysing *Lady Chatterley's Lover* and its proletarian successors, it is worth briefly summarising the post-Strike writing of Galsworthy and Wells. Galsworthy describes the General Strike in the opening chapters of *Swan Song* (1928), the sixth novel of the *Forsyte Saga* sequence. In their essay 'Writers and the General Strike' (1976), Adrian Mellor, Chris Pawling and Colin Sparks summarise the activities of Soames's daughter and her husband:

> Thus, in *Swan Song*, Soames's son-in-law, Michael, argues that the strikers should be given 'every possible excuse to wink the other eye', whilst his wife, Fleur, does her bit by taking time off from running a canteen for blacklegs in order to undermine the pickets 'with surreptitious coffee dashed with rum, at odd hours of their wearisome vigils'. (Mellor et al. 1976: 342)

Somewhat humourlessly, they conclude that Galsworthy is an unashamedly ideological advocate of national consensus. Of the following passage, in which Soames witnesses the arrival of tanks along the embankment, they allow only that it reflects his creator's unease at the use of force by Churchill:

> 'That'll astonish their weak nerves!' thought Soames, as the tank crawled, grunching, out of sight. He could hear another coming; but with a sudden feeling that it would be too much of a good thing, he turned on his heel. A sort of extravagance about them, when he remembered the blank-looking crowd around his car that afternoon, not a weapon among the lot, nor even a revolutionary look in their eyes!
>
> 'No *body* in the strike!' These great crawling monsters! Were the Government trying to pretend that there was? Playing the strong man! Something in Soames revolted slightly. Hang it! This was England, not Russia, or Italy! They might be right, but he didn't like it! Too – too military! (Galsworthy 2001: 585)

However, there is more than unease with specific individuals and excessive force here. This passage represents an explicit rejection of the militarised European totalitarianism that had developed since the end of the war and was to expand over the subsequent decade. The message is anti-fascist and anticipates the broad Popular-Front sentiments that eventually came to dominate British public opinion and forced a reluctant National Government to stand up to Hitler. Viewed from this perspective, Fleur's running of a canteen during the General Strike and serving working-class strikers as well as middle-class volunteers is the forerunner of the kind of role she might have played on the home front of the Second World War.

Wells wrote directly about the General Strike in *Meanwhile* (1927) and, like Lawrence, relates it to questions of sexuality and gender. The novel is predicated on the idea that a utopian world will be achieved in the future in which all troublesome issues of property and sexual relations will be solved but 'meanwhile' we have to deal practically with issues such as the Strike. So while the philandering coal-owner Philip Rylance turns against his own class and the prophet-like philosopher Sempack's sympathies are also with the miners, nevertheless we are told:

> There is no solution in all that strife and passion. It is just a dog-fight. The minds of people have to be adjusted to new ideas before there is an end to this sweating of men in the darkness. People have to realise

that winning coal is a public service, like the high road and the post office. A service that has to be paid for and taken care of [. . .] Some day it will be clear to everyone, as it is clear to any properly informed person now, that if the state paid all the costs of exploiting coal in the country and handed the stuff out at prices like – say ten shillings a ton, the stimulation of every sort of production would be so great [. . .] as to yield a profit, a quite big profit, to the whole community. (Wells 1962: 33)

The novel is characterised by 'inept characterization and [a] didactic tone' (Mellor et al. 1976: 344) and the fundamental contradiction that 'the Strike is meant to be happening "meanwhile" the future is being prepared, but the novel is a meanwhile to class conflict, the very social struggle' that will bring about that future (Ferrall and McNeill 2015: 47–8).

Nevertheless, as with Galsworthy's anticipation of an anti-fascist wartime coalition and the cross-class spirit of the Home Front, Wells's novel predicts a cross-class acceptance of the nationalisation of coal not as an aim in itself but as an inevitable stepping stone of progress that is not really worth expending passion upon. In this manner, the trajectory from the defeat of the General Strike to the foundation of the welfare state is more directly demonstrated in the work of the liberal – understood in the widest sense 'as an affiliation to the individual over the collective' (Ferrall and McNeill 2015: 43) – Edwardians, Wells and Galsworthy, than either that of the (late) modernists Lawrence and Woolf or that of proletarian writers such as Greenwood, Brierley, Heslop or Wilkinson. Both of these latter groups of writers were concerned with a much more fundamental reimagination of the symbolic order.

As Ferrall and McNeill show, Woolf wrote most of the 'Time Passes' section of *To the Lighthouse* (1927) during the nine days of the Strike, and its traces can be detected in these pages and the various revisions of the novel, particularly with respect to the character of Charles Tansley: 'the problem of class is "solved" through [. . .] its transformation into purely interpersonal relation' (Ferrall and McNeill 2015: 72). However, the 'interpersonal' is also political and it is possible to see this politics emerging in *A Room of One's Own*, if not as a direct consequence of the Strike then certainly as an echo of Wilkinson's understanding of a change in gender relations in both the social and political spheres resulting from it; one example of which was the equalisation of the age at which men and women could vote in 1928. Like Lawrence and, to a certain extent, Wells, Woolf projects a future in which gender relations are transformed. She imagines a contemporary novel, *Life's Adventure*, by the fictitious Mary Carmichael, detailing how Chloe liked Olivia and they share a laboratory together. Woolf describes the faults of this novel but also suggests that given the context of women's lives in the 1920s, Mary Carmichael 'did not do so badly': 'Give her another hundred years [. . .] give her a room of her own and five hundred a year, let her speak her mind and leave out half that she now puts in, and she will write a better book' (Woolf 2000b: 85). This foreshadows the conclusion of the essay as a whole, that women's writing – as embodied in the idea of a female equivalent to Shakespeare, who would be an author of a women's writing that would by implication be other to the symbolic order – will become possible, providing 'we live another century or so – I am talking of the common life which is the real life and not of the little separate lives which we live as individuals' (Woolf 2000b: 102).

'But don't you care about the future?': *Lady Chatterley's Lover*

As noted above, Lawrence began writing the novel in October 1926 and finished the first draft, which would subsequently be published as *The First Lady Chatterley* (1944), just before the end of November at around the same time as the defeat of the Strike. As Ferrall and McNeill observe, Lawrence would surely have known the outcome of the Strike before he began the second draft, subsequently published as *John Thomas and Lady Jane* (1954), in early December. The third and final version, however, was only begun in November 1927 and finished in the following January (see Ellis 1998: 388). *The First Lady Chatterley* has generally been seen as the most overtly political version not least because Parkin (as the gamekeeper is named in the first two versions) leaves the Chatterleys' estate, Wragby, to work in a Sheffield steel mill and joins the Communist Party. For a long time, the conventional critical response to the trajectory of the drafts of *Lady Chatterley's Lover* was to argue that Lawrence's visit to his native Eastwood during the Strike, as recorded in 'Return to Bestwood', triggered a 'momentary' return on his part to the idea of 'working-class values' as a basis for positive social change, which subsequently collapsed pessimistically into lamentation over the 'dehumanization of the industrial masses' and a retreat into an 'individualistic sexual politics' (Mellor et al. 1976: 347–8).

Ferrall and McNeill have exhaustively reviewed this critical tendency of seeing the progressive revisions of the novel as cumulatively resulting in, according to various critics, a 'declassing', a 'de-proletarianizing' and a 'retreat from history' (Ferrall and McNeill 2015: 84). They provide a very clear illustration of how such a critical orthodoxy is reinforced by the constant repetition of a similar analysis. While such processes of the reproduction of the dominant ideological viewpoint are systemic in the history of institutional literary criticism, they are not normally quite as obvious as they are with respect to *Lady Chatterley's Lover*. On the one hand, Lawrence is a major canonical writer and although his critical value has declined over recent decades, Cambridge University Press are still hugely invested in publishing his complete works edition and biographical and critical studies. On the other hand, *Lady Chatterley's Lover* still contains more overt class politics and antagonism than most canonical English literature. The normal solution applied to the question of what to do with books containing class politics and antagonism is to isolate them in a sub-canon or -category such as 'working-class writing' where they can be safely quarantined from (other) literature. However, because the novel is by Lawrence and because it is also explicitly about gender and sex, it is not so easily contained by categorisation; nor can it be so easily dismissed as bad as Mitchison's similarly intersectional *We Have Been Warned*. Therefore, it is easier to insist, across repeated iterations, that because the class politics of *Lady Chatterley's Lover* are superficially less overt than those of *The First Lady Chatterley* that there is a progressive reduction of class politics in favour of pastoral 'romance' across the three drafts. Against this orthodoxy, Ferrall and McNeill's dissenting opinion is that the successive revisions intensify both the sex and the politics so that the simultaneous effect is 'politics not just becoming more sexualised but sex also more politicised' (Ferrall and McNeill 2015: 84).

They discuss a number of ways in which the class politics become more marked across the drafts. For example, the scene in which Clifford Chatterley's wheelchair gets stuck in the woods and the gamekeeper has to rescue him begins with a discussion between Connie and Clifford about a possible strike in which '[a]s the versions progress, [. . .] Connie increasingly challenges her husband's political views' (Ferrall and McNeill 2015: 97). In *The First Lady Chatterley*,

Connie – she is actually called Constance in the first two versions of the novel but Connie is here used throughout for clarity – echoes Lawrence's concern in 'Return to Bestwood' when she asks Clifford: 'Do you think there *must* be a war between the classes?' (Lawrence 1973a: 103). He replies in the negative but insists that 'the few must govern the many' and goes on to explain that if you pulled down Wragby, then you would also have pulled down decency, dignity and godliness: 'Do you think any miner's dwelling would have had a piano, for example – the old example – if Wragby hadn't helped to bring pianos into being three hundred years ago?' (Lawrence 1973a: 104). Connie realises that she agrees with this analysis: 'Suddenly she knew *really* why she didn't want to bear children in a miner's dwelling or bring them up in a gamekeeper's cottage' (Lawrence 1973a: 104). In *Lady Chatterley's Lover*, the corresponding scene is no longer haunted by the fear of a coming class war but nonetheless demonstrates a much more fundamental class antagonism:

> 'No wonder the men hate you,' she said.
> 'They don't!' he replied. 'And don't fall into error: in your sense of the word, they are *not* men. They are animals you don't understand and never could. Don't thrust your illusions on other people. The masses were always the same, and will always be the same. Nero's slaves were extremely little different from our colliers [. . .]' (Lawrence 1994: 182)

Not only does Connie not find herself agreeing with her husband as she does in *The First Lady Chatterley* but she subsequently vehemently disassociates herself from such class politics: 'Why my father is ten times the human being you are: you *gentleman*!' (Lawrence 1994: 194). As Ferrall and McNeill note, while most critics find Clifford to become nastier across the versions, they do not generally notice how this nastiness 'is increasingly a function of his class' (Ferrall and McNeill 2015: 98), or that Connie's response is increasingly a rejection of that class.

As mentioned above, *The First Lady Chatterley* was written while the miners were still on strike; once the Strike was defeated then the possibility of a war between the classes, which concerned Lawrence so much, receded and consequently ceased to be a significant component of the later drafts. In 'Return to Bestwood', Lawrence related this fear to the contradictions of respectable working-class life as embodied by his mother's simultaneous expression of desire to 'get on' and gratitude to the upper classes. This 'structure of feeling' is present in *The First Lady Chatterley*, both in minor details, such as Clifford's assertion that pianos illustrate how culture originates in the upper class and then finds its way out to the masses, and in the most significant scene to be deleted from the final version: Connie's tea with the Tewsons, the working-class family that Parkin is staying with in Sheffield. The tea, itself, in which the best white cloth and crockery are laden with 'tinned salmon and boiled ham, tinned peaches and tinned strawberries, though it was fruit season: brown bread and butter, and white, and currant loaf – besides various home-made cakes and pastries' (Lawrence 1973a: 190) signifies that the Tewsons are 'decent working-class people' (Lawrence 1973a: 192). In an echo of the earlier scene with Clifford in the woods, Bill Tewson asks Connie if she thinks there is much difference between her sort of people and his. Although she answers in the negative, she realises as the conversation continues that Tewson not only thinks that there is a difference but that he wants it confirmed because it is in some way part of his respectable working-class belief set. Tewson wants to believe that 'masters' like Clifford will willingly give up some of their coal royalties in order partially to even up things with the men because it is the decent, respectable thing to do. At the same time, Tewson is also in the process of questioning his own beliefs because of his interaction with socialists and communists at work in the Steel Mill, and their claim that the 'masters' have no feeling for anybody. Eventually, Parkin can stand this no longer:

> 'Pff! [. . .] Hold they face! Even up a bit! – Why, they'd rather be hung an' drawn an' quartered rather then even up a bit [. . .] They don't think as we're the same as they are. They don't think as we're the same flesh an' blood. – An' they're right, They're nobbut sort of fishes, an' what they've laid hold on they'll keep, if you tear 'em to bits to get it from 'em.' (Lawrence 1973a: 197)

Connie sits through this diatribe in irritation and depression: 'This kind of hatred got on her nerves' (Lawrence 1973a: 197). Here, Connie's point of view and the narration coalesce and we can be sure that this is Lawrence rejecting such class hatred because of his fear of a class war. Yet at the same time, Parkin is only voicing Lawrence's own understanding of the logical consequences of the breakdown of the respectable working-class structure of feeling due to its inherent contradictions. Between them, the two main characters provide a means of dramatising the concerns expressed in 'Return to Bestwood'. However, the consequence of the defeat of the Strike in the real world is not to diminish the class politics of the succeeding drafts of the novel but to liberate them from Lawrence's fear of violent conflict. Therefore, by *Lady Chatterley's Lover*, Connie is no longer put off by hate for her husband's class-based actions but actually shares it, as evidenced by the passage quoted above.

The trajectory through the drafts is therefore one of Parkin/Mellors and Connie coming together politically in opposition to Clifford and the class structure he represents. This progression is supported by the changes in the text, such as the name change from Constance to Connie and the diminution of the ironic distance that Connie maintains around herself throughout *The First Lady Chatterley*. This latter can be seen in the alterations to the depiction of the tea with the Tewsons in *John Thomas and Lady Jane*. Here, Connie interacts much more directly with the family and their children and as a consequence the scene is not so obviously directed to the purpose of a symbolic examination of respectable working-class culture itself. In *The First Lady Chatterley*, Connie reacts to Tewson's tirade concerning how she is obviously a bit more 'free' in her attitudes than Clifford because she is the daughter of an artist with amused detachment that they take 'her visit for a sort of bohemian curiosity' (Lawrence 1973a: 192). In *John Thomas and Lady Jane*, without the distance and detachment, she feels as though 'she was being put on a very precise shelf of class-distinction, a little lower than Clifford' (Lawrence 1973b: 362). The fact that she takes things more personally and even mentally winces at the way Mrs Tewson says 'Money' is indicative that Lawrence has rewritten the scene as a realistic account of what such an encounter might actually be like if the upper-class protagonist was genuinely committed to interaction with the working-class family. In keeping with the realignment between Connie and Parkin, in this version it is Tewson who is insistent on the incompatibility of the classes due to the masters only caring for their own mind. Parkin expresses none of the hatred of the previous version and instead asserts that there are only two types of people in the world: 'them as 'as got money, an' them as is after it' (Lawrence 1973b: 365). When Tewson jokes that both he and Parkin belong to the second category, Parkin demurs that all he wants is enough to feed and keep himself.

Taken alone and even more so in contrast to *The First Lady Chatterley*, this might seem as a contemptuous rejection of the legitimacy of the class struggle, but it is still in full accordance with the overall argument of 'Return to Bestwood', in which Lawrence comments of the struggle over property:

> I know I want to own a few things: my personal things. But I also know I want to own no more than those. I don't want to own a house, nor land, nor a motor-car, nor shares in anything. I don't want a fortune – not even an assured income. (Lawrence 1971: 155)

What has happened between drafts is that rather than the two main characters expressing the two sides of Lawrence's thinking, they are now united against hatred and for a utopian vision of freedom in the future.

It is only through this possible future that the wider crisis which the novel locates in society can be resolved, but this future is only convincingly possible if we can genuinely imagine Connie and Parkin/Mellors being able to live together. This is difficult in *The First Lady Chatterley* because Lawrence's need to work through his thinking on respectable working-class society involves him allocating his own ironical scepticism to Connie and the trenchant class-antipathy to Parkin. While the ending is optimistic, it depends on Connie aligning herself with working-class people and a working-class politics through the kind of ironic accommodation that Lawrence is trying to problematise as the source of what is wrong with modernity because it amounts to refusing to take the crisis of the age seriously. In *John Thomas and Lady Jane*, Lawrence solves this problem of the convincingness of Connie's and Parkin's future together by allowing them to share a rejection of hatred which potentially aligns them both with the utopian vision of a world without property relations. However, in this version with no prospect of them living in a working-class community, it is not clear how they will live together and the closing passages of the book feature them in a clinch in a field and having an awkward encounter with another gamekeeper. Furthermore, given that Parkin is now no longer required to be aligned with a working-class militancy in order to work through the themes of the novel, there is no real purpose served by him going to Sheffield. Rather unsurprisingly, he finds the experience unhappy and decides to leave and find farm work. Therefore, in the final version of *Lady*

Chatterley's Lover, the Sheffield scenes are simply omitted because they are of no use in showing the possibility of Mellors and Connie being able to live together. The net effect is that there is less direct representation of working-class life in the final version of the novel but this can be seen as a move from describing the world, to an exploration of the possibility of changing it.

Returning to the different versions of the scene in which Clifford's wheelchair gets stuck in the woods, it is possible to see the kind of changes that Lawrence envisions happening in the world from the different accounts of how the chair is pushed up the hill. In *The First Lady Chatterley*, Parkin on his own has to push Clifford 'slowly up the incline' (Lawrence 1973a: 113); while in *John Thomas and Lady Jane*, Connie insists on helping him push in 'a hard voice, determined and dangerous' and as their hands brush against each other, she thinks 'I'm going to sleep with him tonight!' (Lawrence 1973b: 218). In *Lady Chatterley's Lover*, the fleeting moment of ease between the two men when they discuss the mechanical aspects of the chair – what Connie thinks of as the 'freemasonry of men' in regard to machinery (Lawrence 1973a: 111, 1973b: 214) – which happens in both earlier versions is omitted and when Connie helps Mellors push, they deliberately lock their hands together:

> Shoving with his left hand, he laid his right on her round white wrist, softly enfolding her wrist, with caress. And the flamy sort of strength went down his back and his loins, reviving him. And she, panting, bent suddenly and kissed his hand. Meanwhile the back of Clifford's head was held sleek and motionless, just in front of them. (Lawrence 1994: 192)

This image of the interlinked couple pushing Clifford, who will shortly afterwards be berated by Connie for being a gentleman rather than a human being, is on one level symbolic of the subjugation of workers and women under patriarchal capitalism. On another level, Clifford's helplessness in the woods suggests that they may safely be considered a space outside the patriarchal order, in which Mellors and Connie can meet freely to construct a different mode of life.

The woods are not just presented as a pastoral idyll but also as an enchanted space right from the beginning of the novel:

it was all like a dream: or rather, it was like the simulacrum of reality. The oak-leaves to her were like the oak-leaves seen ruffling in a mirror, she herself was a figure somebody had read about, picking primroses that were only shadows, or memories, or words. (Lawrence 1994: 18)

When Connie looks at herself naked in her mirror – in a scene that we will see repeated in texts by Gibbon and Sommerfield – after having seen Mellors bathing behind his cottage, she finds her body meaningless, dull and opaque. Trapped in the overtly patriarchal world of Clifford and his male friends, who she has to listen to talking while she sits sewing in the evenings at Wragby, she is constrained in the symbolic order and cut off from the landscape of the imaginary that surrounds her and in which she might find herself beyond patriarchal binary thought in the kind of post-scarcity emotional economy prefigured in aspects of Mitchison's *We Have Been Warned*. In this manner, *Lady Chatterley's Lover* starts like a fairy tale or a fantasy and it can also be read according to John Clute's schema of the four stages of fantasy: wrongness, thinning, recognition, return (see Clute 2011: 26, 114–16). The opening paragraph of the novel, quoted at the beginning of this chapter, states that the age is caught in crisis and this 'wrongness' is felt in the 'thinning' of life; not just in Connie's experience of the sensations of meaninglessness and of existing in only a simulacrum of reality but also in the novel's critique of the emptiness of modern life for the masses and Mellors's despair at the common people's confusion of spending with living.

The majority of the novel, though, is concerned with 'recognition': the discovery of one's true self and a return to meaning. Connie and Mellors recognise themselves as the reflection of each other, as anticipated by that scene where Connie goes from seeing his nakedness to looking at her own, and then repeated on the occasions when they look upon each other naked. This recognition operates on a number of levels. First, it is implicitly intersectional in that the equivalence between them is that as a working-class man and a woman neither can fully participate in the symbolic order. Because of his own transposition from the working class to literary society, Lawrence was aware of this shared outsider status and he was capable of demonstrating this awareness very succinctly, as in the passage from *The First Lady Chatterley* discussing how Connie's sister Hilda, with an MP husband, had conquered all of the political world apart from the aristocratic men with permanent civil service positions who actually ran everything: 'They had made her *know* she was plebeian' (Lawrence 1973a: 135). Second, the relationship between Connie and Mellors is intersubjective; neither constructs their identity at the expense of the other. Third, there is an autobiografictional equivalence in that both are versions of Lawrence himself, which leads to moments where Connie's free indirect discourse blurs with narrative comments expressing viewpoints indistinguishable from that of Mellors, such as in the car journey through the mining districts. Fourth, the novel operates as a version of Empsonian pastoral but one which is balanced in the respect that both are the more complex person in different senses and therefore both are pushed into independence. All of these forms of recognition are visible in the scenes in which Connie attempts to speak dialect:

> 'An' slaip wi' me,' he said, 'it needs that. When sholt come?'
> 'When sholl I?' she said.
> 'Nay,' he said, 'tha canna do't. – When sholt come then?'
> ''Appen Sunday,' she said.
> ''Appen a' Sunday! Ay!'
> 'Ay!' she said.
> He laughed at her quickly.
> 'Nay, tha canna,' he protested.
> 'Why canna I?' she said.
> He laughed. Her attempts at the dialogue were so ludicrous somehow. (Lawrence 1994: 177)

Mellors's capacity to switch from standard English to dialect marks him out throughout the novel as the possessor of an Empsonian double attitude and Connie's attempts to do the same represent the point at which she comes fully to share this double attitude. This is not a passive act on Connie's part. Mellors's laughter is partly a way for him to deal with her penetration of his selfhood. Equally, a similar but reverse dynamic operates in those scenes in which Mellors uses four-letter words: '"An' if tha shits an' if tha pisses, I'm glad. I don't want a woman as couldna shit nor piss." Connie could not help a sudden snort of astonished laughter' (Lawrence 1994: 223). As Tony Pinkney observes: 'This snort of laughter is the novel's mockery of its own mythic pretensions, of its claim to have found the utopian language of immediacy' (Pinkney 1990: 146). By such devices, *Lady Chatterley's Lover* does not bring in the absolute too prematurely. It is a novel written in the knowledge that 'there's a bad time coming'

(Lawrence 1994: 300) but in the belief that living in a mutual relationship between two people open to each other holds open the possibility of a transfigured future.

The miners chaff them as do women's work

Lady Chatterley's Lover serves as a useful point of comparison with another novel dealing with gender relations in a mining area, explicitly concerned with the General Strike and its aftermath: Ellen Wilkinson's *Clash*. While upper-class Connie chooses the working-class gamekeeper Mellors over her modern writer husband, Clifford, Wilkinson's working-class protagonist, Joan, chooses the socialist movement over modern, Bloomsbury writer, Anthony Dacre. While *Clash* is more consciously proletarian, *Lady Chatterley's Lover*, with its woodland settings, is more consciously pastoral; but in both cases because the principal protagonist is a woman who – in accordance with Empson's formula of proletarian literature as pastoral – is learning by 'imagining the feelings' of a man, the net effect is that she gains a traditionally masculine agency without having to abandon her womanhood. It is not so obvious to see how this would work in reverse. Male involvement as equal partners alongside women in the political struggle, as implicitly advocated by *Clash*, is only a temporary solution deferring the question of what a liberated masculinity would actually be like to some as yet unspecified future. This question of what the role of men should be, given the change in women's status and the eclipse of the miners as the role models for working-class masculinity, is a constant subtext of 1930s proletarian writing.

Clash anticipates the complex interweaving of class and gender across different social milieux that would mark much political fiction of the 1930s. The extent to which it describes a newly emerged social context becomes clear when it is compared with Ethel Carnie Holdsworth's *This Slavery*, which was first published in serial form between 1923 and 1924 but is set a few years before the First World War. While both novels combine romance with class politics in order to pursue an intersectional politics – *This Slavery* is equally concerned with both economic and sexual slavery – the options open to their female protagonists are radically different. Carnie Holdsworth's Hester and Rachael Martin, cotton mill workers out of work due to a factory fire, choose different paths leading to the former prostituting herself in a loveless marriage while the latter becomes a socialist activist and orator who is imprisoned for incitement. The politics of *This Slavery* are sophisticated – Rachel eschews respectability, relates the social construction of gender to property relations and imagines a world in which people only have to work three hours a day – but the novel's melodramatic ending in which Hester dies in order to avert bloodshed between striking workers and the militia is indicative of the fact that there is no prospect of a satisfactory resolution for the sisters other than to hope for the day when '"This Slavery" will pass' (Carnie Holdsworth 2011: 250). In contrast, Wilkinson's Joan Craig, a trade union official, is the beneficiary of a society in which women have the right to vote and the organised working class have the realistic possibility of gaining political power by electing a Labour government. She is represented as a person with the agency to act on her own desires and, by the end of the novel, is allowed to choose between her two upper-class suitors and continue her career without any melodramatic consequences. Not only is Joan a sought-after political speaker but she is able to initiate and organise a Women's Relief Distribution Committee in a mining area, which functions as a public sphere for the discussion of socialist and feminist ideas including birth control. The productiveness of this organisational work is repeatedly contrasted with the pointlessness of the miners continuing to strike in a situation where 'there is no hope of winning' (Wilkinson 2004: 145). The prevailing tone of the novel is therefore one of optimism for a future in which things are done differently.

One of the members of Joan's Relief Committee in *Clash* cheerfully answers the question of how she can possibly fit in all this extra work on top of running a house and family by pointing out that because her husband is on strike 'he can turn the mangle and wash the floors. So long as I don't ask him to do anything the neighbours can see him doing, like windows or steps, he's very handy. The miners chaff them as do women's work' (Wilkinson 2004: 149). Following the financial crash of 1929 and the subsequent depression, the rise of mass unemployment exacerbated this kind of gender anxiety as it left men at home with time on their hands. Jack Cook, the unemployed miner protagonist of *Means-Test Man*, stretches out gardening tasks to keep himself from idleness but also helps round the house. While completing the weekly chore of 'blackleading' the fireplace he wonders what would happen if his male neighbours saw him engaged in such domestic labours:

To the miners he would have become a woman, working in the home, providing for it with money which came from a pool into which all the bread-winners in the land threw a determined, compulsory amount. But he had become so accustomed to doing this, black-leading, scrubbing, bed-making and bread-baking at times, tidying round, that he could not imagine himself doing any other work; his wife too, left things to him now quite naturally. (Brierley 2011: 23)

Jane Cook might accept Jack's housework naturally but this does not preclude her issuing commands or from checking that he has completed tasks satisfactorily. Under the stress of the impending monthly visit of the means-test man, who will demand to go through all their personal details, the relationship of the Cooks frequently reaches a Lawrencian intensity. From Jack's perspective, Jane's concerns for 'money, nice clothes, variety in food, opportunity for pleasure' are depressingly material: 'the woman was strong in her, it pained her to be compelled to lag behind her kind [. . .] But where he was touched was far, far deeper, in the very springs of life' (Brierley 2011: 161–2). However, the text does not necessarily endorse his viewpoint, as it also shows Jane's resistance. In an earlier argument, Jane sees the 'strength and power' in Jack's gaze:

the long, long fact of the inferiority of woman. Through him could come pain to her, physical and mental, he could beat or despise her if she stayed with him, there was only horror waiting if she went into the world and left him. (Brierley 2011: 107)

The tension of this moment is still with them when they go to bed, lying beside each other not speaking, but it is Jane who feels triumphant when he falls asleep first: 'She had outstayed him for all his secret strength' (Brierley 2011: 126).

The subject of the novel, therefore, is only ostensibly the indignity of being unemployed and subjected to means testing; it is far more profoundly concerned with charting an ongoing shift in gender relations that is highlighted by this context and the intense subjective focus of Brierley's writing. As Carole Snee notes, the fact that '[Jack] and his wife are forced by external factors to modify their relationship, and to break with the separation of conjugal roles which traditionally operates within their own community' demystifies the way in which 'certain social relations [. . .] institutionalise sexual divisions' (Snee 1979: 179). However, the novel does not just blame these relations on capitalism and class division but also on masculine identity. The admission that Jack 'sometimes vowed religiously that the day he got a safe job he'd give her the biggest hiding any woman ever had, just to show her who was really who' (Brierley 2011: 205) reveals how the traditional division of labour between men and women had underpinned a hierarchical relationship that was enforced through violence. However, despite moments of hatred, the overall logic of the novel, which also includes Jack's pleasure in sharing the caring for his schoolboy son, suggests that a rebalancing of the Cooks' marriage is taking place. Life will not simply revert to its former course when work is restored but will become something different as foreshadowed by the way Jane smiles wanly and meets her husband's gaze after confirming to their son that she will come on a Sunday picnic with them in her new homemade dress: 'The child dropped on the rug and turned head over heels, while the faces of his parents moved into greater seriousness' (Brierley 2011: 282).

In contrast to Jack Cook slowly moving away from the learnt behaviour of the working-class man, Harry Hardcastle in *Love on the Dole* comes to the realisation that he does not want to become one in the first place: 'Try as he would he could not bring himself to think himself a man. Did he lack some masculine quality which others possessed?' (Greenwood 1969: 75). Harry's failed attempts to become a man function in the manner of Empson's description of the simple person in pastoral becoming 'a clumsy fool who yet has better "sense" than his betters, and can say things more fundamentally true' (Empson 1995: 18). Harry eventually finds peace with himself not, as he had once dreamed, through operating a lathe but as a caring house husband 'making up the fire' and 'putting fresh newspaper on the table' while waiting for his pregnant wife, Helen, to come home: 'Ah ne'er thought Ah'd be one of them fellers whose wives went out t' work' (Greenwood 1969: 230). In a short but telling scene, he becomes very embarrassed when picking up his wife's wages after she has gone into labour; the message that gender relations are changing is made clear to the reader. Significantly, however, this novel which reached a wider audience than any other work of proletarian literature through numerous reprints, a highly successful stage adaptation and then a film version, did not just promote companionate marriages but a more liberated form of female agency in the shape of Harry's sister, Sally. After her preferred partner, the Marxist Larry Meath dies from injuries sustained on a political demonstration, Sally chooses to become the kept woman of local bookmaker, Sam Grundy. This is not, as implied by the film version, a desperate measure intended to demonstrate how pitiful the plight of the unemployed was at the time; Sally is no fallen angel. Rather she embodies a powerful rejection of traditional working-class values:

> 'It's sick Ah am o' codgin owld clothes t' mek'em luk summat like. An' sick Ah am o' workin' week after week an' seein' nowt for it. Ah'm sick o' never havin' nowt but what'a bin in pawnshop [. . .] Yaaa, who cares what folk say? There's none Ah know as wouldn't swap places wi' me if they'd chance. Y'd have me wed, wouldn't y'? Then tell me where's feller around here as can afford it? Them as is workin' ain't able t' keep themselves, ne'er heed a wife. Luk at y'self . . . An luk at our Harry. On workhouse relief an' ain't even got a bed as he can call his own. Ah'd be fit t' call y' daughter if Ah was like that, an' a tribe o' kids like Mrs Cranford's at me skirts. [. . .] Well, can y' get our Harry a job? *I* can an' Ah'm not respectable.' (Greenwood 1969: 246)

Although this is a revolt against the values of her own community, Sally is not entirely isolated. The supports she gets – as indeed is also true of Harry and Helen – comes from a circle of Dickensian-sounding older women – Mrs Bull, Mrs Doorbell, Mrs Nattle – who operate their little economic side lines of organising trips to the pawnshop for their more respectable neighbours and selling spirits illegally. As Haywood comments, 'so from the outset the novel challenges the dominant masculine ideology that positions women in the role of submissively servicing men's needs' (Haywood 1997: 51). *Love on the Dole* certainly privileges such forms of resistance over organised class politics but it does not present the clash between these two gendered spheres as a conflict as is done implicitly in *Means-Test Man* or explicitly in Gibbon's *Grey Granite*, as discussed in the next chapter. Instead, Harry's detachment from this masculine ideology is played largely for good-humoured laughs. More generally, the combination of romance, melodrama and Dickensian humour in the novel makes it somewhat atypical for the proletarian literature of the time but probably helps explain its immense popularity. However, in other respects, such as its representation of the daily cycle of proletarian experience and its presentation of both male and female viewpoint protagonists, *Love on the Dole* is typical of proletarian literature, in the broad sense of that term which became established in the 1930s as a consequence of the defeat of the General Strike.

In this context, 'the task for a politically engaged narrative [was] to programme working-class readers primed for class action [through the] "education of desire"' but, on the other hand, the defeat of the Strike complicated 'the project of educating desire in ways that play[ed] out [...] through an association of political action and sexuality' (Ferrall and McNeill 2015: 144). Ferrall and McNeill cite Wilkinson as the obvious example of a writer who successfully fused political and sexual desire into 'a new politicised and gendered imagination for struggles to come' (Ferrall and McNeill 2015: 145). However, the work of Harold Heslop, another miner writer, takes the contrasting stance of situating the questions of gender and sexuality in opposition to the industrial class struggle. When sexuality is problematised as a force disrupting the class struggle, the only route open to it is sublimation into work as in the opening passage of Heslop's *Last Cage Down* (1935):

> The whole being of a man must be in tune with the silver rock before him and the frowning strata about him. He must know when to kirve, when to knick, when to smash down the 'caunch'. He must make this dead coal speak, speak with many tongues of coal, weep as a woman weeps when she mourns. If he is skilful he will make the coal leap voluntarily from its fastness with a shriek of joy [...]
> (Heslop 1984: 3)

The only other time Jim Cameron feels like a proper man is when he is with Betty, the barmaid from the Red Lion: 'She was a likeable lass, one with whom a man could become a man because she was essentially a woman possessed of the rich virtues and treasures of a woman' (Heslop 1984: 55). This rhetorical excess is consciously employed by Heslop; the point is that Cameron's sense of self-importance is a weakness in comparison to the political leadership which will eventually be provided by the communist Joe Frost. However, just because we realise that Cameron is a deliberately romanticised version of the heroic worker does not automatically function to demythologise that representation.

As Empson notes, to argue that a representation is a myth is not the same as saying that it is nonsense:

> the facts of the life of a nation, for instance, the way public opinion swings round, are very strange indeed, and probably a half-magical

idea is the quickest way to the truth. People who consider that the Worker group of sentiments is misleading in contemporary politics tend to use the word 'romantic' as a missile; unless they merely mean 'false' this is quite off the point; what they ought to do is produce a rival myth [. . .] (Empson 1995: 20)

The context of Empson's discussion was that the Conservative-dominated National Government were successfully producing exactly such a 'rival myth' to proletarian propaganda by appropriating the figure of the 'Worker' and presenting him in posters as

a stringy but tough, vital but not over-strong, cockney type [. . .] one feels it is fair to take him as a type of the English skilled worker, and it cuts out the communist feelings about the worker merely to look at him. (Empson 1995: 20)

What was needed, therefore, was yet another rival myth, which is what Heslop was actually trying to produce in the figure of Frost; a fact that was recognised by Alick West in *Crisis and Criticism* (1937), in which he devotes the final chapter to presenting Heslop as the successor to James Joyce in representing the pinnacle of Western literary development. The problem is that Frost is not particularly convincing. While his description as 'one of that new breed of men, who read diligently, who owned a radio' (Heslop 1984: 42) suggests him as a forerunner of the new classless culture which Orwell described, he is simply too anaemic a character, especially when placed alongside the larger-than-life Cameron, to signify any real difference from the National Government's propaganda of the 'English skilled worker'. Empson's analysis of the consequences of that propaganda applies equally to the versions of the myth provided by both Heslop and Orwell: 'To accept the picture is to feel that the skilled worker's interests are bound up with his place in the class system and the success of British foreign policy in finding markets' (Empson 1995: 20). This mythic formula certainly played a part, alongside more progressive impulses, in enabling the 1945 political settlement through its symbolic reconciliation of the figure of the 'Worker' with British capitalist interests rather than with communist ones.

Unless proletarian texts could successfully detach their male viewpoint protagonists from masculine ideology – whether in the humorous manner of *Love on the Dole* or through a more complex mutual intersubjective exchange as in *Lady Chatterley's Lover* – there was always the danger that the oppositional position they were trying to present would simply collapse back into the ruling ideology. Awareness of this problem led to some sophisticated representational strategies. For example, critics such as Klaus and Cunningham, as discussed in the Introduction to this book, are both contemptuous of James Barke's protagonist, Jock MacKelvie, in *Major Operation* (1936), who seems the epitome of the proletcult worker-hero, in his role as a leader in the unemployed movement: 'All the past in his life contributed to the present. He had always instinctively been on the right side of the battle. He found he had no serious errors to combat: no grave ideological faults to overcome' (Barke 1955: 131). However, in practice, we come to link him increasingly to the middle-class George Anderson as the novel progresses. At first, they trace separate paths across the modernist cityscape of Glasgow until they literally collide when Anderson tries to force his way across the street through an unemployed march. Subsequently, both end up in hospital together, where across extensive passages MacKelvie slowly converts Anderson to the cause. Thus MacKelvie's self-assured certainty becomes presented as one half of a unit completed by Anderson's self-reflective uncertainty. At the end of the novel, Anderson dies defending the fallen MacKelvie from a mounted police charge and thereby completes a strange timeloop by which MacKelvie's certainty is now explained through the history of the novel even though he has always displayed it.

The symmetry of this homosocial relationship is complicated by the novel's problematic depiction of gender and sexual relationships. MacKelvie's wife Jean is depicted as strong and resourceful, a socialist before her husband was, and yet she only rarely appears as a viewpoint figure. She is shown as instigating sex with MacKelvie and there is a nice moment when she thinks to herself that her brother-in-law 'could have been better managed' (Barke 1955: 283). However, more regularly, she is represented as someone whom MacKelvie has to placate. On the other hand, during the long key hospital sequences it is the working-class nurses who have the upper hand; a situation which Barke seems simultaneously fascinated and appalled by. The novel sets up the opportunity to reconcile these elements when Anderson, now out of hospital and a socialist, has tea with the nurse, Marion MacLean, who fell in love with him while looking after him. However, he spurns her offer of sex and she, the most interesting character in the book, leaves the story. Clearly, Barke was aware of the need to incorporate working-class female agency into his panoramic vision of class conflict in the modernist city but somehow could not quite manage to bring himself to confront the full implications of such a move. In contrast, the next two chapters analyse the respective work of two male proletarian writers who were prepared to make this move: Lewis Grassic Gibbon and John Sommerfield.

Chapter 3

'She Had Finished with Men Forever': Lewis Grassic Gibbon's *Grey Granite*

Not all revolutionary writers

In February 1935, the month that he died, Gibbon contributed to the discussion in *Left Review*, on the statement of aims of the Writers International (British Section) – notionally the parent body of the journal – by describing its claims, that English literature and theatre had been decadent for the past twenty years and showed a culture in collapse, as 'bolshevik blah': 'Neither in fiction, sociological writing, biography (to take only three departments) was there work done half so well in any Victorian or Edwardian period of equal length' (Gibbon 1935: 179). He castigated 'revolutionary' writers for not only failing to read their contemporaries but nonetheless still criticising them with 'bad Marxian patter and the single adjective "bourgeois"'; before adding 'Not all revolutionary writers (I am a revolutionary writer) are cretins' (Gibbon 1935: 179). Instead of organising writers into the three categories suggested in the statement of aims – anti-fascists, those expressing the class struggle, and those defending the Soviet Union – he suggested restricting membership of a union of revolutionary writers to those who could prove their work was of literary value and then setting them the task of properly analysing contemporary literature and its constituent movements. Ironically, ten pages further on in the same issue, Gibbon's *Grey Granite* (1934) was being praised by John Lehmann as 'an extremely remarkable and courageous attempt' by a 'bourgeois intellectual' to write proletarian literature (Lehmann 1935: 190).

Gibbon was in fact the son of a crofter who identified himself as being of 'peasant stock' (Gibbon 2001: 83) but because he was not from the industrial proletariat, a rigid binary perspective would situate him as bourgeois. As an exception to Andy Croft's argument that the term 'proletarian literature' was not generally used by communists and their allies by 1935, Lehmann's review is a useful indicator of the persistence of such binary viewpoints, and the confusion they created, on the left following the 1934 Soviet Congress's adoption of the concept of 'socialist realism'. For he clearly sees the novel as an almost exemplary committed account of the class struggle by a bourgeois writer that appears 'intensely real and authentic' (Lehmann 1935: 191). Apart, that is, from the 'obvious faults' of the protagonist, Ewan Tavendale, being a humourless prig who treats his girlfriend in a horrifying manner and the more general problem of the monotony of 'the dominant, rather emotional mood' (Lehmann 1935: 191). In short, Lehmann assumes that the novel is a work of socialist realism and therefore tailors his review to match the expected criteria of such. What is noticeable, though, is how much the narrow 'proletcult' sense of proletarian literature still underpins his concept of socialist realism. Lehmann's opening question might have been written a decade earlier:

> It is an interesting problem – and one which LEFT REVIEW should help in time to solve – how far a proletarian literature, that is a literature written from the standpoint of class-conscious workers, can exist in the structure of still undefeated capitalism. (Lehmann 1935: 190)

A year later, James Barke's much longer critical appreciation of *A Scots Quair* – the trilogy of which *Grey Granite* was the third volume, alongside *Sunset Song* (1932) and *Cloud Howe* (1933) – details similar criticisms of the 'strained and monotonous' tone and Ewan's 'contemptible' behaviour towards his sweetheart, before concluding that despite his 'honourable intentions', Gibbon's 'lack of knowledge, his lack of experience of the day-to-day actualities of the workers' struggle, prevented him from presenting a true and powerfully convincing picture of working-class life' (Barke 1936: 222–4). At its best, *A Scots Quair* is 'a worthy forerunner' of 'the novel that will be written by workers for workers' (Barke 1936: 225). Here, the 'proletcult' sense of proletarian literature is not so much underpinning socialist realism as supplanting it again.

So powerful is this narrow sense of proletarian literature that it has continued to negatively determine reception of the novel over the subsequent years. In 1946, Hugh MacDiarmid wrote an essay about Gibbon for *Our Time*, the postwar successor to *Left Review*, and notes that despite Gibbon's general proficiency in socialist realism, he was much less successful in *Grey Granite* 'in his portrayal of city life than in his handling of the rural scenes of his boyhood' (MacDiarmid 1948: 307). Half a century later, Ian A. Bell noted Gibbon's 'lack of engagement with urban working-class lives' (Bell 2000: 185) and summed up *Grey Granite*:

> Although the book ends with Ewan heading south to embark on a solitary life of political activism, the collective experience of the workplace remains drastically under-recorded by the author, and the narrative concludes with an elegiac return to a rural environment. (Bell 2000: 186)

The legacy of the narrow sense of 'proletarian literature' leads to a tradition of men reading *Grey Granite* as a flawed work because it does not successfully represent revolutionary male subjectivity. But this is not particularly surprising as *A Scots Quair* – which was always conceived as a trilogy – is mainly about a woman, 'Chris-alone, Chris-herself, with Chris Guthrie, Chris Tavendale, Chris Colquhoun dead' (Gibbon 1986: 317). Chris – shorn of her father's and husbands' names – is the chief viewpoint protagonist of the trilogy even in *Grey Granite* despite a fair proportion of that novel being told from her son Ewan's perspective. As Deirdre Burton observes in 'A Feminist Reading of *A Scots Quair*' (1984), while the novels 'clearly describe the nature and extent of the oppression of the working class, they also do not suggest that the mobilised Left have anything like an adequate vision with which to transform existing power relations' (Burton 1984: 40). There is a tendency among male critics of *Grey Granite* to read Gibbon's depiction of the 'mobilised Left' as evidence of a failure to understand the industrial working class rather than as a trenchant critique of narrow proletarian politics. From this perspective, the novel's continual switches to Chris's stream of consciousness and relationships with other women appear unnecessarily strained and emotional, and 'she soon ceases to be of interest' (Barke 1936: 223). Unsurprisingly, therefore, most of the best critical work on the novel has been written by feminists.

Of course, there is no necessary contradiction between feminism and 'revolutionary writing'; indeed, as critics such as Burton suggest, and as Gibbon himself strongly implies in his writing, only an intersectional approach is capable of challenging capitalist power relations. Moreover, as Gibbon's response to the statement of aims by the Writers International (British Section) suggests, the way to write intersectionally was by drawing on the unprecedented literary achievements of the previous twenty years' work, by which he clearly means modernism in today's broad sense of the term, and analysing the most effective techniques and tendencies within it. As discussed below, this is what Gibbon was doing himself and it culminated in *Grey Granite*. Analysing the novel in this respect, reveals a proletarian-modernist trajectory from the work of Joyce and Lawrence that, unlike the version outlined in West's *Crisis and Criticism* as leading to the work of Harold Heslop, would not now appear to be a dead end but actually lead on through Gibbon to contemporary literature in Scotland, such as James Robertson's *And the Land Lay Still* (2010).

In her essay, 'Modernism and Marxism in *A Scots Quair*', Margery Palmer McCulloch cites Gibbon's own discussion of his work from the essay 'Literary Lights', which appeared in *Scottish Scene* (1934) – the book which Gibbon wrote with Hugh MacDiarmid:

> The technique of Lewis Grassic Gibbon in his trilogy *A Scots Quair* – of which only Parts I and II, *Sunset Song* and *Cloud Howe*, have yet been published – is to mould the English language into the rhythms and cadences of Scots spoken speech, and to inject into the English vocabulary such minimum number of words from Braid Scots as that remodelling requires. His scene so far has been a comparatively uncrowded and simple one – the countryside and village of modern Scotland. Whether his technique is adequate to compass and express the life of an industrialised Scots town in all its complexity is yet to be demonstrated; whether his peculiar style may not become either intolerably mannered or degenerate, in the fashion of Joyce, into the unfortunate unintelligibilities of a literary second childhood, is also in question. (Gibbon, qtd in McCulloch 2003: 28)

McCulloch discusses this allusion to Joyce, pondering whether it is being used ironically 'to forestall criticism of [Gibbon's] own experimentation' and noting that Gibbon is, elsewhere in the same essay, more positive about Joyce (McCulloch 2003: 28). Moreover, contra McCulloch, Gibbon is not necessarily indicting *Ulysses* here because, while she is correct in pointing out that *Finnegans Wake* (1939) had yet to be published, he is most probably referring to the drafts that were published as instalments of 'Work in Progress' in journals such as *Transition* and the *Transatlantic Review* throughout the 1920s and 1930s. The Joyce of *Ulysses* is held out as a future aspiration for those Scottish writers not experimenting with incorporating the rhythm of Scots within their prose:

> Nearly every Scots writer of the past writing in orthodox English has been not only incurably second-rate, but incurably behind the times. [. . .] At such rate of progress among the Anglo-Scots one may guess that in another fifty years or so a Scots Virginia Woolf will astound the Scottish scene, a Scots James Joyce electrify it. (Gibbon 1934: 126–7)

The scorn directed at his fellow Scots authors is no different to that he directed at his fellow revolutionary writers and for the same reason: their failure to realise the importance of moving on from the innovations of Joyce and Woolf rather than ignoring or attacking them. Furthermore, Gibbon's point is both that without embracing the experimental innovations of modernism it will be at least fifty years before Scottish literature will have a transformative societal impact (as arguably happened exactly according to his schedule in the 1980s) and that without including industrial class relations within its depiction of the sum of social reality modernist innovation will degenerate into meaningless strings of words. In other words, the question was both what modernist technique could do for writing proletarian literature (in the widest sense) and what proletarian literature could do for modernism. The answer was to be provided by *Grey Granite*, with its blurring of the distinction between the voices of narrator, characters and readers within a rhythmic Scottish free indirect discourse. Its success would suggest that the future of modernism and proletarian literature lay together in a proletarian-modernist blend that would evade both such a narrow focus on working-class authenticity as to be limiting and a pluralistic approach so open-ended as to be unintelligible. From this perspective of recognising, as McCulloch does, that Gibbon was trying to do something new, *Grey Granite* is not the partial failure that Barke, MacDiarmid and others labelled it:

What is so significant about *A Scots Quair* itself is the way in which he has succeeded in marrying a modernist fictional form with a Marxist exploration of contemporary and historical force, an exploration more often conducted in fiction through socialist-realist methodology. (McCulloch 2003: 29)

For McCulloch, this innovative blend works especially well for *Grey Granite* because it enables the trilogy's focus on women in general, and Chris in particular, to offer 'an alternative, even sceptical perspective on Ewan's ideological commitments' that renders 'the book's ending as an open one' (McCulloch 2003: 38). In *Scottish Modernism and Its Contexts 1918–1959* (2009), McCulloch relates this openness to a sense of 'history in the making' (McCulloch 2009: 143) in *A Scots Quair*, which corresponds to the understanding of Mitchison and Sommerfield, in respect of *We Have Been Warned* and *May Day*, that they were writing historical novels about their own times. This sense is particularly acute in *A Scots Quair* because the human history of social development from the land via small towns to the industrial city is effectively compressed into a period of a little less than a quarter of a century across the three books. One consequence of this compression is that it highlights Raymond Williams's conception of 'metropolitan perception' – the awareness of changed social relations, the mutability of conventions, and a new sense of different social possibilities – as in part a product of the continued immigration into the city of people from rural or otherwise more traditional societies, in some cases with memory of precapitalist social relations or at least the vestiges of such (see R. Williams 1996: 39–47). The adaptation of Chris and Ewan to the city in *Grey Granite* is both a process of acquiring a metropolitan perception and a demonstration of how that metropolitan perception folds history into everyday life.

The resultant metropolitan everyday life combines the historical trace of unalienated precapitalist social relations with the new sense of different social possibilities into what might be considered, following the analysis of Jameson, either to be a weak utopian feeling situated in 'the relatively feeble life of desire and fantasy' or a more socially resistant moment of being from which the future might be excavated: 'Utopia, which combines the not-yet-being of the future with the textual existence of the present is no less willing of the archaeologies we are willing to grant to the [historical] trace' (Jameson 2005: xv–xvi). Metropolitan perception within urban everyday life is typically represented in modernist works, such as *Ulysses*, *Mrs Dalloway* or *Major Operation*, through free indirect discourse as a particular subject moves through the city environment. This combined sense of movement, both physical and of the stream of consciousness, suggests the possibility of a liberated future. However, there is always the danger, as Williams suggests, that the sense of new possibilities might overwhelm the trace of precapitalist social relations with a desire for a degree of self-liberation that can never 'be achieved in a settled relationship or in a society' (R. Williams 1996: 57). Similarly, it might also be a desire for a liberation that cannot be achieved across the whole of a society in an egalitarian manner; it might only be achievable by a minority ruling class, such as the property-owning bourgeoisie, supported by a disempowered lower class, the wage-earning proletariat. Moreover, even the intersubjective relationships in *Mrs Dalloway* and *Ulysses* – leaving aside the gender and Irish contexts of these works – might be seen as nonetheless maintaining, and even dependent on, the class differences between Clarissa and Smith or Stephen and Bloom; with only the subjectivity of the first of each pair fully liberated. Indeed, arguably, the use of the class differentials in those novels to affirm the self-consciousness of the principal subjects functions no differently at a structural level to the Hegelian dialectic of lordship and bondage (see Hegel 1977: 104–19). There are parallels with Shakespeare's *Henry V* in which Henry's self-consciousness as king is in part a product of his younger self's apparently equal intersubjective relationships, which retrospectively appear to be much more a case of 'negative identification' as Williams defines it. A similar relationship is also revealed in Mass-Observation's account of the coronation of George VI, *May the Twelfth* (1937), which, like *Ulysses* and *Mrs Dalloway*, focuses on a single day. On the one hand, the book suggests utopian possibilities in the apparently liberated independence of the holiday crowds lining the streets through which the royal procession passes; on the other hand, in its demonstration of the continuing 'magical power of the symbol of the monarchy' (Madge 1937: 33) in the twentieth century it indicates how such possibilities are reincorporated into the traditional hierarchies of British public life:

> It could be argued that this type of independence [of the coronation crowds] only ever exists through the social relationship with the monarch: that the King's pure consciousness of being-for-self, and hence his authority to rule, is guaranteed precisely by the independence

of the masses' being-for-others, and *vice versa*. Therefore, *May the Twelfth* holds the independence of the coronation crowds open at exactly the moment when its public manifestation was required in order to legitimate the new King [. . .] (Hubble 2010: 126)

Part of the problem here is the tendency of any distinct narrating voice to uphold the values of self-conscious bourgeois subjectivity, not so much in the manner in which the upper-class voice-over of some documentary films of the period undermines the potentially radical working-class representation, but rather in the way that the implied narration mythologises that representation so that it signifies, for example, the dignity of labour as opposed to an anti-bourgeois proletarian consciousness. In this respect, Empson criticised John Grierson's film *Drifters* (1929), despite its qualities as proletarian pastoral, for being essentially, a '"high-brow" picture' (Empson 1935: 15). Similarly, despite the efforts of MO in *May the Twelfth* to avoid such narration (with the exception of the footnotes), even its very attempt to do this suggests a certain type of hierarchical narrative position. As discussed in the Introduction to this book, Williams regarded such modernist practices as bearing out the tendency of anti-bourgeois bourgeois revolts to produce increasingly bourgeois positions. The cases where this type of anti-bourgeois revolt does not end up in a more bourgeois position are those in which the artist has another identity which is liberated from the bourgeois hierarchy through the revolt, such as Joyce's Irishness or Woolf's feminism. These examples – and that of Gibbon – make it clear that the main reason that there are no major English modernists is that the modernist revolt against bourgeois subjectivity was mainly a revolt against the Victorian and Edwardian English patriarchal bourgeois subjectivity that was hegemonic in Britain. If you were a bourgeois Englishman, the only thing you could achieve through modernist revolt was to become a highbrow but you could not escape your implication in hegemonic bourgeois Englishness; indeed, some immigrants, such as Eliot, were actually able to use modernist revolt as a means of gaining hegemonic bourgeois Englishness. Orwell partially escaped through the genius of using modernist techniques and all seven of what Saunders calls the levels of narrative construction to create himself as a character who was read as a plain-talking average sensual man, a better-educated version of George Bowling, the protagonist of his *Coming Up for Air* (1939). Lawrence was from the working class but could have been absorbed fully into the bourgeoisie if it was not for the fact that the narration of his major novels – *The Rainbow* (1915), *Women in Love* (1921) and *Lady Chatterley's Lover* – was blended with the free indirect discourse of his major female protagonists so that it does not hold up the values of the patriarchal order.

Gibbon followed after Lawrence's example in terms of the gender of his main protagonist but he also made two other key aesthetic choices: his use of a version of Scots as a medium for prose fiction and his frequent use of narration in the second person. As McCulloch notes, until Gibbon, the Scots revival had been almost entirely in poetry: 'Fiction had continued to be written in English, or, following the example of Walter Scott, written with an English-language narrative voice accompanied by dialogue for country-dwellers or lower-class characters in either a rural or urban dialect of Scots' (McCulloch 2009: 133). By his moulding of English into the rhythm and cadence of Scots and introduction of 'such minimum words from Braid Scots as that remodelling requires', Gibbon was able to replace the English-language narrative voice, anticipating James Kelman's use of similar strategies half a century later in order to get 'rid of a whole value system' (qtd in McCulloch 2009: 133). In the process, Gibbon created a new medium for a modern fiction that was 'rooted in Scottish everyday life' (McCulloch 2009: 133). Consequently, any utopian possibility of liberation opened up by the metropolitan perception of *Grey Granite* is not connected to individualist bourgeois subjectivity because the narrative voice is made up of many personal and community perspectives woven in together with no linguistic hierarchy.

You see I'm awfully common myself

The different narrative perspectives are periodically presented to the readers in the second person, as though drawing them in to participate directly in the novel's intersubjective weave of consciousness. This textual strategy is used throughout the three volumes; particularly when new or significant experiences are being represented, as for example the well-known and oft-quoted passage first outlining Chris's duality in *Sunset Song*:

> So that was Chris and her reading and schooling, two Chrisses there were that fought for her heart and tormented her. You hated the land

and the coarse speak of the folk and learning was brave and fine one day and the next you'd waken with the peewits crying across the hills, deep and deep, crying in the heart of you and the smell of the earth in your face, almost you'd cry for that, the beauty of it and the sweetness of the Scottish land and skies. (Gibbon 1986: 37)

Readers, men or women, Scots or English, are pitched headfirst into the narrative voice of the trilogy and forced to view their surroundings from Chris's perspectives. The fact that the English Chris and the Scottish Chris are held in tension creates a situation similar to the double attitude of pastoral as identified by Empson. The main difference is that Chris always already embodies both the simple and the complex; she does not have to abandon her specialised feelings to imagine those of the simple person because she can see from both perspectives anyway. Making her the readers' point of identification with the novels, supplemented by second-person passages written from the more general perspective of a community member, allows readers to share that double attitude. As Empson explains in his discussion of John Gay's *The Beggar's Opera* (1728) in *Some Versions of Pastoral*, the double attitude of characters in pastoral can lead to 'Comic Primness, the double irony in the acceptance of a convention' (Empson 1995: 72). This is not critical irony in which somebody pretends to believe in something in order to make the other person see that there is something wrong with it but a more complex position in which the speaker simultaneously accepts and rejects the convention they are ironicising and so is forced into a position of isolation and therefore independence. Such comic primness is more frequently displayed in the general second-person narration or by independently minded characters such as Long Rob of the Mill or Ake Ogilvie than by Chris, although the following passage from *Grey Granite* provides a rare example:

[Ellen] and Ewan were indifferent, polite, Chris thought them too much alike to take heed of each other. But Miss Lyon couldn't abide [Ellen] at all, and would sniff as she watched her, Just a Vulgar Flirt, she didn't let me take Liberties with *her*. She told this to Chris after breakfast one day, didn't Mrs. Colquhoun think the Johns girl Common? And Chris smiled at her sweet. *I don't know, Miss Lyon. You see I'm awfully common myself.* (Gibbon 1986: 392)

On one level, Chris's reply illustrates what Empson would describe as second level comic primness. Chris is being critically ironic in that the implication of her retort is that both Miss Lyon and the social conventions of correct behaviour she upholds are wrong. Nevertheless, her reply does not actually contradict Miss Lyons so much as to confirm the arbitrariness of the convention which she does not actually challenge, suggesting that she herself is still comfortable with complying with this convention that she does not actually believe in. Empson suggests that this would be the basis for a '"critical" comedy' (Empson 1995: 171) and indeed Gibbon does use mealtimes in the boarding house for such critical comedy, which often serves to expose the hypocrisy of the petty bourgeois boarders. However, the scene also demonstrates third level comic primness in that Chris is displaying what Empson describes as

> Ironical Humility, whose simplest gambit is to say, 'I am not clever, educated, well born', or what not (as if you had a low standard to judge by), and then to imply that your standards are so high in the matter that the person you are humbling yourself before is quite out of sight. (Empson 1995: 171)

What makes this different to the second level is that Chris's statement that she is common carries with it a sense of precapitalist social relations for the reader who is aware that she comes from the organic rural community depicted in *Sunset Song*. On another level completely, therefore, Chris is not accepting Miss Lyon's sense of social propriety at all but implicitly advancing an alternative set of social values which are not entirely rooted in class relations because they still contain the trace of an unalienated experience. It is in this respect, more generally, that Chris is pushed into isolation and independence throughout the trilogy; her growing dual awareness means that she becomes increasingly ill at ease with social conventions because her consciousness of their difference from the alternative social values she holds becomes unbearable.

Early in *Grey Granite*, second-person narration is combined with Chris's free indirect discourse to communicate to the reader that her status has changed from being the minister's wife in a small town – as she was in *Cloud Howe*, which was itself a significant change from her life on a smallholding in *Sunset Song* – to having become the junior partner in running a boarding house in the industrial city of

Duncairn: 'At half-past five the clock would go *birr!* in the narrow long room you had ta'en for yourself [. . .]' (Gibbon 1986: 362). And so starts a long description of a day of preparing meals, administering to boarders and cleaning bedrooms. However, the narrative then cuts to an unemployed worker:

> On the Broo since the War and five kids to keep, eating off you head – och, why did you live? – never a minute of quiet to yourself, nothing but the girnings of the wife for more silver, the kids half-barefoot, half-fed, oh hell. (Gibbon 1986: 369)

And then to his wife: 'Hardly believe it was him you had wed, that had been a gey bit spark in his time, hearty and bonny, liked you well: and had hit you, the bloody brute coming drunk from the pub [. . .]' (Gibbon 1986: 370).

Significantly, Gibbon never allows the narrative voice of the urban consciousness of the city to become equated solely with a masculine proletarian viewpoint and this leaves a space, certainly at the beginning of the novel, for Chris to be linked to this collective voice. However, the surrounding third person narrative contextualises this second-person narrative so that we see areas of identity and difference. For example, at the same time as we are being presented with this urban narration, Ewan is being treated as a toff by the other apprentices at the engineering works where he is now based and finally gets involved in a fight with them. The section describing his return to work afterwards – when he becomes accepted and involved in union meetings – begins and ends with second-person narration from an unknown apprentice, who is later identified as Bob. This starts off 'you couldn't but wonder what Tavendale would do [. . .]' and ends up on first-name terms with the 'funny chap [. . .] but you'd like him to tea some Saturday night' (Gibbon 1986: 389, 391). Until this point, Ewan has been an enigmatic figure but now he is aligned, despite his difference, with both the workers and the general narrative voice of the novel. The same run of pages includes Chris's mealtime exchange with Miss Lyons as discussed above, but also an earlier encounter with a working man in which she gets him reluctantly to return a sixpence to her:

> *There you are, mistress. Enjoy your money while you have it. There's a time coming when your class won't have it long.*

> Chris's temper quite went with her a minute, silly fool, the heat she supposed, she didn't care:
>
> *My class? It was digging its living in sweat while yours lay down with a whine in the dirt. Good-bye.* (Gibbon 1986: 377)

Here, Chris's independence is asserted not against petty-bourgeois snobbishness but against a worker. It is a response triggered by a loss of temper but it also indirectly makes the point that the labour of the industrial working class is not the only source of material value historically or even in a modern industrial society. Chris does not accept that the labour of the industrial working class gives them an agency in history which outweighs her earlier memories of an unalienated connection with the land. From this point on, she is very rarely a focaliser for second-person narration again, while Ewan increasingly comes to fulfil this function.

This transfer of roles by which Ewan becomes one with the workers and Chris gradually becomes isolated is finalised by the march organised by the communist Jim Trease in protest against the means test. This begins with a return to the second-person stream of consciousness of the anonymous unemployed worker describing how he gets involved in the march despite just going to watch and pretending not to hear the shouts from the communists to join up: 'And a man'd look shame-faced at another childe, and smoke his pipe and never let on till Big Jim himself came habbering along, crying you out by your Christian name, and you couldn't well do anything else but join' (Gibbon 1986: 393). McCulloch analyses this passage to show how the man's perspective is also a group perspective which furthermore incorporates the perspective of his wife and all the wives, before reflecting the change of mood by which he and the other men get swept up in the passion of the march as 'memories of his past army service come flooding into his present thoughts' (McCulloch 2009: 142). This passion leads them to attack the police when they are prevented from getting to the town hall and they are only saved from the retaliatory mounted charge when Ewan, who is just passing by and not even on the march, directs them to a brewery lorry full of empty bottles with which they can fight back.

While this is a vividly described dramatic scene which engages the reader directly in the action, it can also be read as a critique of the tactics of the communists and working-class movement at the time. As Walter Benjamin noted in his essay, originally published in the same year as *Grey Granite*, 'The Work of Art in the Age of Mechanical Reproduction' (1936):

> The growing proletarianisation of modern man and the increasing formation of masses are two aspects of the same process. Fascism attempts to organise the newly created proletarian masses without affecting the property structure which the masses strive to eliminate. Fascism sees its salvation in giving these masses not their right, but instead a chance to express themselves. (Benjamin 1992: 234)

Benjamin's broader argument was that as a consequence of the rise of cinema – itself a product of metropolitan perception – and the general shift in ways of seeing resulting from watching films, mass society generated a new mode of participation in which the masses fulfilled a desire to be brought face to face with themselves by taking part in mass rallies, parades, marches and war. Gibbon's account of the march is psychologically acute in the way it replicates the process by which mass participation in an event is generated. The men look at each other and see themselves reflected, which they enjoy because they feel that they are being given expression, and then they are reminded of similar feelings from marching during the war. Participation in the march creates a collective identity, like that of the army, which is based not on everyday knowledge but on a temporary sense of being at one with each other and, therefore, of being in possession of an agency, which is in reality false because there has been no accompanying change in their material circumstances.

Gibbon's criticism is not just directed at communist tactics and aestheticised politics but is also a gendered critique of male behaviour, as is made clear from the description of the men, in various bloodied states, reliving the fight through the night afterwards in the tenements, while the women look on in disbelief. When asked what the use of more fighting is, the anonymous second-person focaliser says you only have to die once and it would be worth it with your fist in a policeman's guts. However, in this passage, the second-person narrative, which by definition is gender neutral, can also be seen to challenge gender norms, as arguably it does throughout the trilogy. The women feel sick to see their particular man, face dripping with blood, whispering '*I'm fine, lass, fine*': 'Oh God you could greet if it wasn't that when you did that you would die . . .' (Gibbon 1986: 398). This creates a momentary confusion in the reader as to whose thoughts are being focalised. It comes immediately after the man speaking and so there is a possibility that it might be his thoughts but in the context of the paragraph, however, it is probably the focalised thoughts of a woman. Or, at least, that is the way that readers with gendered consciousnesses are likely to reconcile the passage with their worldview. On the other hand, the two mentions of death in quick succession suggest both that masculinity is something to be demonstrated primarily by being prepared to die for it and that the desire for such a death is itself a primary ingredient of that masculinity. Readers of *A Scots Quair* are already aware of this idea from the way that the men in *Sunset Song* are unable to resist the compulsive need to set off to die in the First World War. A similar compulsion is echoed later in *Grey Granite* in the account of an evening spent together by Ewan and Trease, who become great comrades following the march and its aftermath, in the unacknowledged but implicitly shared understanding that 'they *are* the workers', which is reinforced because, with Mrs Trease out at the cinema, they are men together. Then Mrs Trease comes back singing 'Ta-ra-ra, 'way down in Omaha':

> Trease twinkled at Ewan: That's what you get. Not revolutionary songs but Ta-ra-ra, 'way down in Omaha. Mrs. Trease said Fegs, revolutionary songs gave her a pain in the stomach, they were nearly as dreich as hymns, the only difference being that they promised you hell on earth instead of in hell.
>
> And Ewan sat and looked on and spoke now and then, and liked them well enough, knowing that if it suited the party purpose Trease would betray him to the police tomorrow, use anything and everything that might happen to him as propaganda and publicity, without caring a fig for liking or aught else. So he'd deal with Mrs. Trease, if it came to that . . . (Gibbon 1986: 482)

While Gibbon never gives Ewan anything but his full imaginative conviction, this passage – perhaps more than any other in the novel – exposes exactly the inadequacies of the male fantasy of mutual betrayal and death which underpins homosocial relationships and maintains women as objects.

Time she went home herself

Ferrall and McNeill are surely correct when they argue that the heterogeneous narrative blend of free indirect discourse in *Grey Granite* reflects a conscious decision by Gibbon to give voice to a variety of competing ideological commitments and co-existing social claims from a position that is to 'the left of "official" Communism' (Ferrall and McNeill 2015: 135–6). Although, to be clear, this position does not reduce to an ultra-leftist advocacy of direct proletarian agency; rather Gibbon is criticising the narrow proletarian outlook of the Communist Party during the 'class against class' period. He is also completely scathing about the Labour Party and notions of a gradual road to socialism. The account of the failure of the General Strike at the end of *Cloud Howe*, interwoven with Chris's miscarriage, was designed to shatter such progressivist illusions: 'What and who is to replace them, however, is a question the novel leaves open to debate' (Ferrall and McNeill 2015: 136).

On the one hand, as McCulloch notes, the age difference between Gibbon, born in 1901, and other major modernists means that unlike Joyce, Lawrence, Woolf or MacDiarmid, the decisive change in human relationships from his perspective occurred neither in 1910 nor as part of the direct experience of the First World War, but rather as a result of the Russian Revolution in 1917 and his subsequent involvement with the foundation of the Aberdeen Soviet in 1918 and in the political ferment of Red Clydeside in 1919. As a consequence, he had a clear conception of the potential of revolutionary socialism to generate wholesale social change by overturning class society. On the other hand, Gibbon's feminist politics and his linked belief in diffusionist theories of a Neolithic golden age – both of which feature in his two science fiction novels (written under his real name of James Leslie Mitchell), *Three Go Back* (1932) and *Gay Hunter* (1934) – gave him a perspective similar to that advanced by Benjamin in 'Theses on the Philosophy of History' (1950). Benjamin describes history as an angel being blown backwards out of paradise by the storm of progress, so that when we look back on a chain of events, the angel 'sees one single chain of catastrophe which keeps piling wreckage upon wreckage and hurls it in front of his feet' (Benjamin 1992: 249). In Gibbon's first book, *Hanno, or, The Future of Exploration* (1928), having invoked the myths of Avalon and Atlantis, he discussed exploration as the search for an equivalent post-scarcity utopia for humanity to return to, before concluding 'Looking up at the night upon the untrodden starfields, it needs no robust faith to believe that in the Future of Exploration lies the Future of Mankind' (Gibbon 1928: 94). His concept of exploration was not, therefore, one of colonial expansion or the instrumental acquisition of wealth and raw materials, but of a utopian desire to find a location in which to revive the unalienated social relations of the past. This is reinforced by his *Nine Against the Unknown* (1934), published in the same month as *Grey Granite*, which seeks to distinguish between the ideals of the explorers themselves, such as Vasco da Gama and Mungo Park, and the exploitative motives of those who sent or funded them. As Ian Campbell notes, Mitchell repeatedly turns to the idea of 'the fortunate isles – the dream of an undiscovered, unexplored, "undeveloped" source of riches or beauty' (Campbell 2000: xiii), which could inaugurate a new golden age far away from the spoilage and ravening exploitation of civilisation. Both *Hanno* and *Nine Against the Unknown* are prefaced with part of Tennyson's *Ulysses* (1842), culminating in these four lines:

> To sail beyond the sunset and the baths
> Of all the western stars, until I die.
> It may be that the gulfs will wash us down:
> It may be we shall touch the happy isles.

Similar ideas underpin the ending of *Grey Granite* with Chris sitting alone at sunset on the hillside above Cairndhu, where she was born, until the lights in the little towns go out and she can no longer feel the touch of the rain or hear the sound of the lapwings going by. This is normally interpreted as her death but it might also be seen as indicating that somehow she has reached the utopian haven of the 'happy isles' just 'beyond the sunset'. The penultimate sentence of the novel – 'Time she went home herself' (Gibbon 1986: 496) – would therefore be referring to home in the sense of the golden age. We know from the earlier visit to Cairndhu of Chris, Ewan and Ellen that on the hill is an 'old Pict fort built by the men of antique time, a holy place before Christ was born' (Gibbon 1986: 386). However, suggesting that home is really the Neolithic past is not necessarily regressive because as Ellen points out, '*If there was once a time without gods and classes couldn't there be that time again?*' (Gibbon

1986: 387). The ending of the novel, therefore, is directly connected to one of the key political discussions in the trilogy; for it is in this earlier scene that Ewan first expresses socialist ideas in his complaint concerning civilisation as a calamity from the point of view of that ancient society. Rather than bringing him closer to Ellen, this triggers a disagreement between them that anticipates their irrevocable split later in the novel. While Ewan thinks the prospect of a golden age to come is of no concern to him because he will not live to see it and he has his own life to lead, Ellen castigates his complacency in the face of capitalist crisis and the rise of fascism. Ewan's rejoinder – '*They won't rule me. I'm myself*' (Gibbon 1986: 387) – is a straightforward assertion of nineteenth-century bourgeois male self-consciousness. When Ellen responds by pointing out that everyone is a consequence and a product 'of our fathers and mothers and the things we've read and depended upon' (Gibbon 1986: 387), he just shrugs and asks what that has to do with it.

Later, during the scene in which they split up, this same division re-emerges. Their final argument is triggered by Ellen's leaving the Communist Party because otherwise she will lose her job and also because she is 'sick of being without decent clothes, without the money I earn myself, pretty things that are my mine, that I've worked for' (Gibbon 1986: 490). While the content of this complaint is very similar to Sally Hardcastle's defiant rejection of respectability in *Love on the Dole*, the text does suggest Ellen's hypocrisy in saying that they could justify having a comfortable life together with a car and a flat, by working for the Labour Party. However, this is a recognisably human hypocrisy, which includes a desire to be connected to other people and to society. Elsewhere in the trilogy such hypocrisies are treated with a humorous but critical irony. Ewan's hostile response – '*I can get a prostitute anywhere*' (Gibbon 1986: 490) – is clearly meant to be experienced as brutal and shocking by the reader as well as by Ellen herself. It is an indication not of his commitment to communism but of his commitment to the idea of himself as a revolutionary. At this point, Ewan's behaviour resembles the kind of modernist desire for liberation that Williams suggests cannot be achieved in a settled relationship or in a society. Indeed, Ewan's position is indistinguishable from that of those modernists, such as Nietzsche, whose rejection of the family was not really to do with property relations but a misogynist rejection of women and children because they undermine a male sense of pure, subjective liberty. Ironically, far from being independent, such positions are little more than a distillation of the restrictive, traditional patriarchal values from which women like Ellen and Sally are struggling to free themselves. Through this stark moment of rupture between Ewan and Ellen, the political trajectories that have been running through the trilogy come into focus.

Although the General Strike comes at the end of *Cloud Howe*, Gibbon had originally conceived of it, as Ferrall and McNeill (2015) note, as the climactic event in the whole novel sequence. By June 1931, when Gibbon signed a memorandum of agreement with his publisher concerning the planned trilogy (see Malcolm 2016: 86), the collapse of the Strike, and with it the idea that had circulated ever since the Russian Revolution that the millennium was in reach, appeared to be the defining event of the postwar years to date but already it was becoming apparent that the consequences – not least in the apportioning of blame between communists and labourites – were more significant than the event itself. Therefore, 'instead of offering a myth of betrayal', *Grey Granite* focuses on the Strike's aftermath by examining it as an 'unresolved strategic and rhetorical challenge' (Ferrall and NcNeill 2015: 140). One element of this examination is the inclusion of Ewan, whose 'character development is in fact shaped along exactly the same lines as that of the archetypal socialist realist hero' in a novel that is unlike a socialist realist novel (Malcolm 2016: 116–17). However, there is no sudden disjunction between *Cloud Howe* and *Grey Granite* as Ewan represents the call made by his stepfather Robert in his last sermon for 'a stark, sure creed that will cut like a knife' (Gibbon 1986: 350) and, therefore, also the breakdown of Robert's Christian socialist fantasies of a Kingdom of Heaven on Earth, which have determined the unreal quality of so much of the middle novel. In this respect, similarly to *Lady Chatterley's Lover*, *A Scots Quair* follows John Clute's schema of the four stages of fantasy: wrongness, thinning, recognition, return. *Sunset Song* traces the 'wrongness' of the break-up of the organic rural community, *Cloud Howe* the 'thinning' of social life, and *Grey Granite* the 'recognition' of self-realisation and the final 'return' home.

Those critics who recognise the continuity in the trilogy, and therefore do not read *Grey Granite* as a failed socialist realist novel in the manner of Barke or MacDiarmid, tend to see Ewan and Chris as representing contending but not necessarily opposed forces, with the balance finally tipping in Chris's favour. As Douglas Young suggests, it is significant that the book ends not with Ewan but with 'Chris and her return to the land' (Young 1973: 135). William Malcolm captures more of the novel's complexity: 'Where Ewan ends trying to conquer history, Chris finally is at one with nature and triumphs over the forces of time' (Malcolm 2016: 123). Perhaps surprisingly, David Smith's reading in *Socialist Propaganda in the Twentieth-Century British Novel* (1978) is the most ingenious – possibly because, rather than in spite, of his book's overall anti-communist framing[1] – in its reconciling of the communist content with the deeper sense of history associated with Chris:

> What finally emerges, however, is not so much a clash of irreconcilable opposites, as a dual tension, a philosophy which can see communism both as necessary, inevitable, and the only possible hope for the future, and at the same time can draw back in resignation and see it as but one part in a larger cycle of history which will in its turn be superseded – possibly having accomplished no more than the revolutionary creeds of the past. (Smith 1978: 127)

These readings taken together do seem to go some way to unpacking the strategic and rhetorical challenge of not just the General Strike but the novel itself. There is clearly an intention on Gibbon's part to create a dual tension in the novel and yet it is difficult to reconcile Ewan's position with that of the emphasis of the ending on Chris unless one simply implies, as Young does, that Gibbon was not able to manage it as satisfactorily as he wanted to. If we assume that the privileging of Chris's viewpoint over Ewan's is deliberate, as the scenes analysed above make clear, then we are confronted by a number of possible ways this can be accounted for; two of which are demonstrated by Malcolm's and Smith's different readings.

The endings of the other novels examined in depth in this book have been unpacked through autobiografictional readings and there is no question that it would make interpreting the end of *Grey Granite* easier if, as with the case of Mitchison for example, we knew Gibbon's subsequent political trajectory and how he continued to develop his politicised aesthetics in subsequent works. Given the relative proximity of their age and background in the rural community of the Mearns,

Chris is clearly the main point of autobiographical identification in the text, with Gibbon also drawing on his wife's experiences to supplement his own. However, as a self-proclaimed revolutionary writer, he is also invested in Ewan. Therefore, in textually working out both Chris's and Ewan's processes of self-realisation, Gibbon was working though his own double attitude to Scotland and class politics. Feeling the weight of the arguments on all sides, as in Empson's account of comic primness, was pushing him into a position of political isolation and independence of thought. There is a case for arguing that it is this self-realisation which leads to the otherwise somewhat surprising and seemingly abrupt declaration at the end of the novel that the central tension is between 'FREEDOM and GOD' (Gibbon 1986: 495).

The context for this revelation is 'the last supper' of Chris and Ewan before both leave Duncairn, she for Cairndhu and he as leader of a hunger strike. They talk of Segget, the small town in which they lived during the events of *Cloud Howe*, and Ewan finally recognises that in his conversion to communism he has found the clear, sharp creed that his stepfather talked of the day that he died. In other words, he is motivated by faith but this is a faith which Chris rejects: *'The world's sought faith for thousands of years and found only death or unease in them. Yours is just another dark cloud to me – or a great rock you're trying to push up a hill'* (Gibbon 1986: 495). This is a judgement on Ewan's masochistic denial of the social life around him and an indictment of communism as a narrow creed. The effect of this on Ewan is to bring him out from behind the tenets of communism so that he speaks 'openly and honestly, kindly and wise' in the realisation that the opposition between Chris and himself is, in fact, that between 'FREEDOM and GOD'. At this moment, therefore, Ewan is between the second and third sorts of comic primness because he is now – temporarily at least – fully aware that communism is simply a convention which is offering him a possibility for an otherwise unrealisable self-liberation from the intersubjective ties of society; indeed, a darkly comic critical irony. In this respect, Ewan's future remains ambiguous as we do not know if he will slip back into sheltering behind the conventions of communism or if he will develop a broader independence of thought. This latter, of course, would not necessarily lead to him leaving the Communist Party but might entail him continuing to pursue social revolution with a more independent mindset; an opportunity which became possible historically because of the transition from the 'class against class' policy to the advocacy of a Popular Front. A variety of possible sequels featuring Ewan can be imagined.

Paradoxically, Chris's 'freedom' – despite its connection to the idea of a classless golden age which may yet come again – seems more final; especially if it were to be read as a return to oneness with nature, which, after all, is just another way of thinking about death. It makes little sense to criticise, in effect, a narrow proletarian universality for bringing in the absolute too prematurely, while proclaiming a different kind of universality. As Empson says:

> Once you have said that everything is One it is obvious that literature is the same as propaganda. Once you have said that no truth can be known beyond the immediate dialectical process of history it is obvious that all contemporary artists must prepare the same fashionplate. (Empson 1995: 24)

However, the novel is never didactic in this manner and, furthermore, Chris is explicitly identified with 'FREEDOM'. One way of resolving this paradox is to consider whether Chris has literally, rather than metaphorically, returned home to the golden age. The last sentence of the novel is precise on the fact that she is still sitting on the hill even as she no longer feels the touch of the rain. The alternative interpretation to her being dead would be that the universe around her has changed while she continues to sit on the hill. Such a reading suggests that rather than close with the merging of the self into the material world, *Grey Granite* ends with a transformation of that world into what Cairns Craig calls 'a universe of which the self need no longer be afraid' (Craig 1999: 69). For such a universe to function, it would have to be outside the symbolic order of patriarchy so that it enabled the type of intersubjective selfhood discussed in the Introduction to this book with respect to Mitchison's *We Have Been Warned*. With no need to give up the claim for imaginary identity with other possible subject and object positions, such a universe would be free of the gendered and political constraints of the 1930s. Such a universe would also have a post-scarcity emotional economy so that Chris's love and desire would no longer be exhausted as it is across the course of the trilogy. Her closing vision of 'the land' as 'enduring, encompassing'

(Gibbon 1986: 496) suggests it as a magical other-worldly space superimposed on the mundane world. In conjunction with the trilogy's structure of wrongness, thinning, recognition and return, and its opening which mentions 'gryphons and such-like beasts' (Gibbon 1986: 15), this idea of 'the land' indicates how *A Scots Quair* may be read as containing similar fantasy elements to *We Have Been Warned* and *Lady Chatterley's Lover*. While Gibbon does not explicitly address the issues of gender and sexuality at the trilogy's close, Chris's experiences throughout the text suggest that his overall intention is to provide what would now be called an intersectional feminist analysis of society, which also bears comparison with Mitchison's and Lawrence's novels.

Seeing mirrored her face

Gibbon's obvious feminism was first pointed out by Burton over thirty years ago:

> Reading Lewis Grassic Gibbon's famous trilogy in the early 1980s, I found I was having to remind myself continually that I was *not* reading a work by a modern female writer, who wrote from a woman's cultural experience, and with a strong political commitment to specifically feminist perspectives on major socialist issues. (Burton 1984: 35)

A refreshing tone of delighted surprise permeates Burton's chapter, which is the standout contribution to Hawthorn's collection, *The British Working-Class Novel in the Twentieth Century* (1984), and evinces a sense of enlightened breakthrough which is the hallmark of the best criticism. Significantly, the previous secondary work which she draws on the most is Jenny Wolmark's 'Problems of Tone in *A Scots Quair*' (1981) published in *Red Letters*, the Communist Party journal discussed in the Introduction to this book. Rather as with Carole Snee's analysis of *Means-Test Man* in that journal, Wolmark ultimately endorses a narrow conception of proletarian literature but only after highlighting a number of key points of ideological uncertainty and contradiction in the text centred on the opposed perspectives of Chris and Ewan. Wolmark explains this contradiction as a product of liberal ideology's inability to cope with the economic crisis of capitalism in the 1930s and argues that this is manifested in *Grey Granite* by the clash between what she sees as Ewan's radical politics and Chris's 'conservative idealization of the past' (Wolmark 1981: 17). However, she is nonetheless aware of the obvious disjunction between Ewan's professed political position and the 'sentimentality and overstatement' of certain scenes such as the account of the evening spent together by Ewan and Trease: 'Gibbon seems unable to present Ewan's total commitment to socialism and the working class in anything other than abstract terms, so that the fiction itself serves to undermine the very ideology it seeks to support' (Wolmark 1981: 20). The reason why Burton values Wolmark's analysis, despite coming to radically different conclusions, is because it problematises reading *A Scots Quair* as a conventional work of socialist realism by identifying the points of contradiction in the text, which are not simply treated as arising from Gibbon's supposed shortcomings – such as his alleged lack of knowledge of the industrial working class – but seen as the reflection of a deeper hegemonic crisis in monopoly capitalism.

Burton draws on this analysis of the contradictions in the text as support for her first impressions of the trilogy as a feminist work in order to argue that Gibbon both deliberately exposes Ewan as a person of 'limited vision, limited growth – both personal and political' and more generally recognises how 'patriarchal attitudes have consistently excluded women, their experiences, their insights, their work from all radical movements and activities except their own' (Burton 1984: 45). In this respect, she reads the alignment of Chris with the alternative universe of the golden age outside of the gendered and political constraints of the 1930s as prefiguring the 'feminist personal-political experiential cosmology' emerging in the 1980s across disciplines from history to ecology and concludes that the trilogy offers us knowledge 'beyond the confines of both capitalism and patriarchy' (Burton 1984: 43, 46). What is perhaps most significant about Burton's reading of the trilogy is the way that she focuses on how Gibbon represents Chris's split subjectivity in various ways, including constituting her body parts as objects of her own gaze, frequently in scenes where she examines her own reflection in a mirror or standing water. Burton describes such features as 'characteristic of women's writing in this century' (Burton 1984: 38). However, the very same features have been criticised by other female critics as a 'voyeuristic' means of displaying the female body to the male gaze (see Murray 2003: 59–60). Isobel Murray is probably correct in suggesting that in practice young women do not continually undress in cold bedrooms to inspect themselves in front of a mirror or at least that they do not linger unnecessarily while doing so. While Pamela Fox agrees with Burton that Chris experiencing herself in such scenes 'as an object of desire (as well as desiring subject)' is true to female subjectivity, she also finds potentially disturbing what she sees as the tendency of the trilogy to present Chris as a sexual object for the consumption of its readers (Fox 1994: 199). Significantly, Fox, who interprets the end of *Grey Granite* as marking Chris's final withdrawal from class community into personal experience, finds this bodily objectification 'uncomfortably reminiscent of Lawrencian women like Anna Brangwen' (Fox 1994: 200). This discomfort at men writing women in this way is perhaps understandable given the overriding way in which patriarchal society tends to constrain depictions of women's sexuality to either objectification or threat; but such criticisms also inhibit the capacity of male writers to identify with subject positions outside the patriarchal order.

Both Murray and Fox seem to miss the important qualification in Burton's argument, which is that 'the quality of the trilogy that allows it to be radical in terms of sexual as well as class politics is, however, that it foregrounds the female point of view [. . .]' (Burton 1984: 46). The point about these mirror scenes, whether they are in Gibbon's *A Scots Quair* or Lawrence's novels, is that the female body is only available to the male gaze when that gaze is focalised through a female point of view. It is not clear that inhabiting the female subject position of Chris, which is a fundamental challenge to any male reader of the trilogy, allows the male gaze to function as normal. Male readers that do not make the effort to inhabit Chris's subject position, such as Barke, simply lose interest rather than become titillated by her and tend to view the trilogy as flawed socialist realism. However, those that do identify with Chris are going to experience any sexual desire for her body in the mirror scenes in quite complex ways. The fact that Chris does not experience shame while contemplating herself as a sexual object problematises any simple masculine enjoyment of her body because it diminishes the possibility for that male reader of transferring any sense of guilt on to her. This guilt would arise first from recognising that one is in a voyeuristic situation (within a woman's private bedroom) and gazing sexually at that woman's body and then simultaneously experiencing that gaze from the perspective of the woman who is the object of that gaze. Because Chris does not lower her eyes, or blush, but calmly gazes back, the normal subject–object relationship of the male gaze is disrupted and confused. It is not clear who is the subject and who is the object in these scenes. Moreover, this subversion of traditional gender relations is not only implicit but also explicit in some of Gibbon's passages. For example, in *Grey Granite*, Chris tears off her clothes and looks 'at herself, as of old, with cool scrutiny, seeing mirrored her face with the broad cheek-bones, seeing the long white lines of thigh and waist and knee, not very much need to envy men' (Gibbon 1986: 382). Her looking at her body is superimposed with her memories of looking at men's bodies and anyone reading this scene is briefly immersed in a web of identifications and objectifications simultaneously involving different gender permutations. Chris's immediate thought – '*The queer years that I've been with you!*' – might have a different meaning for readers following the rise of Queer Studies than for most of its contemporary audience but, nonetheless, the feeling of uncanniness thereby generated creates a similar spark of self-recognition for anyone sufficiently invested in her viewpoint.

The process of male reader identification with Chris might be seen as similar to the experience of shame and self-recognition undergone by Dione in Mitchison's *We Have Been Warned* and theorised by Lynd. This is a double feeling by which the reader might feel shame at experiencing Chris's self-consciousness of being simultaneously desired object and desiring subject and then further shame at this feeling of being ashamed by a woman's complex sexuality. As discussed in the Introduction to this book, Lynd argues that shame helps answer questions of identity by providing a means of more fully apprehending the nature of the society and world to which we belong by making us aware of transcultural values. In the case of *A Scots Quair*, the transcultural values would be those lying 'beyond the sunset' in the alternative universe accessed by Chris at the end of *Grey Granite*; the knowledge which Burton describes as 'beyond the confines of both capitalism and patriarchy' (Burton 1984: 46). Knowledge of these transcultural values are only accessible for anyone by moving beyond the patriarchal order and the route provided for readers to achieve this goal is through identification with Chris and the processes by which she comes by turns to realise that, in the words of Ma Cleghorn, men 'never live at all' and that she, herself, is 'finished with men forever' (Gibbon 1986: 409, 447). 'Men', in this context, does not necessarily mean biological men but those inhabiting the subject position of patriarchy and the male gaze, without consciousness of themselves as also being objects. By going beyond the double shame caused by identification with Chris in the trilogy's mirror scenes, male readers might recognise and embrace the wider possibilities of going beyond being 'men', in the sense referred to by Chris, and opening themselves to a post-binary imaginary identification with all possible positions in the world. Because of this 'alignment of a multiplistic subjectivity with the feminine', Alison Lumsden argues that *A Scots Quair* can be considered as an example of *écriture feminine* (Lumsden 2003: 42–4).

Moreover, given, as suggested above, that *A Scots Quair* is also a work of autobiografiction, Gibbon must clearly have opened himself to a similar process of identification. As Glenda Norquay points out, Gibbon consistently uses intelligent, strong female characters as focalisers in his fiction:

> Whether because of a personal fascination, the centrality to his life of an intellectually dynamic marriage, or a recognition that women in this period serve to embody the modern moment and therefore presented the richest subject for fiction, both the novels of James Leslie Mitchell and the fiction of Lewis Grassic Gibbon operate through a particularly powerful attention to women and women's issues. (Norquay 2015: 76–7)

While the female protagonists and main characters of his fiction written as Mitchell are often emancipated new women, the characters drawn by Gibbon are more likely to be seen as products of their social context and rather than be exceptional are shown to achieve agency through a variety of different ways. In this manner, Gibbon shows a 'complex understanding of the components of female subjectivity' and through this develops a conception of identity formation which 'would appear to extend beyond patterning a gendered self' (Norquay 2015: 81–2). By identifying himself with feminine subjectivity, Gibbon found an answer to both the proletarian question of how to express a post-capitalist culture and the modernist question of how to identify a collective that would support a liberated identity:

> To read the author's fascination with women viewing their own bodies as voyeuristic is, in this context, to embody the sexual puritanism, repression and corruption that the novel is arguing against. An actively self-regarding sexuality becomes vital and political in this reimagining of modernity. (Norquay 2015: 84)

Implying that the scenes in which Chris looks at herself in the mirror are a voyeuristic presentation of her as a sexual object for consumption by a male readership shares structural similarities with the now discredited theory that transgender women are motivated to become women because of their experience of 'autogynephilia' – sexual arousal or fantasies involving imagining oneself as a woman (see Serrano 2010). Such theories exist solely to delegitimise not just transgender women's status as women but also any deviation from an essentialist adherence to a gender binary, assigned at birth according to biological markers, which underpins the symbolic functioning of the patriarchal order. Without moving beyond that binary, it is impossible to escape from that symbolic order. This is the reason why authors such as Gibbon, Lawrence and Sommerfield (as discussed in the next chapter) employ mirror scenes featuring female protagonists as complex sites of autobiografictional identification. Of course, it is a wider literary trope of the period and part of the process identified by Rita Felski by which 'an imaginary identification with the feminine emerged as a key stratagem in the literary avant-garde subversion of sexual and textual norms' (qtd in Norquay 2015: 88). However, its functioning within the proletarian literature of these authors is not just a subversive tool of a form of liberation which might – as Williams feared – never be compatible with any form of liveable society, but connected to the possibility of building new societies beyond the traditional hierarchies and patriarchal structures of existing capitalist society. As Norquay concludes of Gibbon, 'that project to imagine a different world, a project with women at its centre, shapes all his fiction' (Norquay 2015: 88).

Note

1. For an argument that 'anti-communism' should be understood as a cultural formation in its own right that is unrestricted by a coherent ideology and therefore almost uniquely attuned to even the slightest fluctuations in literature's social and political environment, see the introduction and articles in the special 'Literatures of Anti-Communism' issue of *Literature & History*, 24: 1 (Spring 2015).

Chapter 4

'The Raw Material of History': John Sommerfield's *May Day*

> The everyday consciousness that things could be different

John Sommerfield's *May Day* (1936) may be considered as the culmination of the trend of proletarian literature, by writers such as Gibbon, Greenwood, Lawrence, Mitchison and Wilkinson, considered so far in this book. One of the key contexts remains the General Strike of 1926 and the central concern is as much with gender relations as those of class. Unlike those other writers, Sommerfield was a communist who went on to fight in the Spanish Civil War. Furthermore, *May Day* includes relatively extensive scenes set in the factory workplace it is centred around; in contrast, we merely learn in *The First Lady Chatterley* that Parkin is working in a Steel Mill, we never see inside the factory gates in *Grey Granite*, and although we hear about Harry Hardcastle's joy at becoming a lathe operator, little action is set inside the factory in *Love on the Dole*. In this respect, the depiction of active class struggle in *May Day* represents an intensification of the conflict that features in these earlier novels. However, as Stuart Laing notes, the fates of the two Seton brothers in *May Day* parallel those of Greenwood's and Gibbon's characters:

> In the May Day march which forms the climax of the novel one brother (like Larry in *Love on the Dole*) dies after being struck by a policeman, while the other (like Ewan in *Grey Granite*) simultaneously takes a leading part and finds his uncertain political commitment becoming firm. (Laing 1980: 147)

While the focus on the significance of May Day itself as a temporal rallying point for the dream of the classless society to come is also a feature of Mitchison's *We Have Been Warned* (see Mitchison 2012: 172–87), *May Day* is actually a transitional novel marking the point at which the proletarian literature of the decade following the General Strike switches from dealing with the aftermath of defeat to encompassing the rapid social change of the 1930s and anticipating the politics and representational forms of the Popular Front, which would dominate the second half of the decade.

The action of *May Day*, as a prefatory note to the novel informs us, 'takes place between the morning of April the twenty-ninth and the early afternoon of May the first a few years hence' (Sommerfield 1936: ix). However, Sommerfield quickly quashes any notion that he is intending a work of prediction by suggesting that the reader should 'view the situations depicted as belonging to an *average* year between 1930–40 rather than to any definite date' (Sommerfield 1936: ix). The resultant mild temporal dislocation is heightened by Sommerfield's use of cinematic techniques, particularly montage and close-up, to depict a broad cross-section of London lives interlinked through the network of social relations surrounding the focal point of Langfier's factory. In this respect, Sommerfield anticipates Alick West's call for a literature that shows the world of individuals both to lie within the society they live in and to be shaped by the conflicts around the capitalist production process. As with *Grey Granite* and the examples examined in Chapter 2, *May Day* attempts to fuse political and sexual desire into 'a new politicised and gendered imagination' (Ferrall and McNeill 2015: 145). Sommerfield differs from Gibbon, though, in that he includes women workers within his proletarian framework rather than allowing an opposition such as that between Ewan and Chris to develop. Not only are women, such as Ivy Cutford, a significant component of the factory workforce but, as Ronald Paul notes, despite critics' tendencies to view *May Day* in terms of the relationships between the male protagonists, it is the 'complex intersectional web of gender and class, of action and reaction among the women that gives the novel its particular dynamic' (Paul 2012: 124).

This is not to suggest that the novel does not register conventionally gendered differences of political consciousness as, for example, in the relationship between John Seton, a carpenter in the factory workshop and his wife, Martine. Paul suggests that 'there is an emotional strain between these two people with John feeling drawn to the trade-union struggle at work and Martine acting as a break [sic] on his militancy by her dreams of domestic bliss' (Paul 2012: 125). John feels guilty towards Martine because he knows that she wants to feel safe from poverty and aspires to 'a nice home with bright curtains and new furniture [. . .] [t]o think her husband was a "Red" would fill her life with a perpetual sense of danger' (Sommerfield 1936: 27). This couple are the second and third of the novel's dozens of named protagonists to be introduced to us, immediately following the opening scenes in which John's seaman brother James sails up the Thames as his ship returns to port after a long voyage. Given that work as a seaman and a carpenter (making stage scenery) had been Sommerfield's two main occupations since leaving University College School in Hampstead at the age of sixteen, it is clear that the Seton brothers function to some extent as an autobiografictional presence in the text. Although both are politicised, there is a crucial difference between James as a rootless individual on shore leave and John as a rooted member of a collective workplace. Read purely through the relative trajectories of the two brothers, the implicit message of *May Day* might be taken to be that the individualism represented by James has to die – he is bludgeoned to death by a policeman close to the novel's climax – so that collective protest can generate 'a new phase of class struggle' (Sommerfield 1936: 245).[1] Indeed, Brian McKenna has argued that the novel's ending is simply an explicit espousal of the Communist Party line at the time, as evidenced by the following passage which he describes as 'so over-appropriate' as to 'border on the badly written' (McKenna 1996: 377):

> The workers seethe around the base of the Arch like an angry sea, and the noise comes up to the men at the top like the sound of a storm as James's flag-draped body is held up and saluted by a hundred thousand clenched fists raised in the air, a hundred thousand shouts of 'Red Front.' (Sommerfield 1936: 242)

McKenna uses this example as part of his wider assertion that traditional 'monologic' left-wing novels were often more effective than apparently 'polyphonic' texts such as *Grey Granite* or *May Day*, which are 'vulnerable to critique on other grounds (such as sensationalism, sentimentality, lack of insight into bourgeois characters, or whatever)'

(McKenna 1996: 384). However, the fact that he describes James as the 'main character' highlights how his reading of *May Day* is dependent on judging it against what he takes to be the traditional norms of the novel (McKenna 1996: 376).

It seems more plausible to interpret this aspect of the novel as autobiografiction, as a means of Sommerfield performatively completing his own transition from individual adventurer to communist, rather than as an expression of narrow propaganda. However, what is particularly significant about this autobiografictional element of the novel is that apart from the aforementioned fact that John is part of the local community and his brother is not, there is nothing else which particularly distinguishes John in any way from the other characters in the novel, all of whom are occupying positions defined by their position in the network of social relations surrounding the particular means of production embodied by Langfier's factory. It is noticeable that the first three times that John's name is mentioned in the novel, it is linked with Martine's as part of the unit 'John and Martine' (Sommerfield 1936: 8–9). In fact, the pair of them are linked not only with each other but also with 'the baby, and Mick the dog' as equally the producers of the 'four breathing rhythms' that are the only sound in their little room under the eaves before the early-morning alarm clock rings (Sommerfield 1936: 8). On the one hand, the scene presents an Edenic harmony that pre-exists whatever emotional strains the capitalist system will place upon it during the course of the day, while on the other hand it serves as the first of many everyday moments within the novel in which the possibility of social relationships existing outside the mediation of capital is made visible. These everyday moments arise when either the memory trace of unalienated experience becomes conscious, such as when John remembers a day in the country with Martine as he cycles to work (Sommerfield 1936: 13), or when personal interaction is so immediate that externally imposed social relations cease to have purchase, such as the scene where John senses Martine sitting next to him in the cinema and the resultant bodily awareness releases him from the spell of 'the romance of chorus girls and big business men' (Sommerfield 1936: 90):

> But the world is *not* so, was the burden of his thoughts. It was not all love and breasts and the romance of big business. For me the factory is the world, the house we live in, the May Day demonstration, David's messing his napkin, Langfier's car, the price of tobacco and

food, pain and fatigue and going to the lavatory. Life is a struggle for us, life is a battle under the long shadows of the factory chimneys. (Sommerfield 1936: 91)

Here, the irruption of the immediacy of the everyday provides John with a vantage point outside capitalist social relations from which to gain an overview of them and relate them to a materialist view that is not derived from theory but actual lived experience. Later, in bed, where they make love naked and with no sense of sexual shame – a state of affairs that is clearly ascribed by the text as due to Martine's influence on John – their bodily awareness of each other results in a perfect intersubjective moment in which both become fully conscious of themselves through total acceptance of the other: 'Clasped in each other's arms, their mouths and bodies locked, they sighed into consciousness of their separate selves' (Sommerfield 1936: 106). Furthermore, far from John and Martine being presented to us as exceptional, we are told that 'their sighs were echoed far and wide' in thousands of rooms across London emphasising the point that there is a collective basis to everyday experience that offers an alternative to social structures mediated by property relations.

Applying this potentially transformative everyday context to the passage discussed by Paul as demonstrating an 'emotional strain' between John and Martine, it becomes possible to read John's 'inner ache of disloyalty to Martine' not as the sign of an opposition between them but as a register of how much her concerns have become his concerns. It is significant that Martine is not actually present during these scenes, rather John is thinking about her while at work discussing factory politics with colleagues. The overall logic of the passage, therefore, is not that gender perspectives are irreconcilable with those of class but that the two categories of experience need always to be held in dialogue with each other. By picturing Martine's facial reaction to being confronted with the uncertainty and potential poverty consequent on his taking strike action, John is instantly reminded of how she looked when her labour pains began and of the bodily experience of walking to the hospital with her; the moment when he first realised that poverty and unemployment were not '"misfortunes" coming from the sky like thunderbolts' but the consequences of the capitalist system (Sommerfield 1936: 27). Therefore, while the relationship between John and Martine is represented unequally to the extent that it is John that is afforded the subjective consciousness and Martine who functions as the constant reminder of everyday bodily existence, its purpose in showing class and gender concerns as inextricably entwined is nonetheless central to the novel's overall project. The relationship also serves, as Elinor Taylor notes, to demonstrate the links between commodities and labour through Martine's desire for an armchair made of the artificial leather produced by Langfier's (Taylor 2014: 67–8). In a scene that does feature Martine's point of view, the 'leathery' armchair features as part of her vision 'small and distinct, as through the wrong end of a telescope, [of] a little house with shining windows and very bright red-and-white check curtains' (Sommerfield 1936: 118). This daydream is not denigrated in anyway by the narrative or represented in terms of the shame that, as discussed in the Introduction to this book, Pamela Fox identifies as often attached to female working-class material desire. On the contrary, it is actually the novel's only concrete projection of what future life might look like if society was orientated towards meeting social needs. While this sense of the centrality of such desires, typically gendered as female, to the realisation of a future society is implicit rather than explicit in *May Day*, it becomes more explicit in Sommerfield's later work such as *Trouble in Porter Street* (1939) in which the impetus for a successful rent strike is Rosie Dixon's desire for a better standard of living and the possibility of going on a proper holiday; this novella is further discussed in the next chapter. His postwar novel, *The Inheritance* (1956), features Betty Lidstone, a wife and a trade unionist, who acts as both the subjective consciousness and the embodiment of the novel's hopes for a socialist future. Far from being the doctrinaire communist of the period that critics like McKenna and David Smith identify, Sommerfield stands out amongst the leftist intelligentsia of the 1930s and afterwards because of his relaxed attitude to the material desires of women in and of the masses in general.[2] This can be seen most clearly in his 'Author's Note for 1984 Edition' of *May Day*, which might have been expected to have referred to the renewed need for struggle in the Thatcherite period but instead focused on how class relations had been transformed since the 1930s so that only 'the truly rich and powerful can still carry on more or less as if nothing had really changed' (Sommerfield 1984a: xviii). Indeed, one might even think that Sommerfield is suggesting that the politics he gave expression to in *May Day* was somehow successful in fulfilling the dreams and desires of those like John and Martine: 'The material circumstances and social climate of everyday life in this country now would have seemed unbelievable to the people depicted in *May Day*' (Sommerfield 1984a: xix).

However, it needs to be emphasised that while John and Martine are obviously on one level intended to be representative of young working-class couples, their role in the text is not simply to signify this particular social type but to illustrate, in the way that the novel links them to other protagonists, how everyone is potentially connected in a manner that transcends social types. So, for example, in the scene where their lovemaking is set in the context of that of thousands of others across London, the focus shifts to one of the factory workers, Molly Davis, gasping despite failing to reach orgasm with her unnamed lover. The tenderness she nonetheless 'feels for the sake of her lover's pleasure' still carries her sufficiently outside capitalist time and space for its unwelcome reinvasion of her consciousness to feel 'like the suddenly remembered ticking of a clock to one tortured with insomnia' (Sommerfield 1936: 107). What links the working-class characters in the novel is this heightened sensitivity to everyday moments outside calendar time which they possess precisely because these are their only waking moments when not subject to the internalised rhythms of the factory in the form of 'the endless song of the machines and the sense of strain and hurry' (Sommerfield 1936: 108). In turn, the consciousness of these characters provides a key for reading the temporal location of the novel's non-working-class characters. So while the former factory worker, Jenny Hardy, who is now maintained in a flat as the mistress to the Works Manager, Dartry, has escaped the machines, she can still remember their noise. Therefore, she is aware of her freedom in a way that Dartry, lying at her side plagued by the spectre of senility and impotence, is not. Without the means of sensing a liberated time, he is reduced to torturing himself with 'visions of impotent desire' (Sommerfield 1936: 108). Here, Sommerfield demonstrates a deft psychological analysis of the limits of masculine bourgeois subjectivity with Dartry's position anticipating that of the Lacanian neurotic 'imagin[ing] that the Other demands his castration' (Lacan 1980: 323). Ironically, his fear of the risks of offering himself as the object of pleasure to his lover prevents him from grasping the freedom that surrounds him and condemns him to an existence equivalent to that of the factory worker under the capitalist system; shuddering 'to the insistent hammerblows of his beating heart' rather than actual machinery (Sommerfield 1936:

108). However, unlike the workers, he has no means of taking collective action to overthrow what is an entirely self-imposed condition and therefore he lacks their agency.

A further night-time contrast in the novel is established with respect to the residual upper-class relationships represented within the household of the factory's owner, Sir Edwin Langfier:

> Tomorrow, thinks Jean the maid, tomorrow . . . we will be together again, we will be clasped in each other's arms under the tree shadows. The day will be too long until that moment . . . if only we had somewhere to go, somewhere of our own where we could be alone and private . . .
> Tomorrow, thinks Langfier. Tomorrow will be another day . . . there is no sense in this procession of days once that I expect nothing from tomorrow that was not in yesterday.
> Tomorrow, thinks Bertha the cook, tomorrow I will make a kedgeree.
> Peter thought about Pamela. Her cheeks are like flowerpetals, he thinks. They have a bloom that I am frightened to touch, to spoil. Also I wish to possess her with the utmost shamelessness.
> Lady Langfier dreamed the incoherent dreams of a child. (Sommerfield 1936: 188–9)

This is more than just a parody of *Mrs Dalloway*. Rather, in line with the way that *May Day* employs the devices of Woolf's novel to show the connectedness of people from different backgrounds in London, Sommerfield also seeks to relate Woolf's representation of time as subjectively experienced to the proletarian time inhabited by the factory workers. Here, the point is not so much to demonstrate the impoverishment of a non-proletarian consciousness for someone working in the production process such as Dartry, but to illustrate how those outside the production process yearn for a means of transforming calendar time so that tomorrow will be different. The overall logic of *May Day* is in accordance with the Marxist idea that it is proletarian subjectivity and experience which generates the agency that makes the transformation of society possible for the benefit of all. However, what distinguishes the novel is Sommerfield's understanding of not only how Woolfian techniques make it possible to show the interaction of different subjectivities across society, but also how widespread people's desire for a different kind of time is. It is this unconscious agreement uncovered by the adoption of a Woolfian approach that justifies the final sentence of the main narrative of *May Day*: 'Everyone has agreed on the need for a big change' (Sommerfield 1936: 242).

Working women's historical agency

Of course, British society did undergo a big change in the decade following *May Day*'s publication and that change did revolve around the way in which working-class consciousness became central to both cultural and political representation. In this respect, *May Day* anticipates both the intermodernist mode of representation which arguably became culturally dominant during the Second World War and the changes in British society that marked the postwar decades. The understanding that the novel is related to actually existing change rather than an imaginary set of events necessarily diverts the focus of criticism from its revolutionary themes and imagery, such as the 'hundred thousand shouts of "Red Front"' (Sommerfield 1936: 242) at the novel's close, and other examples of what Sommerfield retrospectively labelled 'early 30s communist romanticism' (Sommerfield 1984a: xviii–xix). Once attention is turned to the novel's representation of those social trends which did continue across the wartime and postwar years and contribute to the transformation of Britain that Sommerfield saw so clearly in 1984, then it becomes clear that the most significant factual feature of *May Day* is its focus on the emergence of politicised women factory workers during the course of the 1930s. Following the equalisation of the voting franchise in 1928 and the change in labour patterns which saw the opportunity of mechanised factory work preferred to domestic service, there was a marked increase in the self-confidence of young working-class women. As the economy emerged from recession, and as mass-production techniques led to the establishment and rapid expansion of new manufacturing industries, both male and female workers were in demand and consequently had greater bargaining rights than in the previous decades. In this context, as Selina Todd demonstrates in her history of the British working class, *The People* (2014), women were often at the forefront of demands for better pay and conditions, such as the campaign for paid holidays, upsetting the usually male-dominated local union hierarchies, who were still scared of being labelled militants as a result of the failure and aftermath of the General Strike. When women workers at the Wolsey factory in Leicester went on strike in December 1931 over concerns of how the introduction of the mechanised Bedaux system would affect their piece rates, their actions were initially treated dismissively, as Todd records:

> The Wolsey strikers earned themselves the disapproving title of 'Boisterous Workers' in the local press. The epithet suggested that their spontaneous action – there was no single leader – was provoked by the young women's frivolous attitude to work; much was made of their 'singing and dancing' as they formed a picket line outside the factory. Initially, the Leicester Hosiery Union (LHU), which enjoyed a good relationship with Wolsey's management, appeared to agree. It was not until 10 December, three days after the young women had walked out, that the LHU formally agreed to support their dispute. The union leaders had previously avoided the contentious issue of the Bedaux scheme. Their sympathies lay with those skilled, male workers who were not required to undertake automated tasks and so were unlikely to be directly affected by the reforms. (Todd 2014: 103)

However, following the LHU's delayed recognition of the Strike, most of the factory workforce also came out in support, while many of the women joined the union. Although the eventual outcome was a compromise in which the mechanisation went ahead with negotiated piece rates in place, significant bargaining rights were gained for the unskilled and semi-skilled factory work in which not just most of the women but also many men were employed. As a result of this and other struggles, the attitudes of national union leadership to women workers changed so that by the mid-1930s, Britain's largest union, the Transport and General Workers Union (TGWU), was actively targeting the recruitment of women, had a women's page in its magazine and acknowledged in general that 'enthusiasm for dancing, cycling, rambling, football, gymnastics, and other organised sports and pastimes can usefully be diverted into trade union channels' (qtd in Todd 2014: 106).

Acknowledgement and understanding of this wider process of women's involvement in factories and the union movement, and the debate surrounding it, is often missing from the frequent citation by critics of part or all of the following passage from *May Day*:

> Blondes and brunettes, beauties and uglies, good girls and bad girls, virgins and tarts, so much flesh, so many thoughts and feelings, so

many drab, cheerless destinies, so many who might have been born at some time in some other place to live the lives of human beings. At least once the moment will come in each of these lives when they will stop and think, 'What have we born for, why do we live as we do, toiling only to eat, eating only to toil . . .' This moment may come and be forgotten in an instant, or it may be a sudden revelation altering the whole course of a life.

These silly girls with their synthetic Hollywood dreams, their pathetic silk stockings and lipsticks, their foolish strivings to escape from the cramped monotony of their lives, are the raw material of history. When their moment of deep discontent comes to them in a mass, taking form in their class leaders, then there are revolutions. What happens to the revolutions depends upon other facts – automatic lathes for instance. (Sommerfield 1936: 30)

The first paragraph up to the end of the penultimate sentence is reproduced by Klaus as evidence of Sommerfield's tendency to 'simply enumerate' details of London life rather than 'flesh' them out in 'concrete experience' (Klaus 1979: 151), whereas the first sentence of the second paragraph has been quoted by critics seeking to denigrate Sommerfield himself. David Smith cites it as representative of Sommerfield's 'dubious' attitude to his characters, who he implies are merely instrumental with regards to the novel's propagandist aims (Smith 1978: 66). Peter Gurney includes it in a footnote as support for a lengthy analysis of one of the pub reports that Sommerfield wrote for Mass-Observation, in which he concludes that Sommerfield displays a typical middle-class disgust in his attitude to working-class women (Gurney 1997: 275n.).[3] Commenting on this accusation, James Hinton has noted, correctly, that Gurney is patently wrong to accuse Sommerfield of middle-class fastidiousness but suggests instead that the claim that he was guilty of masculine arrogance is borne out by 'May Day, which combines a realistic (if over-politicised) account of working-class life with a relentlessly sexualised treatment of the female characters' (Hinton 2013: 35n.). Even Ronald Paul, who quotes the full passage in his account of how May Day demonstrates the intersectional relationship between class and gender, criticises the 'predominantly masculinist point-of-view' on display here and, because he interprets Sommerfield as saying that this mass of women can only be led forward by male 'class leaders', insists that 'there is therefore no irony intended in the description of these women as the physical "raw material of history"' (Paul 2012: 127–8).

However, the logic of the novel is that it is the 'dreams' and 'foolish strivings to escape' of these young women workers which will provide the hitherto missing catalyst necessary for transformational social change in the same way that the actual influx of women workers in 1930s Britain transformed workplace and trade union practice. Moreover, they find their class leaders within themselves: it is Molly Davis, whom we last encountered in her lover's arms, who jumps up in the mess room and shouts, 'How much longer are we going to stand for this, girls!' after her friend Daisy is injured by one of the machines (Sommerfield 1936: 150). Both Molly and Daisy accompany the communist, Ivy Cutford, in the ultimately successful deputation to gain the support of the men for setting up a Work's Committee. As with the 1931 Wolsey factory strike, it is the women workers who act and initiate the dispute thus demonstrating their possession of agency, which is intrinsically linked to their material and sexual desires. In this respect, Sommerfield's 'sexualised' treatment of his women characters is progressive, despite some of his choices of idiom, because it always acknowledges and never criticises this key component of female subjectivity. By including Molly, who has 'the reputation of being a bit of a tart' (Sommerfield 1936: 150), and the former factory worker turned mistress, Jenny Hardy, within the continuum of women protagonists alongside Martine and Ivy, he evades the discourses of respectability and deservingness which plagued earlier writing about the working class and working-class women in particular. Instead he highlights what links working women's lives under patriarchy and capitalism and demonstrates the importance of having the means to escape the deleterious effects of these twin forms of oppression for a more materially secure future.

As Paul notes, examples like that of Jenny provide 'intersectional points in the novel where the connection between class and gender is shown to be fraught with social and psychological tensions' (Paul 2012: 129–30). Yet these points also indicate the possibility for different forms of living. When the novel returns to Jenny in the early afternoon of the day after her evening with Dartry, we find her mooching around in a kimono contemplating a bath:

> . . . I'll put the bath on in a minute. . . . I do look a sight . . . wish I had something to read . . . be all right if I had some of the girls up here now, they wouldn't half envy the flat and all my dresses: they

must be just packing up dinner now, going back to work feeling slow and heavy and hating to begin. Glad I'm through with that, anything's better, day after day with nothing nice to look forward to, nothing nice to eat or wear . . . wonder if Molly's still there, wonder how she is. . . . I'd like to see her again . . . she was always silly, throwing herself away with men. . . . It must have stopped raining, I'll look . . . such a grey, dull day – wish the sun'd shine, I could go a walk. I do feel mouldy. Maybe I'll call up Jack . . . I don't know . . . don't feel in the mood now . . . it was rotten last night, he made a mess of it the last time, the old fool. . . . I always feel mouldy like this after I've been with him, all nervy and fed up. If I see Jack now I'll have a row with him, I'd like to shout at someone . . . perhaps I'll go to the pictures . . . must put the bath on . . . the time drags so on days like this . . . (Sommerfield 1936: 160–1)

Her stream of consciousness illustrates both the possibilities of a life no longer governed by the factory and the frustration of no longer being part of the collective. Yet, while she is fed up with her situation with Dartry, and not feeling in the mood to see her boyfriend, the overriding sense here is of a modern self-reflexive consciousness waiting for time to become meaningful in order that she can come into her own. Her example indicates how existence will be different outside the social relations of capitalism even though modern consciousness is not in itself sufficient to actually effect the change that will make things different. This suggests that Sommerfield is using these intersectional points in the text to show how modern self-consciousness and class consciousness need to be brought into alignment in order to enable change. This necessity is made most apparent in the case of Ivy Cutford, who might try to 'think of Lenin' while summoning the courage to jump up and make the suggestion of setting up a Work's Committee to her colleagues (Sommerfield 1936: 150–1), but still travels back in the evening from her Communist Party meeting on her 'lonely bus-ride' to her 'lonely little room' with 'an intolerable longing for a lover, a longing to be desired for once instead of liked, to be followed by amorous looks through the soft night' (Sommerfield 1936: 99). Here, the trajectory is not significantly different from the experience of the protagonist of Katherine Mansfield's 'The Tiredness of Rosabel', which was discussed in Chapter 1, but whereas Rosabel's fantasies, desires and aspirations are ultimately designated by that story as the products of a 'tragic optimism', Ivy can fulfil her desires by changing the world so that the type of relationship and life she wants becomes possible.

When Sommerfield describes the women factory workers as the raw material of history, therefore, it is clear that he is not simultaneously precluding them from being the agents of history. Indeed, rather his point seems to be that the very materiality of women, the fact that they can be simultaneously figured as subjects and objects, is what marks them out as possessing a depth and substance lacking from male subjectivity. This intention is perhaps most apparent in the scene where he discusses the daily routine of the capital's female typists collectively engaged in producing written material ranging from business letters to novels, biographies and autobiographies: 'From this record one half of contemporary life can be deduced, and a material history and philosophy of the organisation of society' (Sommerfield 1936: 126). In fact, what Sommerfield is saying is that all recorded history and culture amounts to only half of human experience and the other half lies in 'lonely and incommunicable private lives and thoughts':

> 'I want' is the burden of these thoughts, and the hates and preoccupations are with the circumstances of their lives that give or deny them their desires. Love, happiness, lust, the bearing of children, the wearing of clothes, the ordering of comfortable homes, wealth and romance, travels – of these are the thoughts that dream, that vainly cry 'I want.' (Sommerfield 1936: 127)

As with modernist fiction in general (see Tratner 1995: 48–76), *May Day* makes the unconscious half of human experience visible by making working-class women visible. Sommerfield continues from this passage by seguing into the individual desires of the stenographer of the Langfier's manager, Dartry, and then from her thoughts to his: 'these little typists and these factory girls filled him with a hunting lust, filled him with a desire that the women of other classes could not arouse' (Sommerfield 1936: 127). Therefore, while the novel does not directly address the feminist concerns that explicitly frame Mitchison's *We Have Been Warned* or more implicitly structure Gibbon's *A Scots Quair*, it is nonetheless clearly trying to find a way of representing women as material sexual beings without reducing them purely to the status of sexual object for the male gaze as personified by Dartry. Those critics who fail to see that Sommerfield is not simply presenting his women protagonists as sexualised are, in effect, choosing to occupy the bourgeois subject position of Dartry which is rejected by *May Day*. Indeed, they are missing the point that one of the central concerns of *May Day* is with how to replicate the successful incorporation of female unconsciousness and sexuality by individualist modernist novels into a collectivist novel concerned with society as a whole.

A portrait of the proletarian artist as a young man

As Taylor suggests, to approach *May Day* as simply an example of 'leftist writers' appropriation of modernist techniques' is to risk undervaluing both key aspects of Sommerfield's individual development as a writer and left literary practice in the 1930s (Taylor 2014: 60–1). As discussed, *May Day* incorporates elements of Sommerfield's own life and in this respect it can be read as a continuation of his first novel, *They Die Young* (1930), starting at a similar point to the latter's ending with a protagonist returning to London from the sea. On one level, therefore, the two novels autobiografictionally chart Sommerfield's progress to becoming a part of the communist movement. However, at the same time, the link between *May Day* and its predecessor, which was written before Sommerfield had become a communist, suggests that 'Sommerfield's style, methods and preoccupations were not simply produced by his engagement with Communism' (Taylor 2014: 63).

Sommerfield, the son of the newspaper editor and journalist, Vernon Sommerfield, was educated at University College School in Hampstead, where he was a contemporary of Stephen Spender and Maurice Cornforth. Although he gained much early experience of working-class life and labour once he left school at the age of sixteen, he did not come from the working class and he also had experience of radically different environments such as Wall Street, where he worked for a while before the crash, and the London theatrical scene for which he was building sets. The two novels may be read together as a working through of these differences in experience. Saunders notes that autobiografiction serves as the necessary precondition for 'the emergence of the modernist *Künstlerroman* (or novel about the development of the artist) which coincides with . . . experimentation combining the fictive and the auto/biographical' (Saunders 2010: 11). A close analysis of *They Die Young* suggests that Sommerfield draws on the model of the autobiografictional *Künstlerroman* in order to become an artist by the means of writing a fictional account of himself becoming an artist.

They Die Young is a self-consciously modern novel which begins with the death of Christopher, a poet and actor.[4] Following his recent experiences working as a common seaman, Christopher realises that he has cut himself off from the youthful carefree existence that defined his identity but also that had he grown up retaining those qualities he would have become ridiculous. Forlorn at the realisation that there is no future for him as he still thinks of himself, he accelerates his racing Bentley and overshoots the lip of a quarry to find that 'he had freed himself from dimensions and overtaken the trampling feet of time, so that the past yet lay in the future and he was once again the Christopher of two years ago' (Sommerfield 1930: 11). So the action of the novel forms an endlessly cycling time loop capturing the ending of the 1920s and the mode of living which characterised it, while anticipating the concerns that would dominate the 1930s without being able to conceive of an appropriate way of realising those.

The main part of the novel is set two years earlier, just after Christopher has come down from Oxford – unlike Sommerfield, who left school at sixteen – and, fed up with writing poems in the countryside, decides to take up the invitation of his friend Samuel to go and work with him at a new art theatre in London. The City is depicted as a giddying vortex within which Christopher's life is shown as a swirl of encounters with smart young women and drunken nights with Samuel:

> Pubs. First one then another. Some more. Oneafteranother. upanddown stairs. They were drinking Beer, then they were drinking Sherry, it might have been at the same place or it might have been at another. It was hard to remember.
>   bring us some of your 1868 Sherry.
>   Migawd Samuel. What *have* you done, we can't pay for all that.
>   all what
>   That
>   what That
>   eighteen hundred and sixty-eight sherries. (Sommerfield 1930: 61)

This passage highlights the avant-garde features of *They Die Young*. The lack of speech marks, word play, ellipsis and line breaks functioning to record fragmented consciousness are particularly emphasised here – in a passage clearly influenced by Joyce – to represent drunken experience but they occur throughout the novel, marking it as more overtly modernist in form than *May Day*. Moreover, *They*

Die Young is also explicitly metatextual, referring to Arnold Bennett, Virginia Woolf and James Branch Cabell in the six-page sequence that follows on from this night out (Sommerfield 1930: 66–72). For example, Woolf is invoked playfully to describe Christopher's stream of consciousness while walking up steps in the theatre where he is involved in a play:

> ... And the large extent of his thoughts made the climb of these stairs as crowded with incident as an interminable hundred yards in St. James Park as featured in the works of Mrs. Virginia Woolf; so that when he reached the door of his dressing-room he had passed through far more experiences and emotions than could be suffered in the four or five seconds that it has taken him to ascend from the stage door. (Sommerfield 1930: 69)

In contrast, Cabell is invoked to describe Christopher's relationship to his lover, Chloe Vanderlyn, who also has the lead role in the play:

> Seeing her out there in that brazen glare it was not quite possible to believe that she had lain in his arms – 'so much prostrate, sweating and submissive meat' as, with more realism than delicacy, Mr. Cabell puts it. One could not connect the women out there with such episodes. And indeed what did he know of Miss Chloe Vanderlyn to indicate that she so disported herself? She was a stranger to him and his Chloe. (Sommerfield 1930: 71–2)

By placing these different viewpoints side by side in this carefully designated manner, Sommerfield is able to investigate the relationship between consciousness and body in gendered terms and, more specifically, Christopher's difficulty in relating to women as both subject and object. In the novel's earlier description of his first sleeping with Chloe, he struggles to deal with the demands placed on him by her sexual desire to yield to him: 'The lust had gone out of him and he was the youthful Christopher again. Strange that he should have reduced the overpowering Miss Chloe Vanderlyn to this recumbent and desirous woman. Strange and a little disgusting and alarming [. . .]' (Sommerfield 1930: 42).

The sequence in the theatre suggests that this earlier scene is actually an authorial critique of Christopher's desire to maintain his male subject position rather than a straightforward expression of male disgust at female sexuality. This is made apparent to us though the characters' double status as characters in the play going on in the theatre. So the Christopher who cannot link Miss Chloe Vanderlyn with the physical body he has made love to suddenly finds himself on stage – having automatically responded to his cue – without 'the slightest idea of what he was going to do or say' (Sommerfield 1930: 72). Only when she smiles at him and thus provides the confirmation of the subjectivity that he is incapable of finding within himself does he remember his words.

This authorial illustration of the inadequacy of the male protagonist sets up an interesting dynamic to the text as it pursues the solution of the problem of modernist consciousness across different configurations of both gender relationships and literary styles. For example, crossing the Atlantic to visit his father in New York, Christopher has an intense but chaste relationship with Lucille, a freelance journalist, returning to her home in Virginia after two years in Paris. A momentary equivalence between the couple is indicated as they lie side by side on the bed in her cabin listening to a portable gramophone and reading the current number of *transition* (Sommerfield 1930: 93). However, first the journal and then the music become neglected as Christopher starts to talk about the future and complains that he cannot enjoy the transience of their time together because of the imminence of their separation on arrival. In contrast, Lucille argues that 'other existences are waiting for us when we arrive and when we take them up again this will seem a gap – an interval in coping with being alive' (Sommerfield 1930: 94). All the while, the up-and-down motion of the ship increases to the point where their feet at the bottom of the bed are swinging through virtually 180 degrees relative to their heads. The implication of the passage is that she is aware of, and accepts, this element of relativity, which is constantly present throughout the novel. However, although Christopher is also aware of relativity, he finds it difficult to reconcile it with the linearity demanded by conventional male subjectivity. The difference between the two is further illustrated when they get off the bed and readjust their clothing. Lucille stands in front of the mirror and thinks to herself: 'this affair of planes, curves and surfaces, is my face, It is me – perhaps these features *make* me, or do they but reflect the am that I am . . . Then I see nothing but a reflection of a reflection' (Sommerfield 1930: 96). Christopher tugs his tie straight and smiles at her in the mirror before kissing the back of her neck and departing.

This passage, similarly to the mirror scenes from the work of Lawrence and Gibbon examined in earlier chapters, anticipates subsequent developments in psychoanalytic theory. By showing how self-conscious subjectivity is generated and maintained by the process of self-recognition as the reflected image, and gendering this process, Sommerfield generates his own primitive version of the distinction between a female imaginary and a patriarchal symbolic order. Christopher is capable neither of sharing Lucille's self-recognition and so accepting a transitory and fragmented existence in the world, nor of imposing himself into the reflection as the equivalent of the male adult figure. In effect, he runs away from the choice. Any doubt as to whether Sommerfield is consciously drawing on Freudian models is resolved by the following section of the novel set in New York during which Christopher lives with his father and has an affair with his stepmother, Gerda.

On Christopher's arrival in America, his tycoon father gets him a job in Wall Street, which is described in the novel in terms reminiscent of Fritz Lang's *Metropolis*. The packed subways are 'greedy alimentary tubes of the machines that each morning absorbed men and women, sucked them from their homes and excreted them as digested masses' who strive for dollars and the one hope of 'a parasitic idleness dependent upon [the machine's] functions' (Sommerfield 1930: 120). While Christopher tries to pretend that he might spend his life in New York and become a sleek stockbroker, he finds his eye increasingly drawn to the harbour that can be seen from the windows of his high office and the fantasy of becoming a common sailor 'with flapping trousers and a gob cap at the back of his head', who would sing, fight and get drunk with his shipmates, while sampling local brothels and gaols (Sommerfield 1930: 129). This fantasy, which is driven by Christopher's desire to escape from his own social and familial situation rather than any positive support for the chosen group, corresponds exactly to Raymond Williams's conception of negative identification. However, given that his father is out of town on a business trip and that he is sleeping with his stepmother, Christopher's motivation cannot simply be reduced to an attempt to escape from the law of the father. Indeed, Gerda even brushes aside any suggestion that the relationship might prove awkward on his father's return. However, Christopher, as with Chloe earlier on, resents having his role delimited to being Gerda's means of self-affirmation: 'She was the abstract of desire, angering Christopher that he should be nothing to her but an instrument of gratification' (Sommerfield 1930: 144–5). He remains caught in two minds as to what his role in life should be, reluctant to take on the patriarchal role of the male but also unwilling to accept the more fluid and self-reflexive subject positions of the female world. What attracts him to the possibility of being a sailor is the sense that he will have to follow prescribed 'lines of action' (Sommerfield 1930: 156) and therefore can escape the gendered dichotomy of volition to a third way of letting himself become an object of fate almost, to be swept wherever the dictates of the shipping companies would take him. This whole dynamic of escaping choice, including the actual descriptions of parts of New York, especially the docks and piers and the men there, is similar to John Dos Passos's *Manhattan Transfer* (1925) and *The 42nd Parallel* (1930). While Sommerfield's novel lacks the explicit political consciousness of those works, it has an extra layer of self-awareness as illustrated by the fact that Christopher's first experience of sea life is exactly the sequence of going out with his shipmates, getting drunk, starting a fist fight and getting arrested that he imagined in Wall Street. The purpose of this self-awareness is made evident in the description of the court house: 'Contrasting with the night outside, the place had a fantastic air of an attempt at reality, like a modernistic stage setting that reduces realism to a few representative essentialities, and so achieves a kind of abstraction, a super-reality' (Sommerfield 1930: 175). Here, the passage in effect admits that the logic of the earlier stage sequence discussed above extends throughout the novel. This exposure of scenes in the novel as staged affects how the passages that might otherwise be read as straightforward realism are received. For example, a sequence in which Christopher watches the loading of bananas at docks in the tropics gives rise to an awareness of the horror of endless labour throughout the life cycle for generation after generation (Sommerfield 1930: 204–7), which is subsequently connected to his own experience endlessly scrubbing decks as a seaman:

> A sense of enormous futility rose in him. All over the world people were spending the greater part of their lives in this manner and, what was worse, unthinkingly accepting it as a reasonable proposition that they should continue to do so. Blind to the futility of their unending pointless efforts, doubtless they were happier, but as long as they continued in their blindness so it would continue for their lives and the lives of their children. (Sommerfield 1930: 222)

While Christopher is clearly depressed, the staged nature of the novel deconstructs the realism of the scene or rather it deconstructs the idea that this is somehow a natural condition of the Earth. Rather, capitalism is being shown to be a modernistic stage setting that includes a few representative essentialities to conjure the illusion of reality. While Christopher feels the weight of this illusion of unescapable reality, the construction of the novel lays bare how this reality is artificially imposed. This gives the novel an interesting political stance because it demonstrates the fallacy of choosing labour and imagining this is in fact a choice of reality over a modern life equated with female consciousness. To this end, Christopher's going to sea is not the decisive break from 'false consciousness' that might be imagined if the book's real aim was to assert the value of reality over modernity.

The nature of Christopher, himself, as a character performing on a stage is finally completely exposed in a scene where he finds himself sitting in a café in Montevideo next to a young man with 'a surprisingly English public school sort of voice' (Sommerfield 1930: 270). At the end of their conversation, the man passes his address to Christopher and tells him to look him up the next time he is in London:

> Christopher looked at the piece of paper. In an ornamental but not very readable hand was written 'John Sommerfield, 19, Bark Place, Kensington Gardens, London, W.2.' John Sommerfield... he reflected. I seem to have heard that name somewhere... (Sommerfield 1930: 270)

Having made it clear that his narrative is staged or framed, Sommerfield then breaks that frame in order to acknowledge his own presence for similar reasons to later postmodernists. Like them, he is choosing to move beyond the trick of modernism in which the author gains a level of awareness beyond that of their characters – a third level of Empsonian comic primness by which they elevate themselves. However, he is not merely exposing the device but also more straightforwardly recuperating the autobiografictional impulse which underlies modernism. Christopher is partly Sommerfield and his story of growing self-awareness is partly Sommerfield's story of growing self-awareness. But whereas Christopher becomes afraid of this self-consciousness so that he increasingly comes to regard himself as an observer, rather than the actor, of his own life, Sommerfield is able to move beyond Christopher's failure to give up the subject-centred universe of the male child precisely by projecting it onto the fictional Christopher and killing him off. This is a first step to dealing with the intersubjective problem of the time – the relationship between the I and the we – which this book is concerned with. In *They Die Young*, Sommerfield works out how to move beyond the 'I' and the negative identification which actually prolongs it, even though there is as yet no sense of any 'we'. It is almost as though the performative leap he makes in this process necessitates the step of joining the Communist Party in order to become part of a 'we' and so fulfil his trajectory as a writer with *May Day*. Therefore, *They Die Young* and *May Day* can be seen as reflecting and generating the emergence of a proletarian artist – a process which they show to be not dissimilar to becoming a modernist artist but which involves the additional step of the artist needing to overcome their own individualism.

May Day and documentary

Individualism in *They Die Young* is not just portrayed as a facet of bourgeois subjectivity but equated in particular with male consciousness, which is repeatedly foregrounded by the text as the cause of Christopher's failure to adjust to a modern consciousness as represented by the novel's female characters. *May Day*, therefore, can be seen as fulfilling the two linked aims of enabling men, such as John, who to some extent is representing Sommerfield in the text, to reconcile their own subjectivity with the female consciousness of relativity and temporality while simultaneously awarding that female consciousness, in the material form of women workers, a historical agency. In this respect, Sommerfield is neither appropriating modernist techniques for political ends nor appropriating politics in an instrumental manner to provide a unity for aesthetic fragmentation, but rather writing about the transformation of social relations and consciousness at the level of everyday life. When taken in conjunction with Sommerfield's obvious use of cinematic techniques, this focus on everyday life aligns the novel with the contemporary documentary movement in British fiction and cinema and a number of critics have discussed it within this context (see Feigel 2010: 93–5; Marcus 2010: 92; K. Williams 1996: 132–4). However, as Keith Williams notes, *May Day* differs significantly from 'Griersonian documentary's more heroicised vision' of workers' involvement in the romance of industry precisely by revealing the clash of class interests present within the mechanised everyday routine of the factory (K. Williams 1996: 133). Moreover, Williams also sees Sommerfield as raising 'radical questions about the politics of "panoptic" media perspectives on society': 'The police gyrophane monitoring the workers' march has a literal view over the "living map of London" (p. 209) rivalled only by the imaginative cooperation between the narrator's Vertovian "camera-eye" and the reader' (K. Williams 1996: 134). Sommerfield eschews the omniscient view of society and provides us instead with a network of social relations that are linked as much by stream of consciousness as by economic determination. His alternative approach is indirectly acknowledged by Klaus's observation that *May Day* absorbs the influence of *Mrs Dalloway* better than that of the documentary movement (see Klaus 1979: 150–1). This is because Sommerfield was more directly concerned with including working-class experience within the presentation of everyday life as a potentially transformative site of subjective and intersubjective experience as it is in Woolf's novel (and also in *Ulysses*) than he was with simply trying to represent the working-class experience of the production process in the manner favoured by the Griersonian documentary movement.

While it is true, as Stuart Laing notes, that *May Day* shares significant structural parallels with Walter Ruttman's *Berlin: Symphony of a Great City* (1927) – as does the postwar Edinburgh-set documentary film *Waverley Steps* (1948) for which Sommerfield wrote the screenplay – it does not share the expressionist presentation of that film (see Laing 1980: 149). As suggested by his use of his 'modernistic' theatre experience in *They Die Young*, Sommerfield is not interested in staging reality but rather in showing reality to be staged. In *May Day*'s one scene set in a theatre, the dress rehearsal of 'Backwards and Forwards' is halted by a dispute with the stage staff that turns into 'the twenty-third strike now on in London' (Sommerfield 1936: 142). Here, the message of the novel is encapsulated by first revealing the workers behind the scenes who enable the public performance and then showing that, if they acted collectively, they could choose to organise themselves differently and thus contribute to what would be a different kind of performance. In a similar manner, the everyday scenes and connections highlighted by the novel as a whole reveal a world of possibility for organising social relationships differently. While the novel's close implies that the May Day demonstration, which the workers of Langfier's have walked out of the factory to join, is the forerunner of a revolutionary situation which 'isn't so very different' to that which preceded the General Strike (Sommerfield 1936: 223), the abiding impression of the overall text is that something *has* changed. There is a new consciousness within society that suggests that the remaining vestiges of the Edwardian social order no longer retain a residual dominance. At a symbolic level, therefore, the references to the General Strike indicate not a desire to replicate that moment but rather a sense that the setback of its defeat has now been overcome. *May Day* marks the point of the decisive cultural shift in the second half of the 1930s by which the advent of the 'classless' society later identified by Orwell in 'The Proletarian Writer' (1940) and *The Lion and the Unicorn* (1941) had become apparent. There was still stark inequality but absolute hierarchy was dissolving and relationships between classes and genders were rapidly reconfiguring themselves in the way that Sommerfield captures so vividly. The question now became what configuration they would settle down in again.

Notes

1. This quote is taken from an 'Extract From Opening of Resolution Passed At a Special Meeting of the London District Committee of the Communist Party on May 3rd', which, together with an extract from a newspaper leader dated 2 May editorialising against the disturbances of the day before, is at the end of the original edition of the novel (Sommerfield 1936: 243–5). Neither of these extracts is included in the 1984 (which otherwise has the same pagination as in 1936) or 2010 editions of *May Day*.
2. The passage in which the millions are criticised for 'believing the dope by which they were ruled, exploited, cheated, and swindled' has been cited as evidence of Sommerfield's criticism of mass society but these thoughts are those of a man 'who looked like an intellectual' on a way into the pub for his first drink of the morning and therefore represent a position that Sommerfield is not endorsing but actually satirising (Sommerfield 1936: 142–4).
3. For a discussion of Gurney's analysis of Sommerfield's pub reports, see Hubble 2012b: 144–6.
4. *They Die Young* was published in the USA as *The Death of Christopher*.

Chapter 5

'None of That "My Good Woman" Stuff': Outsider Observations

Factory wheels

In 1940, Virginia Woolf defended the Bloomsbury Group from an accusation of elitism by noting:

> I never went to school or college. My father spent perhaps £100 on my education. When I was a young woman I tried to share the fruits of that very imperfect education with the working classes by teaching literature at Morley College; by holding a Womens Cooperative Guild meeting weekly; and, politically by working for the vote. . . . I did my best to make them [her books] reach a far wider circle than a little private circle of exquisite and cultivated people. And to some extent I succeeded. (Woolf, qtd in Snaith 2000a: 8)

As Anna Snaith suggests, Woolf's confidence in that 'wider circle' was probably based on the eighty-two letters she received from readers of *Three Guineas* (1938), which were eventually collected by Snaith and published in the *Woolf Studies Annual*. While only three correspondents explicitly identified themselves as working class, and another three said they were from a different class background to Woolf, the letters represented a diverse range of response and proof that working women could get hold of her books through libraries. They also indicate that the arguments of *Three Guineas*, which were driven by Woolf's own feminist and pacifist concerns, connected with women in society. Eight years earlier, Woolf had written in her introductory letter (dated May 1930) to Margaret Llewelyn Davies's edited collection of the autobiographical experiences of members of the Women's Co-operative Guild, *Life as We Have Known It* (1931), that:

> These voices are beginning only now to emerge from silence into half articulate speech. These lives are still half hidden in profound obscurity. To express even what is expressed here has been a work of labour and difficulty. The writing has been done in kitchens, at odds and ends of leisure, in the midst of distractions and obstacles [. . .] (Woolf 1975: xxxix)

In this letter, Woolf writes an account of her own interaction with the working women of the Guild beginning with her attendance at a Guild Congress in Newcastle in June 1913 and sitting through speech after speech in the knowledge that she was personally untouched and therefore only had an altruistic interest in 'questions of sanitation and education and wages'. She had felt 'irretrievably cut off' (Woolf 1975: xix). Moreover, everything seemed to some extent irrelevant because no woman in that room, regardless of social class, had a vote. Even imaginatively trying to inhabit the subjectivities of working women by pretending to be Mrs Giles of Durham or Mrs Phillips of Bacup failed because 'One could not be Mrs. Giles of Durham because one's body had never stood at the wash-tub; one's hands had never wrung and scrubbed and chopped up whatever the meat may be that makes a miner's supper' (Woolf 1975: xxi). If she could have met these working women as equals over the wash-tub or in the parlour then perhaps a great friendship would ensue but this sympathy was largely fictitious: 'it was aesthetic sympathy' (Woolf 1975: xxvi).

It is a very interesting piece of writing because, having read the collected accounts of the women in the book, Woolf flirts with writing proletarian scenes concerning wash-tubs and miner husbands but satirises herself sufficiently to make it clear that she is rejecting this kind of easy identification. Her self-reflective account prefigures much of the logic of Empson's later analysis of proletarian literature as a version of pastoral. She notes that Shakespeare would have appreciated the qualities of the industrial working class and that the abiding impression of that 1913 Congress was that 'the "poor," "the working classes," or by whatever name you choose to call them, are not downtrodden, envious and exhausted; they are humorous and vigorous and thoroughly independent' (Woolf 1975: xxvii). It is for this reason that she does not allow herself to fall into the trap of claiming that these people are somehow down to earth or full of life's experience because, as she explicitly states, no one is closer to reality than the artist or the writer. A simple presentation of working-class women as everyday heroes would be a similar form of aestheticised politics as that identified by Empson in connection with use of the 'mythical cultfigure' of the 'Worker'. Woolf deliberately avoids this kind of approach even as she makes a wider argument for these women having become historical agents through their participation in the public sphere of the Guild, first founded in 1883, via their political demands at the 1913 Congress – not just for sanitation and wages, but also for universal suffrage, divorce law reform and the taxation of land values – and on through their campaigning for peace, disarmament and the global spread of co-operative values. Instead, she emphasises her difference from these women but implies that having now read their in-depth accounts, she is able to put this knowledge together with her subjective experience of the faces and voices of the 1913 Congress and feel a complex relationship with them that is not purely imaginative or fictitious. On the one hand, this serves as a warning to middle-class readers of the book not simply to assume a direct connection to its subjects because of the immediacy of the experiences recounted in it. In this respect, her explicit comments on the book not being literature are not some form of critical snobbery but a straightforward warning that there is little of the mediation of experience that one would find in literary fiction or memoirs. On the other hand, through her literary introduction to the collection, constructed in this complex manner as a confessional letter to Llewelyn Davies, she generates a level of mediation designed to push her fellow middle-class readers into meeting the challenge of really examining their own attitudes and relationship to these working-class women. In this respect, Woolf's introduction can itself be seen as a work of proletarian literature designed to hold open the possibility of readers developing a fuller consciousness while warning that this opportunity is only just beginning to emerge and that therefore it would be too premature to expect anything more than the beginning of an awareness of new intersubjective possibilities.

The process that Woolf describes herself as undergoing in the letter is not dissimilar from that which Mitchison's Dione experiences in *We Have Been Warned* when she gives a lift to an unemployed man and declares herself a 'Red' too. That too was not an immediate response but rather the culmination of years-long engagement with progressive causes. As with Dione and Mitchison, Woolf also had a husband who, even if not an MP, was heavily involved in Labour politics. While she does not display the same obsessive compulsion as Mitchison to break down class barriers and live as in the progressive future, there is nevertheless a keen awareness of difference and it is possible to detect a sense of shame underlying the account of her participation in the 1913 Congress of the Women's Co-operative Guild: 'the contradictory and complex feelings which beset the middle-class visitor when forced to sit out a Congress of working women in silence' (Woolf 1975: xxix). What the letter shows is that as well as not falling into a fictitious identification, Woolf did not retreat fully behind societal conventions and the notion of irreconcilable class difference. By 1930, at least, she was facing up to what these experiences had shown her about herself and the implications of rethinking social conventions even if, as she notes, the complex possibility of engaging with the working class was only just beginning to emerge as the media began to give expression to their voices.

Eight years later, however, at the peak of public awareness of the documentary movement and proletarian literature, nobody would have said that working-class voices were only just beginning to emerge. A huge social and cultural shift had taken place and Woolf had changed herself to the extent that, through the publication of *Three Guineas*, she could enter into a correspondence that would continue for the rest of her life with a working-class weaver from Yorkshire, Agnes Smith. As Snaith notes, while Smith begins by commenting on Woolf's omission of working-class women's experience, her letters fulfil that function and 'fill in the silences left by Woolf's consciously limited perspective' (Snaith 2000a: 4). Smith agrees with Woolf's criticism of the 'infantile fixation' of men preventing women from being free and consequently retarding civilisation but insists that these problems 'affect the working woman to a far greater degree' than the daughters of educated men (Snaith 2000b: 99). If she had Woolf's access to books and economic support, she argues, then she would be able to write her own book:

> I might tell you how I went to sleep at night with factory wheels continuing their grinding in my brain as I slept – how I rose at five a.m.: and went out into the blackness of unlighted country lanes or into the whiteness of a howling blizzard – scared sometimes at the

strange shapes I saw as I passed some lighted window – yet going resolutely on – because even strange shapes must be faced if one has to reach the factory at six a.m.: and how I sometimes had to return home suffering from the most damnable sick headaches – and yet turn up again next day. How I hated the noise, the grease, the whirring wheels and was too sick to eat my breakfast – and disliked even the more spiritual loneliness of working with warm hearted lasses, who thought only of boy friends, of dances, weddings, funerals etc – but had no thought for the beauty of words, of wild flowers and sunsets – or if they had, never let me know it talking only of clothes, of gossip, of money etc. (Snaith 2000b: 99–100)

This lyrical passage echoes various aspects of the experience of working-class women captured by the male writers of the works focused on in this book from Gibbon's Chris Guthrie to Sommerfield's description of the factory workers in *May Day*. On the one hand, it suggests a separation between material desires for consumer goods and enjoyable leisure experiences as opposed to the yearning for a more liberated subjectivity. On the other hand, it demonstrates the all-pervading internalised rhythm of the factory. Sommerfield used Woolfian techniques to show the intersubjective connections surrounding the production process and now, through Smith, these connections came back to Woolf, herself; pulsing in time with the constant grind of the factory wheels. With awareness of the beat of that time, it is possible to start thinking about how that time might be transformed into a non-linear time permitting the expansion of more liberated subjectivities. This correspondence with Smith, and the possibilities it opens up, illustrates a wider change in perspective undergone by Woolf over the period since the stages of self-recognition recorded in *A Room of One's Own* and the introductory letter to *Life as We Have Known It*.

What happened in the intervening years was a sequence by which the modernist questions of *A Room of One's Own* were answered in part by the sense of intersubjective possibility generated by reading the memoirs of women workers and thinking about her own relationship to them. If the central point of *Life as We Have Known It* for Woolf was the importance to working women of their access through the Guild to a room 'where they could sit down and think [. . .] and [. . .] remodel their lives, could beat out this reform and that' (Woolf 1975: xxxv–xxxvi), then it is clear that the logical progression from having a room of one's own is participating in a collective undertaking. The eventual decision to write 'a sequel to *A Room of One's Own* – about the sexual life of women: to be called Professions for Women perhaps' (qtd in Leaska 1978: xv) might have occurred to her in the bath but it follows on from the analysis of her introductory letter to *Life as We Have Known It*. 'Professions for Women' was the title of a talk she gave the following day, 21 January 1931, which was subsequently expanded into the draft of the novel-essay, *The Pargiters*, which, in turn, was abandoned and the material reworked into *The Years* (1937) and *Three Guineas*.

In her 'Professions for Women', Woolf describes how she came to pursue her own profession of writing and discusses how she first had to overcome the idea that the way to express her femininity would be through arts and wiles while hiding the fact that she had a mind of her own; a process she refers to as her killing of the 'Angel in the House'. Nevertheless, she continues, she quickly found further restrictions when writing novels. Asking her audience to imagine a girl sitting with a pen but not writing, she explains:

> she had thought of something, something about the body, about the passions which it was unfitting for her as a woman to say. Men, her reason told her, would be shocked. The consciousness of what men will say of a woman who speaks the truth about her passions had roused her from her artist's state of unconsciousness. She could write no more. (Woolf 2000b: 359)

Her point is that while she could overcome her internal policing, she could not yet see how to solve this problem of expressing the 'truth about my own experiences as a body' which was being restricted by the external existence of men (Woolf 2000b: 360). In the draft manuscript of the speech, Woolf further notes that while men are allowed to let their imaginations run further in this regard than women, there are still conventions that apply even to them 'and if a man like Lawrence [...] runs against convention he injures his imagination terribly' (Woolf 1978a: xxxix). Her thoughts here are borne out by the main texts analysed in this book. For example, Norquay suggests of *A Scots Quair*, that 'Gibbon's representation contains a candour perhaps only possible in a male writer at the time' (Norquay 2015: 83). However, *Lady Chatterley's Lover* was not published in an unexpurgated edition in Britain until 1960 and Lawrence was already bitter at the prosecution of *The Rainbow* for obscenity in 1915 and the general treatment of his work. Mitchison was unable to get *We Have Been Warned* published as she wanted it and even the version that did go into print severely damaged her literary reputation. In this context, it is not clear how *The Pargiters* had it ever been completed and published would have been received. As Woolf continues in the draft version of 'Professions for Women':

> The future of fiction depends very much upon what extent men can be educated to stand free speech in women. But whether men can be civilised, what capacities lie dormant in them, how far their condition is the result of re-education or of nature [. . .] lies [. . .] upon the laps of professional women. (Woolf 1978a: xl)

This is an interesting list of interlinked issues. On the one hand, the dominance of self-regarding bourgeois men is restricting what women can discuss and thereby inhibiting the future of fiction. On the other hand, it is up to women to create the environment in which men will allow women to express the truths about their bodies. Yet the most likely way for this environment to be created was by women writing freely. Moreover, would men ever accept this kind of writing if they did not have the same capacity buried within them? Examples like Lawrence, Gibbon and Sommerfield suggest that men did have these capacities, which are revealed in their fiction by the extent to which it approaches the condition of *écriture féminine*. The surest way to imagine a future in which all of these issues were solved thereby enabling a future type of fiction, which would be characterised by open social conventions and the possibility of writing as a woman as discussed in *A Room of One's Own*, was to imagine a future in which everyone wrote as a woman; that is, from a perspective outside the patriarchal order.

As we know, Woolf ended up dividing her project investigating how to achieve a future fiction allowing women to write about the truth of their bodies into a novel and a polemical, theoretical argument. As Hermione Lee notes, 'in a way, *The Years* rewrote her earlier books' but without an 'I' or an 'inward "stream of consciousness"' (Lee 1997: 637). The 'I' was identified with the male consciousness that needed to be superseded and even a stream of consciousness would impede the intersubjective possibilities that the fiction was supposed to hold open. The initial projected historical span of 1880 to 2012 may be seen as beginning in the decade of Woolf's birth and finishing not far short of the time span of one hundred years predicted in *A Room of One's Own* as the time it would take society to reach the point when it would be fully possible to write as a woman. However, the 1880s are also significant as arguably the decade in which the desire for self-liberation in the modernist sense first became widespread. In *England in the Eighteen-Eighties* (1945), Helen Lynd argues that the shift in general philosophy in that decade helped 'to lay down a basis' for a society that would enable positive freedoms (Lynd 1945: 430). Lynd also suggests that those most likely 'to perceive change and to create change' are often 'outsiders' (Lynd 1945: 423). Woolf had used this term in the first essay of the draft of *The Pargiters*, suggesting that outsiders 'can see aspects of things that are not visible from the inside' (Woolf 1978a: 7). Subsequently, in *Three Guineas*, Woolf proposes a 'Society of Outsiders' who will pursue freedom, equality and peace 'with private means in private' and therefore evade the patriarchal system of the public world (Woolf 2000b: 239). Therefore, *The Years* as initially planned might have demonstrated how a transition to the future society, in which women's writing would be possible, happened in the private sphere.

As published, however, the novel concludes in the 'Present Day' of mid-1930s London, but with a sense in the closing pages of the possibility, at least, that the past, present and future might somehow come into conjunction with each other. By implication, this possibility is a product of the purely intersubjective interaction between the various characters in the novel. The various sections of the novel set across the different years represent the changes within intersubjective relations in the private sphere. Through her understanding of the dynamics of such social relations, Woolf anticipates their future development: 'One of these days d'you think you'll be able to see things at the end of the telephone?' (Woolf 1977: 324). The logical end point of trying to organise outside the hierarchies of the public sphere is twenty-first-century digital technology enabling private individuals to connect into new kinds of collectives in a manner analogous to the formation of the Women's Co-operative Guild in the 1880s with its room. Technically, such a meeting room is a public sphere but the crucial point was that only certain people – women belonging to the Guild – were able to enter it; in that respect it would perhaps be better described as a semi-public sphere. However, the crucial aspect of such spaces remains how the different individuals connect within them once freed of the various conventions and social relationships existing outside that space. As Laura Marcus notes of *The Years*:

> As in a film, the telephone functions to connect one character and location to another, but Woolf's use of the technology works primarily to divide her characters into their verbal and visual aspects, and to explore the ways in which separations, whether the literal separations of distance or those of the boundaries between selves, are to be negotiated. (Marcus 2007: 163)

The mediation of the material world by technology is shown to enable the development of a different set of social relationships to those of the nineteenth century.

In *Literature in the First Media Age*, David Trotter argues that in *May Day*, Sommerfield responds similarly to the potential of connective telecommunications technology, such as telephones and the wireless, to transform informal social solidarity into political solidarity inside 'Popular Front semipublic sphere[s]' (Trotter 2013: 212). While Woolf is clearly not aiming to transfer informal intersubjective relations into direct political action in the same way as Sommerfield, there is common ground between their approaches. Both are fascinated by other people and knowing about them. There is a discussion in the 1917 section of *The Years* of how 'we do not know ourselves, ordinary people' (Woolf 1977: 279). As Marcus notes, '1937, the year of the novel's publication, was also the year in which the Mass-Observation movement was founded, as a project to record everyday life and the "anthropology of ourselves"' (Marcus 2007: 170). This general constellation of interest between Woolf, Mass-Observation and Sommerfield (who was to work for Mass-Observation) apparently accords with Jed Esty's argument that the 1930s were marked by an anthropological turn to a concern with defining the nation which reduced a major literary culture to a minor one. However, the projects of all three can alternatively be considered as primarily concerned with establishing new intersubjective forms of social relationships. While calling for an anthropology of British society, Mass-Observation invited its respondents to think about the extent to which they were both part of, and part outside, that society. Their aim was not to produce definitive accounts of ordinary British life but rather to engage ordinary people with other ordinary people in ways that bypassed the official public organisation of society. In this manner they sought to reconcile individualism to possible collectives without subsuming it; diminishing potential feelings of isolation and alienation while supporting self-reflection and promoting its development into a conscious self-reflexivity. Therefore, in some respects at least, Mass-Observation functioned as a version of a Woolfian 'Society of Outsiders'. It is true that, as discussed in the section below, they were part of the cultural formation that underpinned the postwar formation of the welfare state. They also worked for the government during the war. However, as discussed in the last section of this chapter, the diaries they collected from individual people during the war, including Mitchison, demonstrate on a large scale the pursuit of freedom, equality and peace 'with private means in private' that Woolf called for in *Three Guineas*. Reading these diaries, some of which were continued long after the war ended, gives an idea of what *The Years* might look like if extended beyond its 1930s 'present day'. As James Hinton notes, through these accounts, it is possible to chart 'the changing relationships between men and women in the intimate sphere' which only became apparent publicly in the 1960s and 1970s (Hinton 2010: 8).

In a working-class home

The emergence of the postwar British welfare state out of the wartime production economy via the landslide victory of the Labour Party in the 1945 General Election seemed to bear out Orwell's 1940 prediction that the existence of proletarian literature was a sign of transition to a classless society. However, less than a decade later, his protagonist Winston Smith was living under a dystopian totalitarian regime and writing in his secret diary: 'if there is hope [. . .] it lies in the proles' (Orwell 1976: 69). In *Nineteen Eighty-Four* (1949), Orwell was articulating Cold War concerns and not directly criticising the Labour government or the British welfare state, but what is interesting about his representation of the 'proles' is the way that they are figured as an almost unknowable separate 'other' to the middle-class Winston. The humour of this, as in the scene where Winston tries to get an old man in a pub to talk about the days before the revolution, is often at Winston's expense and there are strong reasons for reading the whole novel as darkly satirical rather than any straightforward warning of the threat of totalitarianism. It is conceivable that Orwell was connecting with a working-class readership at the expense of middle-class intellectuals but nevertheless there is no representation of what a classless society would look like in *Nineteen Eighty-Four*. Moreover, the descriptions of proletarians in the novel never quite escape a pantomimic air. There are versions of pastoral but at the level of a low comedy; the equivalent of what Empson described as 'custard-pie farce' (Empson 1995: 170).

This tendency of Orwell was noticed by postwar critics. For example, in *The Uses of Literacy* (1957), Richard Hoggart points out that 'Orwell never quite lost the habit of seeing the working-classes through the cosy-fug of an Edwardian music-hall' (Hoggart 1968: 15). However, this did not prevent Orwell's arguments becoming very influential following the huge popular success of both *Animal Farm* (1945) and *Nineteen Eighty-Four* (1949). According to Raymond Williams:

> In the Britain of the fifties, along every road you moved, the figure of Orwell seemed to be waiting. If you tried to develop a new kind of popular cultural analysis, there was Orwell; if you wanted to report on work or ordinary life there was Orwell; if you engaged in any kind of socialist argument, there was an enormously inflated statue of Orwell warning you to go back. (Williams 1979: 384)

In his book on Orwell, Williams further argued that Orwell's novels of the 1930s, notably *Keep the Aspidistra Flying* (1936) and *Coming Up for Air* (1939), 'created the style of the drifting anti-hero English novel of the fifties' (R. Williams 1991: 87) such as those written by John Wain and Kingsley Amis. Therefore, Orwell was a significant influence on exactly the style of writing which Angus Wilson considered 'inferior in reality and depth to Virginia Woolf's' (Wilson 1983a: 133). If, as this book argues, a transformative mode of proletarian-modernist writing emerged across the early decades of the twentieth century to become increasingly publicly visible by the mid-1930s, then the 1950s represents the point by which that strand of writing appears to have become disassociated into its individual components again. However, in reality, the transformation in modes of writing was rather more complex than this suggests. As discussed in the Introduction to this book, while most of the self-consciously working-class writing of that period also followed the anti-hero model identified by Williams, ultimately, it served to promote universally the kind of liberated masculinity that had only been available to bourgeois men in the nineteenth century. This development represented a partial dissemination of modernist self-reflexivity through proletarian literature and related versions of pastoral, also dependent on what Empson described as the 'double attitude of the artist to the worker, of the complex man to the simple one' (Empson 1995: 19), such as Orwell's 1930s novels, but also work by Wells, Lawrence and Joyce. Aspects of this masculine liberation undoubtedly tended towards the phenomena of 'mobile privatisation' and the 'rejection of all forms of social reproduction' that concerned Williams in *The Politics of Modernism*, and may be seen as a move away from the social community underpinning proletarian values.

One way of tracing these developments, including the othering of the proletarian community, in the literature of the 1950s back to the 1930s is by analysing Orwell's *The Road to Wigan Pier* (1937). As Ben Clarke argues, *Wigan Pier* is 'a self-reflexive work, focusing on the relation between observer and observed' which 'constructs a powerful, selective myth of the industrial proletariat' (Clarke 2007: 42, 53). By 'myth of the proletariat', Clarke means that, rather than follow Marxist thought and see the value of the proletariat as lying in its potential to emancipate society as a whole by seizing the means of production, Orwell identified that value as residing in the social relations of actually existing working-class communities which he saw as a sufficient basis for a future socialist society. This myth can also be seen as a form of the 'rival myth' which Empson suggested was the only way to counter the myth of the 'Worker' as deployed by both communists and Tories. John Gross suggests that Orwell created exactly such a rival myth in his essays on Dickens, Donald McGill, boys' comics and so on: 'it would be hard for anyone who went along with the main drift of these essays to respond with much conviction to the square-jawed stereotypes of the revolutionary poster' (Gross 1973: 289). *Wigan Pier* would therefore be Orwell's earliest use of such a rival myth. In place of the nobility and heroism of the imaginary category of the 'Worker', Orwell offers something equally imaginary but different:

> In a working-class home – I am not thinking at the moment of the unemployed, but of the comparatively prosperous homes – you breathe a warm, decent, deeply human atmosphere which it is not so

easy to find elsewhere [. . .] I have often been struck by the peculiar easy completeness, the perfect symmetry as it were, of a working-class interior at its best. Especially on winter evenings after tea, when the fire glows in the open range and dances mirrored in the steel fender, when Father, in shirt-sleeves, sits in the rocking chair at one side of the fire reading the racing finals, and Mother sits on the other with her sewing, and the children are happy with a pennorth of mint humbugs, and the dog lolls roasting himself on the rag mat – it is a good place to be in, provided that you can be not only in it but sufficiently *of* it to be taken for granted. (Orwell 1998: 107–8)

The problem, of course, is that Orwell is not sufficiently of it to be taken for granted. As with Woolf's reflections on her experience at the 1913 Congress of the Women's Co-operative Guild, an element of self-parody may be detected in his account of what is essentially an imaginative identification. Unlike Woolf, however, he does not proceed to explain why this kind of identification is difficult but instead relies on readers spotting the fact that, as John Roberts argues, '[the book] is a *satire*, a satire in fact at the expense of the portentous claims of the new social anthropology and the middle-class documentary movement as a whole' (Roberts 1998: 66).Therefore *Wigan Pier* closes with Orwell's otherwise patently absurd exhortation to his fellow 'sinking' middle-class readers not to worry about becoming part of the working class because it will not be 'so dreadful as we feared, for, after all, we have nothing to lose but our aitches' (Orwell 1998: 215). Such satire is in accord with his professed disdain for Popular Front politics up until his apparent conversion following the Nazi–Soviet Pact in August 1939.[1] However, while this satire might or might not have been obvious at the time, it certainly became much less obvious – as did the equally satiric nature of parts of *Homage to Catalonia* (1938) (see Hubble 2012c: 33–43) – following the success of the postwar novels and Orwell's ascension to the status of prophet. Once the satiric intent is misunderstood then it is much easier to read the books as advocating the positions they are satirising; an approach which is aided by the fact that Orwell was in any case partly attracted to such positions. His way of distancing himself from them was by ironically adopting them and thereby, as Saunders argues, 'turning himself inside out':

> instead of opening out the workings of the man of imagination, Orwell wants to make himself transparent (as he wanted to make language transparent) so we can see society, and social injustice. He

has to be the man of compassion and common decency, but what this shows is what unites him to the common man, not what separates him. (Saunders 2010: 510)

Arguably, there remained a man of imagination, Eric Blair, behind the public version of Orwell but by the time his readership opened out in the postwar years, there was only this public persona left and his work therefore differed sharply in effect from the dominant strand of modernist autobiografiction.

It was not always so. Orwell's first English publication was 'The Spike', which appeared in the *Adelphi* in April 1931 under his real name of Blair. The working-class writer Jack Common was part of the *Adelphi* circle and recalled: 'One name that interested me was that of "E. A. Blair" . . . he had a legend. He was a rebel, he was a tramp, he belonged to the underworld of poverty. A man to look out for then, a man to meet' (Common 1984: 139). When the desired meeting did take place, Common saw through the act, describing Orwell as 'an *enfant terrible* in decay', a 'phoney' and an 'amateur pauper'; but there was also an element of mutual interaction to the encounter:

> It was his turn to be suspicious of me. How come that a poorly-educated, hard-up, working-class dialect-speaker such as me came to be employed by a literary-philosophical Bloomsbury magazine? While out of work I explained, I wrote various pieces including one sent to John Middleton Murry, founder of *The Adelphi*; that led to a meeting, the promise of a job some day.
>
> Eric nodded. He was putting me down as a vagary of Murry's romantic idealism and cranky enthusiasm, I felt. So I asked how he came to write for *The Adelphi*. When in Burma he was a subscriber, being interested in the debates of the intellectuals. But he was not a loyal supporter of the Murry crusades. Often the magazine disgusted him. Then he used to prop it up against a tree and fire his rifle at it. (I wanted him to put this in the birthday symposium but he didn't.)
>
> This story, a careless confiding as it was, warmed my imagination towards the man. We parted that day, me to dearest wife and he to dungeon, much better known to each other, the more so for not having been taken in. (Common 1984: 140)

Orwell no more really wanted to be the rebel tramp than Common really wanted to 'interpenetrate the middle class via the literary intelligentsia', to use the terminology of *Wigan Pier* (Orwell 1998: 152). However, they recognised that they were both obliged to conform to these types in order to have any sort of voice in the public sphere and through this mutual recognition they became good friends; but Orwell never represented this kind of interaction between classes in his books, with the possible exception of the trench scenes in *Homage to Catalonia*. Instead, these books have functioned since the publication of *Nineteen Eighty-Four* to demonstrate the heroic quality and independence of the Orwell persona.

By contrast, Common both accepted that he was part of the mass and simultaneously revolted against the idea of the mass. Thus his efforts were directed at trying to change the nature of the mass rather than trying to escape from it through his literary connections. To this end, he wrote a large number of articles throughout the 1930s for the *Adelphi* (often under the by-line of 'The Sweeper Up') and other publications. He was among the first to see that traditional working-class culture had no future. He argued that the skilled working class, which had roots stretching back into artisanal traditions, was being bypassed by the changes in the state and society following the First World War, so that unskilled but collectively organised workers such as the railwaymen – the 'pease-pudding men'[2] – were becoming what might be termed the new labour aristocracy. These were the workers who could afford the rents on the new housing estates and consumer goods such as radiograms, who developed educated cultural interests and encouraged their children to get on at schools:

> The pease-pudding man is now safely ensconced in his five-roomed semi-detached, his garden is about him, the world's classics of music and literature are on his shelves, his job is a permanent one reasonably likely to be well-paid. He is, you might say, in the position of the moderately comfortable petty-bourgeois; he might set out as his predecessors in the class above him did, to impose his views and habits on the world about him. He doesn't, though. There is the catch. His present position depends on his maintaining his proletarian loyalties and yet delimiting them. Let him play the individualist game in authentic bourgeois fashion, and he's down. It is power of striking and standing by his mates, not his enterprise, which keeps him afloat. On the other hand, if he permits class loyalty to run away with him, he must unite with the unemployed and the unions of the starved crafts: it means

sharing their poverty sooner or later. To do that successfully means finding a communal formula which will be a true crystallisation of the proletarian ethic. That's what is needed, a second crystallisation, trade unionism being the first. (Common 1980: 39)

Thus Common's work was directed towards a project very much in keeping with the logic of the proletarian-modernist position outlined in this book; the founding of 'a cultural consciousness which squares with [working-class] communal experience' which could continue after the old working-class communities no longer existed (Common 1980: 39).

Orwell and Common corresponded frequently throughout the period in which *Wigan Pier* was being written and it is perhaps possible to reconstruct a reading of the text that contributes to the proletarian-modernist position. Using analytical categories analogous to Empson's, the situation of Orwell's working-class interior may be seen as matching that of the first level of comic primness: a celebration of a life freely lived underneath conventions. Opposed to this is the middle-class hypocrisy characteristic of the second level of comic primness – an insincere adherence to conventions, which Orwell attacks in part two of *Wigan Pier*: 'the outer-suburban creeping Jesus . . . who goes about saying "Why must we level *down*? Why not level *up*?" and proposes to level the working class "up" (up to his own standard) by means of hygiene, fruit-juice, birth-control, poetry etc' (Orwell 1998: 150). This incorporates a criticism of what Orwell and Common referred to as class-breaking: the implicit desire to destroy working-class culture. Rather than purely attacking the patronising attitudes of middle-class socialists, Orwell tries to show this grouping that they, themselves, are part of the wider process in which the whole middle class is becoming part of a mass-mechanised society:

> It is only romantic fools who flatter themselves that they have escaped, like the literary gent in his Tudor cottage with bathroom h and c, and the he-man who goes off to live a primitive life in the jungle with a Mannlicher rifle and four wagon-loads of tinned food' (Orwell 1998: 203)

To this end he offers his own public persona as a representative model for an ironic accommodation with modern life and the 'sinking' of everyone into the working class. It is precisely this final qualification which raises Orwell's comic primness from the second to the third level as he simultaneously accepts and revolts against middle-class conventions, while holding open the everyday plenitude of the working-class interior – the promise of 'a good place to be in' – against the coming 'bleak world' (Orwell 1998: 108, 156).

However, the problem with the particular working-class interior he offered to his readers was that it was hopelessly out of date; a composite memory of those he 'sometimes saw in [his] childhood before the [First World War]' (Orwell 1998: 52). Idealised, and with clearly delineated gender roles, it suggests a bygone traditional world that has little connection with the semi-detached house of the well-paid railway worker described by Common. It is not coincidental that *Wigan Pier* does not focus on railway workers but on male manual workers and especially miners. As Clarke notes, 'for Orwell, mining communities were stable, cohesive structures, founded upon "traditional" values, which provided their members with stable identities' (Clarke 2007: 53). While that had been true once, though, it was certainly no longer the case following the General Strike. The texts by Lawrence, Wilkinson and Brierley discussed in this book indicate the sharp changes in gender relationships that had been occurring over the previous ten years even in mining communities. Therefore, Orwell's vision of the working-class interior, which was to become much better known in the postwar period than the vast majority of proletarian literature, conceals the gendered and politicised social changes that marked working-class communities in the 1930s. Although it notionally places the working class at the centre of its conception of a good society, *Wigan Pier* upholds class differences. Even while it manifests an admiration for the authenticity of male manual workers, it marginalises the experience of working-class women.

Although Orwell is clearly deploying a version of pastoral in the book, it tends more towards the kind of fairy-tale relationship of the rich and poor that Empson considered to be typical of the old pastoral and less towards the deployment of pastoral by a proletarian literature that enabled emergent social change to be represented to a large public audience in the 1930s. At the same time, however, Orwell's development of what Clarke calls the 'myth of the proletariat' was very powerful and particularly resistant to totalitarian appropriation. This image of the working-class interior, which was also apparent from documentary films, became part of the imaginary landscape of the British 'Home Front' during the Second World War and was to remain a key element of national identity for decades afterwards, featured in innumerable television soap operas and situation comedies. The outdated and nostalgic construction of the 'home' in *Wigan Pier* seems on many levels to be an apt signifier of the stolidity of postwar British culture, which was welcome for many following the anxious uncertainties of the depression-hit 1930s and then the war years. However, the fact that the male protagonists of 1950s novels patterned on Orwell's were always trying to break free from this interior suggests that the easy and traditional gender relationships he depicts were not necessarily reflected in the reality that emerged. Moreover, as the example of Sommerfield demonstrates, it was possible to write pastoral depictions of the domestic interior without occluding the gendered and politicised social changes occurring within the working class.

You'll find us all refusing the landlord's rent

There are many parallels between Orwell and Sommerfield. Both belonged to the literary classes: Orwell was at school with Cyril Connolly and Sommerfield with Stephen Spender. Neither went to university. Orwell was an imperial policeman before working in various casual jobs and tramping. Sommerfield worked as a carpenter and a seaman. Both wrote documentary reports of the Northern working classes and both fought in the Spanish Civil War. Comparing Orwell's *Homage to Catalonia* with Sommerfield's *Volunteer in Spain* (1937), it is clear that they occupied 'very closely related positions that turn on similar aims and assumptions' (Hubble 2015: 64). There were two significant differences between them: Sommerfield was a communist and it is unlikely that anyone ever recollected of him, as Common did of Orwell, 'that no pub ever knew my friend as "Eric", let alone "George"' (Common 1984: 143). For about a year from the summer of 1937, Sommerfield made himself ill through frequent drinking in the pubs of Bolton while recording the reports that went towards Mass-Observation's *The Pub and the People* (1943). All accounts suggest he interacted very easily with the working-class inhabitants of Bolton. The techniques he learnt while working for

Mass-Observation – and even verbatim transcriptions of overheard pub conversations – found their way into the fiction he subsequently wrote, including his novella, *Trouble in Porter Street* (1939), written soon after his return to London from Bolton.

Trouble in Porter Street is a documentary account of the everyday domestic life of a working-class street in West London. Rather than the idealisation of *Wigan Pier*, however, Sommerfield's narrative reflects the nuances of Common's understanding of the changing order within the working class. Porter Street is divided between the significantly better-paid, more prosperous and respectable railway workers and the 'rough' market men. A young couple have married across this divide; Bill is a railwayman on £2 12s. 4d. a week whereas 'all Rosie's family worked in the market. They hadn't wanted her to marry Bill Dixon, but despite her mild looks and ways Rosie has a will of her own, and she got her own way' (Sommerfield 1939: 5). In fact, Rosie getting her own way is a significant factor in the story, which is placed in context through Sommerfield's detailed factual reportage. They have two rooms and a scullery on the ground floor, for which they pay 14s. 10d. a week. Although they have not got any children, the housework is still a full-time job for Rosie and the other women in the street. The fact that the forty-eight houses in the street have only one tap requires each of the street's 127 housewives to fill and carry buckets up and down the broken-down stairs all day long:

> Their life was a continual fight against dirt, the soot from the trains and the dust that seemed to ooze out of the worn floorboards, against the decay of the houses.
>
> Rosie tackled it all cheerfully; she was still young and could hope for better things. Most of the women of the street had started out blithely on this fight, but in the end it wore them down. They were aged by childbearing, by worries about money and unemployment, how to pay the rent and buy new boots for kids; the damp houses gave them rheumatic illnesses, they developed womb troubles from working too soon after having babies. At thirty they were no longer young, the pretty ones looked into a mirror one day and saw that their charm had faded. (Sommerfield 1939: 5–6)

This account of working-class women's health closely mirrors Orwell's reference in *Wigan Pier* to 'the usual exhausted face of the slum girl who is twenty-five and looks forty, thanks to miscarriages and drudgery' (Orwell 1998: 15). Such descriptions were typical of the period (see Clarke 2007: 39–40). It is in consideration of the seemingly inevitable fact of decline that Mrs Bull encourages Sally Hardcastle to make the most of her looks while she can in *Love on the Dole*. However, Sommerfield, as evidenced in *May Day*, was aware of how the expectations of working-class women had changed across the decade as union membership had risen and the entitlement to a week's paid holiday was gradually being implemented from July 1938. Rosie's strong desire for a holiday is not only a reflection of those changed expectations but also an indication that a future in which working-class women do not damage their health through unending drudgery is within reach.

Despite the traditional division of gender roles within their relationship, the Dixons enjoy a companionate marriage. On his one Saturday afternoon off in three, Bill goes shopping with Rosie in his best suit with a white silk scarf round his neck and a cap on the back of his head and his hands in his pockets. She trots beside him, one arm slipped under his and the other clutching her shopping bag and handbag. This always causes comment from the street gossips, two very large, indeterminately aged women who live at numbers three and four Porter Street and are referred to throughout as 'Number Three' and 'Number Four':

> 'There goes Rosie Dixon and 'er 'usband,' the inevitable doorstep gossipers at Number Four would say, adding, 'That dress of 'ers ain't so new as it was once.'
> 'Well 'er 'usband's smart enough anyway,' Number Three would reply. 'A fine built man 'e is. She's a lucky girl.' (Sommerfield 1939: 7)

It is an interesting facet of Sommerfield's approach to documentary – probably a consequence of his experience with Mass-Observation – that there is little authorial comment or implied voiceover in the book. The simple prose narrative is very different to the experimental approach of *May Day* and it functions not to approve or disapprove of different types of behaviour amongst the working-class inhabitants of the street but simply to insert us naturalistically into this environment as though we are part of it. The only hint of an authorial position lies in a very gentle irony: 'The climax of their shopping was the Sunday joint. Rosie always asked Bill's advice on this and he had to have the last word on its final choice; but they invariably got the one that she had decided on' (Sommerfield 1939: 7).

Therefore, although Bill's two main signs of affection are to call Rosie, 'old girl', and to pat her gently, and their respective roles in the relationship correspond to a traditional division in gender terms, Sommerfield is nonetheless presenting a more nuanced account of how these gendered relationships actually functioned in the British working class in the late 1930s. The person who is in control over the dynamic of the relationship is Rosie and it is her dissatisfaction with their life as it is and desire for a holiday which provides the agency that drives the plot. While she wants them to be able to go away on a holiday together, the logic of their finances is that the only item of their expenditure which can be cut to save money is the rent, which of course is not in their control but in the hands of their landlord.

Here Sommerfield steps back from his close-up on this domestic situation to tell us that Porter Street belongs to a concern called the Housing Finance Trust, owned by a 'nervous little gentleman called Levine who lived in a steam-heated baronial mansion in a part of Sussex almost entirely populated by people with incomes of more than five thousand a year' (Sommerfield 1939: 9). As Sommerfield notes, Porter Street had been built ninety-six years earlier in 1842 during which time successive generations of tenants had paid enough rent to buy the street lock, stock and barrel several times over. The same point is made in *Love on the Dole*: 'The identical houses of yesterday remain, still valuable in the estate market even though the cost of their building has been paid for over and over again by successive tenants' (Greenwood 1969: 12). However, Sommerfield's representation of the property relationships underpinning poverty leads neither to the melodrama of Greenwood's novel nor to the nostalgia for a settled past which pervades Orwell's *Wigan Pier*. Even as Sommerfield goes on to detail the ritual of the Sunday roast followed by a fruit pie with custard – 'anything less than this on Sunday would be a calamity and disgrace' (Sommerfield 1939: 21) – he notes that the only people who do not have the day off are the 'housewives' who both cook and wash up afterwards. And all the while, as the contributing moments of everyday life are being itemised, we have Rose's continual refrain 'if only we could get away for a holiday'; 'I would so like an 'oliday' (Sommerfield 1939: 16, 26).

It is in this context that the communist, Mike Bloom, selling copies of the *Daily Worker* door to door enters the story and starts discussing the idea that the rents are too high in Porter Street. Bloom's participation allows Sommerfield to make an argument against anti-Semitism; when one participant of the street complains about their Jewish landlord – the aforementioned Levine – another character is quick to point out that Mike Bloom who came round to help them is also a Jew:

> There's something I'd like to say. I've 'eard this sort of talk about Jewish landlords and bosses before now, I've 'eard some of it in this street. Now let's get this straight. A landlord's a landlord and a worker's a worker, and it don't matter a hoot in hell whether they're Jews or Hindoos or what they are. (Sommerfield 1939: 55–6)

At which point, it should be noted that *Trouble in Porter Street* is communist propaganda. The publisher of the novella, Fore Publications, was set up by Randall and Humphrey Swingler, and owned by a group of communists rather than the Party itself. It was partly designed to replicate the Penguin paperback success of the late 1930s to which end 'Randall Swingler began commissioning "Key Books", a bi-monthly series of pocket-sized 64 page pamphlets' (Croft 1998: 147). Sommerfield as a communist who had fought in Spain, been Secretary of the Chelsea branch of the Party, and a frequent contributor to both *Left Review* and the *Daily Worker*, was asked to write a pamphlet explaining how to run a rent strike but thought instead that 'a story about an actual street and some real people might have a bigger appeal than a pamphlet and might be more effective' (Sommerfield 1984b). *Trouble in Porter Street* went on to sell 'over 80,000 copies' (Croft 1998: 147).

What is really interesting about the book, however, is that it is not the Party which is decisive in the establishment and eventual victory of the rent strike at the conclusion of the story. It is the people of the street, themselves, and especially the women, the housewives, who take decisive actions. When a woman in the street is to be evicted for being in rent arrears, Rosie arranges with Numbers Three and Four to help keep the bailiffs away while support from the Communist Party and the men is gathered. Therefore when the rent collector, three bailiffs and two policemen arrive to evict one woman, they find they are prevented from getting to her door by a group of wives blocking the hallway with the two particularly large women at the front:

> Usually there was something slightly comic and slightly grotesque about these two gossips, but now they seemed grim and menacing. The great spreading bulk of their female flesh opposed the four men with an embodiment of all the patient, endless strength of all the housewives who had laboured from morning to night for all of their lives in the street [. . .] The men experienced an obscure sensation of uneasiness, almost of fear. For a moment they felt dominated by this solid mass of implacable hostility that was so *female*. (Sommerfield 1939: 42)

When Pemberton, the rent collector, summons the courage to address Number Four, 'Listen, my good woman [. . .]', she immediately responds 'None of that "my good woman" stuff, Mr. Pemberton' (Sommerfield 1939: 42–3). A stand-off ensues until the communists arrive and explain that because the landlord has been overcharging, the notice to quit is invalid and the bailiffs are forced to retreat. The moment of resistance when the rent collector and the bailiffs are afraid of the women is foreshadowed by an earlier comment of Rosie's, made when discussing with Bill the idea that the landlord ought to be giving them money for work:

> 'I'd like to see 'im doing my 'ousework for a week,' said Rosie and began to giggle. There was a picture in her mind of an expensively-dressed fat man, with a stiff shirt and collar, down on his knees scrubbing the doorstep. (Sommerfield 1939: 32–3)

In short, the novella despite its gently comic, good-natured presentation is, like *May Day*, an overtly gender-based critique of capitalist society as much as a class-based one and it depends for its effect on mobilising women's consciousness and desires as a source of political agency. Following these symbolic successes of women standing up to men, Rosie goes on to join the local rent strike committee. It is she who proposes the key motion which brings everyone – 'respectable' railwaymen and 'tough' market porters together – and they win the strike and get their rents reduced.

In a spontaneous expression of collective and almost carnivalesque solidarity, as Rosie and her fellow rent strikers spill out onto the street from a celebration in the pub, the kids all start singing an adapted version of the Lambeth Walk:

Any time, any day
Any time you're down our way
You'll find us all
Refusing the landlord's rent. OI! (Sommerfield 1939: 63)

In January 1939, two months earlier than *Trouble in Porter Street*, the Penguin Special *Britain by Mass-Observation* had been published with an extensive chapter discussing the then-current Lambeth Walk dance craze: 'We may learn something about the future of democracy if we take a closer look at the Lambeth Walk' (Madge and Harrisson 1939: 140). Citing the example given by Mass-Observation of the Lambeth Walk being used to break up a Mosleyite demonstration, Ben Highmore suggests that it 'can be seen as the exemplification of a Popular Front culture that comes out of the everyday':

> the discussion of the Lambeth Walk demonstrates another reading of the politics of everyday life distinct from the cultural practices associated with Fascism. It is not a 'scientific' critique of Fascist culture; it too is bound up in ritual and superstition, and for this reason offers an alternative imaginary identification that can be seen as (effectively) resistant to Fascism. (Highmore 2002: 108–9)

The Lambeth Walk offers a rival myth to Fascism, turning not on the chance for people to express themselves by taking part in mass rallies, parades, marches and war, but offering an alternative form of mass participation, as evidenced by the outdoor Lambeth Walk dances that Mass-Observation describe:

> it is not dogmatic and allows for all sorts of improvisations; and it can be seen as a confirmation of festival culture and 'the world turned upside down' ('Men dress up as women or pretend to be animals' [Madge and Harrisson 1939: 145]). (Highmore 2002: 108)

Therefore, while the Lambeth Walk functioned as an Empsonian rival myth like those offered by Orwell in *Wigan Pier* and subsequent well-known essays, it offered a more dynamic model than the outdated and gendered concept of the working-class interior. Because it was based on performance, there was not the same barrier of having to be 'sufficiently *of* it' in order to participate. Charles Madge was no extrovert like Sommerfield, and more reserved than Orwell, but he seems to have had little difficulty in enjoying the intersubjective possibilities offered by the Lambeth Walk:

> Then I went to Lambeth and Christ! What an evening. We had the most wonderful party till two in the morning. Tremendous dancing, tremendous people. All playing piano or accordion by ear. All handing round their glasses of beer for others to drink. Transvestism and fine class-conscious songs. (Madge, qtd in Hubble 2010: 161)

It should be emphasised that Madge and Harrisson were fully aware of (occasional mass-observer) Empson's *Some Versions of Pastoral* and quote from the 'Proletarian Literature' chapter to support their analysis of the Lambeth Walk. In particular, they describe the Lambeth Walk as 'induc[ing] the feelings which Empson calls "pastoral" between rich and poor' (Madge and Harrisson 1939: 169n.). In this respect, like Orwell, they are endorsing a modified version of old pastoral by citing Empson's comments on Bottom and the fairies and the clown being able to speak with the wit of the unconscious. The relationship they envisage is one of critical comedy in which 'the middle classes wish to be Lambethians because it temporarily lets them off a sticky code of manners which they usually feel bound to keep up' (Madge and Harrisson 1939: 174). This is not quite the same as Hoggart's accusation that Orwell only saw 'the working-classes through the cosy-fug of an Edwardian music-hall' (Hoggart 1968: 15). Rather, it suggests something more like a return to the music-hall modernism expressed in the work of Ford and Wells, as discussed in Chapter 1 of this book. If on the one hand this was supported by ironical humour, 'a subtle mode of thought which makes you willing to be ruled by your betters' (Madge and Harrisson 1939: 169n.; Empson 1995: 14), the pastoral relationship still allowed a lot of freedom for the common man underneath the middle-class codes of manners which did not apply to them. Moreover, as Madge speculated, the real attraction of the actual 'Walk' was possibly that 'it combined the aggressive swagger of the hard man with the sway of a slinky woman' (Hubble 2010: 161). Or, rather, the worker in his best suit accompanied by his working-class wife, one arm slipped under his and the other clutching her shopping bag and handbag, in the manner of Bill and Rosie Dixon.

The last page of *Trouble in Porter Street* is laid out in the typical Mass-Observation vox-pop fashion in order to record how 'everyone has something to say':

> Said Bill: 'Another thing – after this there needn't be any more talk of the market chaps and the railway men being against each other.'
> Rosie said: 'Now we'll be able to save up for our 'oliday.'
> Smithy said: 'Hurrah for the Communist Party! They're the lads.'
> Harry Moult said: 'Gorblimey! Now my ole woman'll go and get a wireless on the never-never.'
> Bob Douglas said: 'The next step is to get a proper agreement about repairs and redecorations. And we must start spreading the movement to other streets.'
> [. . .]
> Said Rosie, on her doorstep, very late, as they were going home: 'It should be written down in a book, so that other people can see what we did, and do it themselves.' (Sommerfield 1939: 64)

Of course, people did lead rent strikes themselves, frequently with the support of the Communist Party, but more importantly what 'other people' were to see in bestselling books such as *Trouble in Porter Street* and *Britain by Mass-Observation* was a particular kind of proletarian pastoral which represented a nation with the working class in the foreground, but nonetheless preserved the existing hierarchical class society around it. In this sense, works of this type – and Orwell's too – were part of a wider constellation described by Stuart Hall in 'The Social Eye of *Picture Post*' as prefiguring 'the People's War' and 'the high water-mark of the tide of social democracy as a legitimated "structure of feeling"' (Hall 1972: 78, 108). *Trouble in Porter Street* is illustrated by Sommerfield's artist wife, Molly Moss, who had spent time with him in Bolton also. The style of these illustrations is similar to that of children's books such as Eve Garnett's (self-illustrated) *The Family from One End Street* (1937) and C. Day Lewis's *The Otterbury Incident* (1948), which was illustrated by Edward Ardizzone. Collectively they represent an urban pastoral style which developed in the late 1930s and was to become characteristic of the first two decades after the war. These illustrations are a visual representation of the end point of Sommerfield's pre-war literary evolution from the modernist interiority of *They Die Young* (1930) through the proletarian modernism of *May Day* (1936) and on to *Trouble in Porter Street*'s social-realist pastoral, which became arguably the dominant mode of postwar literary representation in Britain up until the 1970s.

In some ways this progression might be considered a regression. The two novels that Sommerfield wrote before *Trouble in Porter Street* depict female streams of consciousness which are absent from it. Instead, Sommerfield uses the Mass-Observation montage technique to resubmerge part of that female consciousness into an unconsciousness which is revealed to us by juxtaposition rather than explicit presentation. There is no room in *Trouble in Porter Street* for the modern self-reflexive consciousness of *May Day*'s Jenny Hardy, marking time while waiting for the freedom of a future existence beyond the restrictive social conventions and relationships of capitalism. What remains from *May Day* in the novella, however, is narrative from a female point of view and a sense that women are the agents of the political change. Rosie's desire for a holiday, like Martine Seton's aspiration for a nice home with bright curtains and new furniture, holds open a future amounting to more than sitting in front of the fireplace sewing.

The women's perspectives contained in works like *Trouble in Porter Street*, therefore, were as much a feature of the cultural representation of the postwar British welfare state as the valorisation of male manual workers and miners in works like *Wigan Pier*. So while the 'kitchen sink' dramas, soap operas and situation comedies which dominated British cultural production for the three decades after the war did not directly challenge what Empson described as the myth of the 'English skilled worker' and the associated ideology of the national interest, they were often dependent on women's desires as the driving force of the plot, even when this was done for comic effect. Therefore, a space for political agency and a gender-based critique of capitalist class society was held open within the dominant cultural form. In 1968, when 187 women sewing machinists walked out on strike at Ford's Dagenham plant demanding equal pay with men, they became the 'raw material' but equally the agents of history by triggering a sequence of events that would lead to the 1970 Equal Pay Act (see Todd 2014: 287–9).[3] In doing so, they not only retrospectively fulfilled the pragmatic aspirations of proletarian literature such as *Clash*, *Love on the Dole* and *May Day* but they also provided the material for what can be seen as a very late work of both proletarian literature and postwar social-realist pastoral, the film *Made in Dagenham* (2010). *Trouble in Porter Street* also indirectly anticipates another development of the 1970s: the women-led rent strikes, which mushroomed in response to the Conservative government forcing councils to implement rent increases in social housing (see Todd 2014: 303–9). This was one of the routes which brought working-class women into the Women's Movement. In this manner, the working-class interior enshrined at the heart of the post-war welfare state was opened again to the wider possibilities of the post-scarcity emotional economy in Mitchison's imaginary landscape beyond patriarchal binary thought.

One must have contacts with ordinary life

One of the letters written to Woolf following *Three Guineas* was from Mitchison, who began by expressing her admiration for *The Years* but continued by noting the points on which she could not quite agree with Woolf's analysis. In particular, she felt that she would never be able to be indifferent to whether her sons were involved in the next war or that she would be able to stand apart from a revolution even though she knew full well that it would be unlikely to result in the desired outcome. She summarised her objections by stating: 'I can't help thinking that one must have contacts with ordinary life, and once one has them, one can't help doing things in connection with them' (Snaith 2000b: 42). Mitchison had contacts with ordinary life through the Labour Party and the kind of work supporting her husband that she describes Dione performing in *We Have Been Warned*. However, she was also a volunteer for Mass-Observation from its beginning in 1937, having known Tom Harrisson since the early 1930s and also having been a friend of Charles Madge and Kathleen Raine. Her writing for Mass-Observation allowed her to situate herself as an ordinary person as demonstrated by the day-survey she wrote for 12 December 1937:

> Woolworths crowded largely with people wandering about looking at things. Whilst son is parking car Valentine and I get presents for him (pencil rubber). Then get pencils, sweets and games for hanging on tree. While choosing sweets assistant asked twice 'Is this your

little girl?' and beamed at Valentine. Several times I ask if goods are Japanese, but assistants don't seem to know. Can't hear what other people are saying, too much noise. (Mitchison 1986: 53–4)

Such accounts could be placed alongside the day-surveys of other mass-observers to build up a composite map of everyday interactions. Madge analysed these in terms of encounters with other people in either 'Area One', family members and those seen every day in the home or workplace; or 'Area Two', meetings with strangers; or 'Area Three', connections with celebrities or politicians through the media (see Hubble 2010: 127–30). They were trying to map social incidents and the transmission of social behaviour on an everyday basis through the private sphere.

Mitchison's discussion of Mass-Observation in *The Moral Basis of Politics* (1938) is reminiscent of the exchange in *The Years* concerning the need to know ordinary people in order to 'make laws and religions that fit' (Woolf 1977: 279). She suggests that their 'results should be of the utmost importance for politicians' (Mitchison 1971: 320). She classifies the three main social wants of people as security, fun and being able to live to a standard:

> Over all this, Mass Observation should help, for standards of cultural living include not only the furniture of homes, but also amusements, clothes, sexual habits and so on. Thus information on fun would include information on standards. Standards are another way of saying 'what is done' as opposed to 'what isn't done', and it will be seen that they may be used as a bulwark of things as they are. They may also be fixed, to a very large extent, at school. Of course, 'what is done' changes greatly in detail, although it may continue to be part of things as they are. Such changes are adduced to show that, after all, progress is happening, and all that. (Mitchison 1971: 331)

Mitchison wrote this in 1937 during the early period of the organisation. In practice, Mass-Observation never achieved this detailed analysis because they did not have the capacity to analyse the vast quantity of material that they rapidly accumulated. The initial plan was to make British society totally legible precisely in order to help effective government and to provide a means of measuring progress that would otherwise be difficult to trace, as Mitchison's exasperated comment above reflects. However, as Mitchison realised even from the initial investigations, and her direct contact with Harrisson and Madge, what they were also mapping was the social inertia which so frustrated her own desire to live a different, more open style of life: 'we are up against the desire not to be possibly thought strange or deserving to be outcast' (Mitchison 1971: 331).

When, at the outbreak of the war, Mass-Observation called for their volunteers to keep diaries that charted the full duration, Mitchison willingly complied and the huge diary she eventually compiled was subsequently published in edited form as *Among You Taking Notes* (1985). While this is marked throughout by the continued impatient frustration at not being able to live beyond social conventions – 'It is always a bore being ahead of one's time' (Mitchison 2000: 181) – it also functions as an extended form of proletarian literature. Critics such as Gill Plain have portrayed the diary negatively as a 'fiction of equality that Mitchison sought to enact within the "real" world' (Plain 1996: 143). However, this should rather be seen as the true value of the project. Spending the war on her Scottish estate of Carradale allowed her to live out in practice Dione's involvement in the 'feudal democracy' shown in the Scottish scenes of *We Have Been Warned*, as though the imaginary envisioned in that novel actually exists. She did not do this blindly but, as the diary frequently acknowledges, with a self-reflexive questioning of what she was doing as in this passage relating to a meal with some local people:

> I kept on wondering whether I was double-crossing myself, whether this meal at which I was so happy, was really in some way bogus, whether I was just taking refuge among these people out of a romantic or sentimental feeling and possibly out of pique at being criticised by the London highbrows or of being the intellectual inferior of various people. Yet I couldn't make out at what point the sacrament was not genuine; I couldn't see myself not loving these people or being at ease with them. (Mitchison 2000: 46)

There are times when she momentarily sounds like an anthropologist, such as when achieving her goal of being formally invited to tea for the first time at the house of one of her tenants: 'I felt a little like an explorer' (Mitchison 2000: 182). However, she immediately goes on to note that mainly she had just enjoyed herself over the course of the evening, although she cannot help wondering why. On other occasions, she also expresses amazement at experiencing the intersubjective possibilities that were envisioned in *We Have Been Warned*: 'I would never have thought to be so much at ease across so thick a class barrier' (Mitchison 2000: 57).

In 1984, writing the foreword to the published version of her diary, Mitchison expressed sadness on reading it as 'it is full of hope for a new kind of world, for something different, happier, more honest, for a new relationship between people who had been cut off from one another by money, power and class structure' (Mitchison 2000: 12–13). Her sense that this hope was not fulfilled is partly conditioned by the failure of the 1979 devolution referendum to gain a sufficient majority to establish a Scottish Parliament but that context has been significantly transformed since by the successful referendum of 1997, the establishment of a Parliament in 1999, and subsequent events. However, what her retrospective analysis suggests is that her cultural practice was different in form to that which contributed to the postwar welfare state: 'I tried to begin the change [to a more utopian society] with personal relations, but Dick, my husband, working with Beveridge and Cole on the political and economic functions of the welfare state, got much further in the end' (Mitchison 2000: 12–13). Mitchison's focus on personal relations was in keeping with Woolf's call in *Three Guineas* for the pursuit of freedom, equality and peace 'with private means in private'. In this respect, Mitchison's diary may be seen, in common with other Mass-Observation wartime diaries, as demonstrating how widespread social change happened outside the public view through the medium of personal relations (see Hinton 2010; Hubble 2016a). In her Mass-Observation diary presentation of a Scotland as potentially socially transfigured beyond patriarchal binary thought, Mitchison demonstrates a future for the imaginary landscapes that appear at the end of works of proletarian literature such as *Lady Chatterley's Lover*, *A Scots Quair*, *We Have Been Warned* and, even, Woolf's *Between the Acts* (1941):

> It was the night before roads were made, or houses. It was the night that dwellers in caves had watched from some high place among rocks.
> Then the curtain rose. They spoke. (Woolf 1978b: 160)

Notes

1. This conversion is recounted in 'My Country Right or Left' (1940) but it is unlikely that it happened in the manner described. See the discussion in Hubble 2015: 59–62.
2. So called because 'things were dolloped out to them soft as pease-pudding on a paper' (Common 1980: 34).
3. Although the Equal Pay Act received royal assent in May 1970, the Labour Party lost power in a General Election the following month and therefore the Act did not actually come into force until December 1975, after they had come back into power and had a chance to implement it.

Conclusion

The proletarian answer to the modernist question was not the welfare state. The 1945 political settlement ushered in a period in which neither proletarian literature nor modernism flourished. The hopes of writers such as Mitchison, Gibbon, Lawrence and Woolf for moving beyond patriarchal binary thought were not achieved. The 'old pastoral' form of British postwar culture had more in common with the music-hall modernism and Edwardian pastoral of an earlier generation of writers such as Wells, Galsworthy and Ford. Orwell harked back to these models in works like *The Road to Wigan Pier* and *The Lion and the Unicorn*. This is not to say that the period covered by the first three or four postwar decades was a 'bad one to live in' (Orwell 1998: 102). The positive aspects of this period included the centrality of public representations of working-class collectivity, which included some space for the expression of working women's desires and agency as expressed in certain popular works of proletarian literature, such as Greenwood's *Love on the Dole* and Sommerfield's *Trouble in Porter Street*. The political legacy of that period lies in the various equalities legislation it gave rise to, including the 1970 Equal Pay Act. However, there is also another legacy of that period, which dates back to the proletarian-modernist literature of the late 1930s. The spread of self-reflexivity in the private sphere, as shown in Mass-Observation diaries, was a testament to both the democratising of culture embodied by the public visibility of proletarian literature in the 1930s and the influence of modernist writers, such as Woolf. As Hinton notes, *The Common Reader*, *Orlando* and *A Room of One's Own* were all published by Penguin during the period

1939–45: 'Virginia Woolf, we might argue, did more to construct modern selfhood than a far more widely read writer like J. B. Priestley, despite the latter's mastery of the means of mass communication' (Hinton 2008: 219).

In 2017 we have reached a point where the basic features of the welfare state – full employment, paid holidays, family allowances and proper healthcare – are now either gone or under threat. Recognising both that the welfare state is now behind us and that it was in any case problematic in the way it constrained social possibilities of living, leads to the recognition that we need different political objectives or solutions than those we pursued in the past. As Paul Mason points out, in order to rebuild a planned welfare state, it would be necessary to reduce twenty-first-century complexity by enforcing behavioural change at the level of consumption, workplace democracy and investment. Even if this was desirable, the problem would be that the kinds of workplace open to possible democratisation are very much in the minority in a world of zero-hour contracts and nominal self-employment: 'so what happens to the precarious worker with three jobs; or the single mum doing sex work on a web cam? They can't exist' (Mason 2015: 233).

Rather than try and shoehorn society back into a plan, we need a post-capitalist politics that can handle intersectional complexity as well as individual desires. One element of this problem is cultural. We have a cultural understanding of literary history and particularly of working-class fiction that was formed in the cause of the welfare state and which emphasises collectivity, class solidarity, respectability and stability. However, while it might have been possible to see this as part of a long revolution in the 1960s, it no longer looks achievable today. Does that mean we are stuck with capitalism? Mason's response is to argue: 'It is absurd that we are capable of witnessing a 40,000-year-old system of gender oppression begin to dissolve before our eyes and yet still seeing the abolition of a 200-year-old economic system as an unrealistic utopia' (Mason 2015: 290).

One thing that literary scholars can do is help to break down the implicitly gendered opposition between stable, plannable systems and individual desires by reinterpreting literary history. The resources are already in place to do this. On the one hand, as the examples of *Love on the Dole*, *May Day*, *Clash*, *We Have Been Warned* and *Lady Chatterley's Lover* show, women's desires are often the driving force for change in proletarian and left-wing literature. On the other hand, through what we think of as modernism, we have a tradition of literary readings which focus on subjectivity, intersubjectivity, desires and the unconscious. If we combine these two traditions, we can demonstrate a proletarian-modernist focus on the everyday that anticipates an intersectional approach to politics and which can be drawn upon as a resource for today's political situation.

Concentrating on such a project would also help with another modernist-related question. As Latham and Rogers note of the currently dominant institutional and publishing approach to modernism, the New Modernist Studies:

> What was 'new' in the 1990s, however, is now over a decade old [. . .] We are, in some ways, at a moment similar to that of the early 1900s: 'modernism' is conceptually up for grabs in ways that it was not in the mid-1900s, and it is not vilified as it often was in the 1980s. (Latham and Rogers 2015: 151)

It is not necessary to rehearse the various competing planetary, transnational, popular and, even, 'bad' modernisms here to support this point. The most recent Modernist Studies Association annual conference held in Pasadena, 17–20 November 2016, included, amongst the usual varied and wide-ranging programme of papers, seminars and plenary panels, roundtable discussions with suggestive titles such as 'The Limits of the New Modernisms: How Much is Too Much?' and, more bluntly, 'Against Modernist Studies'. To be sure, such questions and reactions have floated around for some years – possibly for the entire duration of the New Modernist Studies – but, in the tense aftermath of Donald Trump's unexpected win in the US presidential elections, the discussions seemed more animated and edgier than previously. The current all-encompassing approach – to a plethora of modernisms rooted in the infinite cultural responses to the multi-faceted experience of modernity that spread globally over the twentieth century – simply cannot hold indefinitely. Regardless of whatever realignments the field undergoes – and the long-term future which might well lie in the more safely periodised category of twentieth-century studies – the concern at the moment must be how to channel the energy and radical analyses which have given the New Modernist Studies momentum into global public engagement with everyday culture. There is a time limit on this as the current spread of isolationist anti-immigrant politics through Europe and the United States is likely to bring an abrupt end to any remaining cultural authority attaching to the West and even tarnish what remains of the allure of Western modernity itself. Of course, that might not be a bad thing and one could further ask, what is the purpose of holding on to modernism? The simple answer to that is that the primary texts, themselves, remain a body of work worth reading. That, after all, is why Anglo-American academic culture currently characterises what would otherwise be more logically labelled 'Early Twentieth-Century Studies' as modernism. The reason why these books are still worth reading is because they tell us about subjectivity and identity and sexuality and gender and ethnicity; they tell us about ourselves. This capacity does not lead to an anthropological turn towards an inward-looking culture, but towards relationships with the other and the intersubjective possibilities of more open, rewarding forms of social life. Such an interest characterises in particular the proletarian-modernist texts focused on in this book. The relevance of proletarian-modernist texts is that they hold open these possibilities to the common people, including those subordinated under a global capitalist system. Therefore if modernist studies, in the context of the current choices facing it, were focused along these lines it would have a chance to connect with the largely female proletariat of the global south and offer its cultural resources in the hope of supporting a greater public agency.

The possible futures imagined by the modernist-proletarian texts considered in this book far exceeded the capacity of state infrastructure and mainstream political imagination. Indeed, what Mitchison had to say of the present was too terrible and shocking for her contemporaries. In a passage struggling to deal with the difficulties of non-monogamous relationships, Dione consoles herself with the thought that conventions will have changed in one hundred years (see Mitchison 2012: 380). The thought is very similar to Woolf's hope that in another hundred years there could be a genuinely women's writing. There is still over a decade to go before that time period elapses but it is already possible to see the social and cultural changes in outline that might enable these possibilities to be realised. It is equally possible to see the development of organised resistance to such change. Awareness of the literary history of proletarian literature might help encourage the cultural and political activity necessary to ensure that these possible futures do come into being.

Bibliography

Barke, James (1936), 'Lewis Grassic Gibbon', *Left Review*, 2 (5): 220–5.
Barke, James [1936] (1955), *Major Operation*, London: Collins.
Barker, Francis, Jay Bernstein, John Coombes, Peter Hulme, David Musselwhite and Jennifer Stone (eds) (1979a), *1936: The Sociology of Literature, Volume 1 – The Politics of Modernism*, Wivenhoe: University of Essex.
Barker, Francis, Jay Bernstein, John Coombes, Peter Hulme, David Musselwhite and Jennifer Stone (eds) (1979b), *1936: The Sociology of Literature, Volume 2 – Practices of Literature and Politics*, Wivenhoe: University of Essex.
Barrett, Michèle and Jean Radford (1979), 'Modernism in the 1930s: Dorothy Richardson and Virginia Woolf', in Francis Barker, Jay Bernstein, John Coombes, Peter Hulme, David Musselwhite and Jennifer Stone (eds), *1936: The Sociology of Literature, Volume 1 – The Politics of Modernism*, Wivenhoe: University of Essex, pp. 252–72.
Bell, Ian A. (2000), '"Work as If You Live in the Early Days of a Better Nation": Scottish Fiction and the Experience of Industry', in H. Gustav Klaus and Stephen Knight (eds), *British Industrial Fictions*, Cardiff: University of Wales Press, pp. 181–92.
Benjamin, Walter (1992), *Illuminations*, trans. Harry Zohn, London: Fontana.
Benton, Jill (1992), *Naomi Mitchison: A Biography*, London: Pandora.
Bluemel, Kristin (2004), *George Orwell and the Radical Eccentrics: Intermodernism in Literary London*, New York and Basingstoke: Palgrave Macmillan.
Bluemel, Kristin (ed.) (2009), *Intermodernism: Literary Culture in Mid-Twentieth-Century Britain*, Edinburgh: Edinburgh University Press.
Bluemel, Kristin [2012] (2015), 'Exemplary Intermodernists: Stevie Smith, Inez Holden, Betty Miller, and Naomi Mitchison', in Maroula Joannou (ed.), *The History of British Women's Writing, 1920–1945*, Basingstoke: Palgrave Macmillan, pp. 40–56.

Bounds, Philip (2012), *British Communism and the Politics of Literature 1928–1939*, Pontypool: Merlin.
Bowlby, Rachel (1988), *Virginia Woolf: Feminist Destinations*, Oxford: Blackwell.
Brierley, Walter [1937] (1990), *Sandwichman*, London: Merlin.
Brierley, Walter [1935] (2011), *Means-Test Man*, Nottingham: Spokesman.
Britton, Derek (1988), *Lady Chatterley: The Making of the Novel*, London: Unwin Hyman.
Burton, Deirdre (1984), 'A Feminist Reading of Lewis Grassic Gibbon's *A Scots Quair*', in Jeremy Hawthorn (ed.), *The British Working-Class Novel in the Twentieth Century*, London: Edward Arnold, pp. 35–46.
Calder, Jenni (1997), *The Nine Lives of Naomi Mitchison*, London: Virago.
Campbell, Ian (2000), 'Introduction', in Lewis Grassic Gibbon, *Nine Against the Unknown*, Edinburgh: Polygon, pp. xi–xvi.
Carnie Holdsworth, Ethel [1923–4] (2011), *This Slavery*, Nottingham: Trent Editions.
Cixous, Hélène [1975] (1981), 'Sorties', in Elaine Marks and Isabelle de Courtivron (eds), *New French Feminisms: An Anthology*, Hemel Hempstead: Harvester Wheatsheaf, pp. 90–8.
Clark, Jon, Margot Heinemann, David Margolies and Carole Snee (eds) (1979), *Culture and Crisis in Britain in the Thirties*, London: Lawrence & Wishart.
Clarke, Ben (2007), *Orwell in Context*, Basingstoke: Palgrave Macmillan.
Clute, John (2011), *Pardon this Intrusion: Fantastika in the World Storm*, Harold Wood: Beccon Publications.
Common, Jack [1935] (1980), 'Pease-pudding Men', in *Revolt Against an Age of Plenty*, Newcastle: Strong Words, pp. 32–41.
Common, Jack (1984), 'Jack Common's Recollections', in Audrey Coppard and Bernard Crick (eds), *Orwell Remembered*, London: Ariel Books, pp. 139–43.
Craig, Cairns (1999), *The Modern Scottish Novel*, Edinburgh: Edinburgh University Press.
Crick, Bernard (1982), *George Orwell: A Life*, Harmondsworth: Penguin.
Croft, Andy (1990), *Red Letter Days: British Fiction in the 1930s*, London: Lawrence & Wishart.
Croft, Andy (1998), 'The Boys Round the Corner: The Story of Fore Publications', in Andy Croft (ed.), *A Weapon in the Struggle: The Cultural History of the Communist Party in Britain*, London: Pluto Press, pp. 142–62.
Croft, Andy (2011), 'Introduction', in Walter Brierley, *Means-Test Man*, Nottingham: Spokesman, pp. vii–xvi.
Cunningham, Valentine (1988), *British Writers of the Thirties*, Oxford: Oxford University Press.

Ellis, David (1998), *D. H. Lawrence: Dying Game 1922–1930*, Cambridge: Cambridge University Press.
Empson, William [1930] (1961), *Seven Types of Ambiguity*, Harmondsworth: Penguin.
Empson, William (1988), *Argufying: Essays on Literature and Culture*, ed. John Haffenden, London: The Hogarth Press.
Empson, William [1935] (1995), *Some Versions of Pastoral*, Harmondsworth: Penguin.
English Studies Group (ESG) (1979), 'Thinking the Thirties', in Francis Barker, Jay Bernstein, John Coombes, Peter Hulme, David Musselwhite and Jennifer Stone (eds), *1936: The Sociology of Literature, Volume 2 – Practices of Literature and Politics*, Wivenhoe: University of Essex, pp. 1–19.
Esty, Jed (2004), *A Shrinking Island: Modernism and National Culture in England*, Princeton: Princeton University Press.
Feigel, Lara (2010), *Literature, Cinema and Politics, 1930–45: Reading Between the Frames*, Edinburgh: Edinburgh University Press.
Ferrall, Charles and Dougal McNeill (2015), *Writing the 1926 General Strike: Literature, Culture, Politics*, New York: Cambridge University Press.
Ford, Ford Madox [as Daniel Chaucer] (1912), *The New Humpty-Dumpty*, London: The Bodley Head.
Ford, Ford Madox [1924–8] (1982), *Parade's End*, Harmondsworth: Penguin.
Ford, Ford Madox [1910] (1984), *A Call: The Tale of Two Passions*, Manchester: Carcanet.
Ford, Ford Madox [1937] (1987), 'D. H. Lawrence', in Sondra J. Stang (ed.), *The Ford Madox Ford Reader*, London: Paladin, pp. 255–63.
Ford, Ford Madox [1915] (1988), *The Good Soldier*, Harmondsworth: Penguin.
Ford, Ford Madox [1905–7] (2003), *England and the English (The Soul of London* [1905], *The Heart of the Country* [1906], *The Spirit of the People* [1907])*, ed. Sara Haslem, Manchester: Carcanet.
Fox, Pamela (1994), *Class Fictions: Shame and Resistance in the British Working-Class Novel, 1890–1945*, Durham, NC and London: Duke University Press.
Galsworthy, John (2001), *The Forsyte Saga: Volume Two (The White Monkey* [1924], *The Silver Spoon* [1926], *Swan Song* [1928])*, Harmondsworth: Penguin.
Gibbon, Lewis Grassic [as James Leslie Mitchell] (1928), *Hanno, or, The Future of Exploration*, London: Kegan Paul, Trench, Trubner.
Gibbon, Lewis Grassic (1935), 'From Lewis Grassic Gibbon', *Left Review*, 1 (5): 179–80.

Gibbon, Lewis Grassic [1946] (1986), *A Scots Quair* (*Sunset Song* [1932], *Cloud Howe* [1933], *Grey Granite* [1934]), Harmondsworth: Penguin.
Gibbon, Lewis Grassic [1934] (2000), *Nine Against the Unknown*, Edinburgh: Polygon.
Gibbon, Lewis Grassic [1934] (2001), 'The Land', in Valentina Bold (ed.), *Smeddum: A Lewis Grassic Gibbon Anthology*, Edinburgh: Canongate, pp. 81–97.
Gloversmith, Frank (ed.) (1980), *Class, Culture and Social Change: A New View of the 1930s*, Brighton: Harvester Press.
Greenwood, Walter [1933] (1969), *Love on the Dole*, Harmondsworth: Penguin.
Gross, John (1979), *The Rise and Fall of the Man of Letters: English Literary Life since 1800*, Harmondsworth: Pelican.
Gurney, Peter (1997), '"Intersex" and "Dirty Girls": Mass-Observation and Working-Class Sexuality in England in the 1930s', *Journal of the History of Sexuality*, 8 (2): 256–90.
Habermas, Jürgen [1962] (1989), *The Structural Transformation of the Public Sphere*, trans. Thomas Burger with Frederick Lawrence, London: Polity Press.
Haffenden, John (2005), *William Empson: Among the Mandarins*, Oxford: Oxford University Press.
Hall, Stuart (1972), 'The Social Eye of *Picture Post*', *Working Papers in Cultural Studies 2*, Birmingham: Centre for Contemporary Cultural Studies, 72–108.
Harding, Jason (2006), 'The Englishness of the *English Review*', in Dennis Brown and Jenny Plastow (eds), *Ford Madox Ford and Englishness*, Amsterdam: Rodopi, pp. 137–45.
Hawthorn, Jeremy (ed.) (1984), *The British Working-Class Novel in the Twentieth Century*, London: Edward Arnold.
Haywood, Ian (1997), *Working-Class Fiction: From Chartism to Trainspotting*, Plymouth: Northcote House.
Hegel, G. W. F. (1977), *Phenomenology of Spirit*, trans. A. V. Miller, Oxford: Oxford University Press.
Heslop, Harold [1935] (1984), *Last Cage Down*, London: Lawrence & Wishart.
Highmore, Ben (2002), *Everyday Life and Cultural Theory*, London: Routledge.
Highmore, Ben (2011), *Ordinary Lives: Studies in the Everyday*, Abingdon: Routledge.
Hinton, James (2008), 'The "Class" Complex': Mass-Observation and Cultural Distinction in Pre-war Britain', *Past and Present*, 199: 207–36.

Hinton, James (2010), *Nine Wartime Lives: Mass-Observation and the Making of the Modern Self*, Oxford and New York: Oxford University Press.

Hinton, James (2013), *The Mass Observers: A History, 1937–1949*, Oxford and New York: Oxford University Press.

Hobsbawm, Eric (1978), 'The Forward March of Labour Halted?', *Marxism Today*, September: 279–86.

Hoggart, Richard [1957] (1968), *The Uses of Literacy*, Harmondsworth: Penguin.

Hubble, Nick (2009), 'The Intermodern Assumption of the Future: William Empson and Mass-Observation', in Kristin Bluemel (ed.), *Intermodernism: Literary Culture in Mid-Twentieth-Century Britain*, Edinburgh: Edinburgh University Press, pp. 171–88.

Hubble, Nick [2006] (2010), *Mass Observation and Everyday Life: Culture, History, Theory*, 2nd edn, Basingstoke: Palgrave Macmillan.

Hubble, Nick (2012a), 'Imagism, Realism, Surrealism: Middlebrow Transformations in the Mass-Observation Project', in Erica Brown and Mary Grover (eds), *Middlebrow Literary Cultures: The Battle of the Brows, 1920–1960*, Basingstoke: Palgrave Macmillan, pp. 202–17.

Hubble, Nick (2012b), 'John Sommerfield and Mass-Observation', *The Space Between: Literature and Culture, 1914–1945*, 8 (1): 131–51.

Hubble, Nick (2012c), 'Orwell and the English Working Class: Lessons in Autobiografiction for the Twenty-First Century', in Richard Lance Keeble (ed.), *Orwell Today*, Bury St Edmunds: Abramis, pp. 30–45.

Hubble, Nick (2013), 'Naomi Mitchison: Fantasy and Intermodern Utopia', in Alice Reeve-Tucker and Nathan Waddell (eds), *Utopianism, Modernism and Literature in the Twentieth Century*, Basingstoke: Palgrave Macmillan, pp. 74–92.

Hubble, Nick (2015), 'Looking Back on the 1930s without Being Anti-Communist: Cornford, Orwell, Spender, Sommerfield', *Literature & History*, 24 (2): 57–72.

Hubble, Nick (2016a), 'Documenting Lives: Mass Observation, Women's Diaries, and Everyday Modernity', in Adam Smyth (ed.), *A History of English Autobiography*, Oxford: Oxford University Press, pp. 345–58.

Hubble, Nick (2016b), 'Common People: Class, Gender and Social Change in the London Fiction of Virginia Woolf, John Sommerfield and Zadie Smith', in Nick Hubble and Philip Tew (eds), *London in Contemporary British Fiction: The City Beyond the City*, London: Bloomsbury Academic, pp. 195–210.

Hynes, Samuel [1972] (1982), *The Auden Generation: Literature and Politics in England in the 1930s*, Princeton: Princeton University Press.

Jameson, Fredric (2005), *Archaeologies of the Future: The Desire Called Utopia and Other Science Fictions*, London: Verso.

Jennings, Humphrey and Charles Madge [1937] (1987), *May the Twelfth: Mass-Observation Day Surveys 1937*, London: Faber & Faber.

Klaus, H. Gustav (1979), 'Socialist Novels of 1936', in Francis Barker, Jay Bernstein, John Coombes, Peter Hulme, David Musselwhite and Jennifer Stone (eds), *1936: The Sociology of Literature, Volume 2 – Practices of Literature and Politics*, Wivenhoe: University of Essex, pp. 143–62.

Klaus, H. Gustav and Stephen Knight (eds) (2000), *British Industrial Fictions*, Cardiff: University of Wales Press.

Lacan, Jacques (1980), *Écrits: A Selection*, trans. Alan Sheridan, London: Tavistock Publications.

Laing, Stuart (1980), 'Presenting "Things as They Are": John Sommerfield's *May Day* and Mass Observation', in Frank Gloversmith (ed.), *Class, Culture and Social Change: A New View of the 1930s*, Brighton: Harvester Press, pp. 142–60.

Latham, Sean and Gayle Rogers (2015), *Modernism: Evolution of an Idea*, London: Bloomsbury Academic.

Lawrence, D. H. (1971), 'Return to Bestwood', in *A Selection from Phoenix*, ed. A. A. H. Inglis, Harmondsworth: Penguin, pp. 146–57.

Lawrence, D. H. [1944] (1973a), *The First Lady Chatterley*, Harmondsworth: Penguin.

Lawrence, D. H. [1954] (1973b), *John Thomas and Lady Jane*, Harmondsworth: Penguin.

Lawrence, D. H. [1928] (1994), *Lady Chatterley's Lover*, ed. Michael Squires, Harmondsworth: Penguin.

Leaska, Mitchell A. (1978), 'Introduction', in Virginia Woolf, *The Pargiters*, London: The Hogarth Press, pp. vii–xxii.

Lee, Hermione (1997), *Virginia Woolf*, London: Vintage.

Lehmann, John (1935), 'Review of *Grey Granite*', *Left Review*, 11 (5): 190–1.

Love on the Dole, film, directed by John Baxter. UK: British National Films, 1941.

Lumsden, Alison (2003), '"Women's Time": Reading the *Quair* as a Feminist Text', in Margery Palmer McCulloch and Sarah M. Dunnigan (eds), *A Flame in the Mearns: Lewis Grassic Gibbon, A Centenary Celebration*, Glasgow: Association of Scottish Literary Studies, pp. 41–53.

Lynd, Helen Merrell (1945), *England in the Eighteen-Eighties: Towards a Social Basis for Freedom*, New York: Oxford University Press.

Lynd, Helen Merrell (1958), *On Shame and the Search for Identity*, London: Routledge & Kegan Paul.

McCulloch, Margery Palmer (2003), 'Modernism and Marxism in *A Scots Quair*', in Margery Palmer McCulloch and Sarah M. Dunnigan (eds), *A Flame in the Mearns: Lewis Grassic Gibbon, A Centenary Celebration*, Glasgow: Association of Scottish Literary Studies, pp. 27–40.

McCulloch, Margery Palmer (2009), *Scottish Modernism and Its Contexts 1918–1959: Literature, National Identity and Cultural Exchange*, Edinburgh: Edinburgh University Press.
McCulloch, Margery Palmer and Sarah M. Dunnigan (eds) (2003), *A Flame in the Mearns: Lewis Grassic Gibbon, A Centenary Celebration*. Glasgow: Association of Scottish Literary Studies.
MacDiarmid, Hugh (1948), 'Lewis Grassic Gibbon: 1901–1935', *Our Time*, 7 (12): 307–8.
McFarlane, Anna (2016), 'Naomi Mitchison's *We Have Been Warned* in Post-Referendum Scotland', *The Bottle Imp*, 19 (June): 1–4.
MacKay, Marina (2007), *Modernism and World War II*, Cambridge: Cambridge University Press.
McKenna, Brian (1996), 'The British Communist Novel of the 1930s and 1940s: A "Party of Equals"? (And Does That Matter?)', *The Review of English Studies*, 47 (187): 369–85.
Madge, Charles (1937), 'Magic and Materialism', *Left Review*, 3 (1): 33–5.
Madge, Charles and Tom Harrisson (1939), *Britain by Mass-Observation*, Harmondsworth: Penguin.
Malcolm, William K. (2016), *Lewis Grassic Gibbon: A Revolutionary Writer*, Edinburgh: Capercaillie Books.
Mansfield, Katherine (1981), *The Collected Stories of Katherine Mansfield*, Harmondsworth: Penguin.
March-Russell, Paul (2015), *Modernism and Science Fiction*, Basingstoke: Palgrave Macmillan.
Marcus, Laura (2007), *The Tenth Muse: Writing about Cinema in the Modernist Period*, Oxford: Oxford University Press.
Marx, Karl and Friedrich Engels (1969), *Basic Writings on Politics and Philosophy*, ed. Lewis S. Feuer, Glasgow: Fontana.
Mason, Paul (2015), *PostCapitalism: A Guide to Our Future*, London: Allen Lane.
Mellor, Adrian, Chris Pawling and Colin Sparks (1976), 'Writers and the General Strike', in Margaret Morris, *The General Strike*, Harmondsworth: Pelican, pp. 338–57.
Miller, Tyrus (1999), *Late Modernism: Politics, Fiction, and the Arts Between the World Wars*, Berkeley: University of California Press.
Mitchison, Naomi [1938] (1971), *The Moral Basis of Politics*, Port Washington, NY: Kennikat Press.
Mitchison, Naomi [1962] (1976), *Memoirs of a Spacewoman*, London: New English Library.
Mitchison, Naomi (1986), *You May Well Ask: A Memoir 1920–1940*, London: Flamingo.
Mitchison, Naomi [1985] (2000), *Among You Taking Notes*, ed. Dorothy Sheridan, London: Phoenix Press.

Mitchison, Naomi [1935] (2012), *We Have Been Warned*, Kilkerran: Kennedy & Boyd.

Moi, Toril (1985), *Sexual/Textual Politics: Feminist Literary Theory*, London: Routledge.

Murray, Isobel (2003), 'Gibbon's Chris: A Celebration with Some Reservations', in Margery Palmer McCulloch and Sarah M. Dunnigan (eds), *A Flame in the Mearns: Lewis Grassic Gibbon, A Centenary Celebration*, Glasgow: Association of Scottish Literary Studies, pp. 54–63.

Murray, Isobel (2012), 'Introduction', in Naomi Mitchison, *We Have Been Warned*, Kilkerran: Kennedy & Boyd, pp. v–xix.

Nicholls, Peter (1995), *Modernisms: A Literary Guide*, Basingstoke: Macmillan.

Norquay, Glenda (2015), 'Lewis Grassic Gibbon and Women', in Scott Lyall (ed.), *The International Companion to Lewis Grassic Gibbon*, Glasgow: Scottish Literature International, pp. 76–88.

Orwell, George [1949] (1976), *Nineteen Eighty-Four*, Harmondsworth: Penguin.

Orwell, George [1937] (1998), *The Road to Wigan Pier*, London: Secker & Warburg.

Orwell, George [1940] (2000a), 'The Proletarian Writer', in *A Patriot After All 1940–1941, Collected Works XII*, ed. Peter Davison, London: Secker & Warburg, pp. 294–9.

Orwell, George [1941] (2000b), *The Lion and the Unicorn*, in *A Patriot After All 1940–1941, Collected Works XII*, ed. Peter Davison, London: Secker & Warburg, pp. 391–434.

Paul, Ronald (2012), '"A big change": Intersectional Class and Gender in John Sommerfield's *May Day*', *Nordic Journal of English Studies*, 11 (2): 120–37.

Pinkney, Tony (1990), *D. H. Lawrence and Modernism*, Iowa City: University of Iowa Press.

Pinkney, Tony [1989] (1996), 'Editor's Introduction: Modernism and Cultural Theory', in Raymond Williams, *The Politics of Modernism*, ed. Tony Pinkney, London: Verso, pp. 1–29.

Plain, Gill (1996), *Women's Fiction of the Second World War: Gender, Power and Resistance*, Edinburgh: Edinburgh University Press.

Reeve-Tucker, Alice and Nathan Waddell (eds) (2013), *Utopianism, Modernism and Literature in the Twentieth Century*, Basingstoke: Palgrave Macmillan.

Roberts, John (1998), *The Art of Interruption: Realism, Photography and the Everyday*, Manchester: Manchester University Press.

Saunders, Max (1996), *Ford Madox Ford: A Dual Life. Volume 1: The World Before the War*, Oxford and New York: Oxford University Press.

Saunders, Max (2010), *Self Impression: Life-Writing, Autobiografiction, and the Forms of Modern Literature*, Oxford and New York: Oxford University Press.

Serrano, Julia (2010), 'The Case Against Autogynephilia', *International Journal of Transgenderism*, 12 (3): 176–87

Smith, David (1978), *Socialist Propaganda in the Twentieth-Century British Novel*, London and Basingstoke: Macmillan.

Smyth, Adam (ed.) (2016), *A History of English Autobiography*, Oxford: Oxford University Press.

Snaith, Anna (2000a), 'Wide Circles: The *Three Guinea* Letters', *Woolf Studies Annual*, 6: 1–10.

Snaith, Anna (ed.) (2000b), '*Three Guineas* Letters', *Woolf Studies Annual*, 6: 17–168.

Snee, Carole (1979), 'Working-Class Literature or Proletarian Writing?', in Jon Clark, Margot Heinemann, David Margolies and Carole Snee (eds), *Culture and Crisis in Britain in the Thirties*, London: Lawrence & Wishart, pp. 165–91.

Sommerfield, John (1930), *They Die Young*, London: Heinemann.

Sommerfield, John (1936), *May Day*, London: Lawrence & Wishart.

Sommerfield, John (1939), *Trouble in Porter Street*, London: Fore Publications.

Sommerfield, John [1939] (1954), *Trouble in Porter Street*, London: Lawrence & Wishart.

Sommerfield, John (1956), *The Inheritance*, London: Heinemann.

Sommerfield, John (1960), *North West Five*, London: Heinemann.

Sommerfield, John (1977), *The Imprinted*, London: London Magazine Editions.

Sommerfield, John [1936] (1984a), *May Day*, London: Lawrence & Wishart.

Sommerfield, John (1984b), Letter to Andrew Whitehead, *London Fictions*, <http://www.londonfictions.com/john-sommerfield-trouble-in-porter-street.html> (last accessed 9 February 2017).

Sommerfield, John [1936] (2010), *May Day*, London: London Books Classics.

Spufford, Francis (2010), *Red Plenty*, London: Faber & Faber.

Taylor, Elinor (2014), '"The Rich Harmonics of Past Time": Memory and Montage in John Sommerfield's *May Day*', *Key Words*, 12: 60–72.

Todd, Selina (2014), *The People: The Rise and Fall of the Working Class, 1910–2010*, London: John Murray.

Tratner, Michael (1995), *Modernism and Mass Politics: Joyce, Woolf, Eliot, Yeats*, Stanford: Stanford University Press.

Trotter, David (1993), *The English Novel in History 1895–1920*, London: Routledge.

Trotter, David (2001), *Paranoid Modernism: Literary Experiment, Psychosis and the Professionalization of English Society*, Oxford: Oxford University Press.
Trotter, David (2013), *Literature in the First Media Age: Britain Between the Wars*, Cambridge, MA: Harvard University Press.
Webster, Roger (1984), '*Love on the Dole* and the Aesthetic of Contradiction', in Jeremy Hawthorn (ed.), *The British Working-Class Novel in the Twentieth Century*, London: Edward Arnold, pp. 49–61.
Wells, H. G. (1932), *The Bulpington of Blup: Adventures, Poses, Stresses, Conflicts, and Disaster in a Contemporary Brain*, London: Hutchinson.
Wells, H. G. (1934), *Experiment in Autobiography: Discoveries and Conclusions of a Very Ordinary Brain (Since 1866)*, vol. 2, London: Gollancz and the Cresset Press.
Wells, H. G. [1927] (1962), *Meanwhile*, London: Ernest Benn.
Wells, H. G. [1909] (1972), *Tono-Bungay*, London: Pan.
West, Alick [1937] (1975), *Crisis and Criticism and Selected Literary Essays*, London: Lawrence & Wishart.
Wilkinson, Ellen [1929] (2004), *Clash*, Nottingham: Trent Editions.
Williams, Keith (1991), 'Joyce's "Chinese Alphabet": *Ulysses* and the Proletarians', in Paul Hyland and Neil Sammells (eds), *Irish Writing: Exile and Subversion*, Basingstoke: Macmillan, pp. 173–87.
Williams, Keith (1996), *British Writers and the Media, 1930–45*, Basingstoke: Macmillan.
Williams, Keith and Steven Mathews (eds) (1997), *Rewriting the Thirties: Modernism and After*, London and New York: Longman.
Williams, Raymond (1979), *Politics and Letters: Interviews with New Left Review*, London: Verso.
Williams, Raymond [1983] (1985), *Towards 2000*, Harmondsworth: Penguin.
Williams, Raymond [1975] (1990), *Television: Technology and Cultural Form*, London: Routledge.
Williams, Raymond [1971] (1991), *Orwell*, Hammersmith: Fontana.
Williams, Raymond [1989] (1996), *The Politics of Modernism*, ed. Tony Pinkney, London: Verso.
Wilson, Angus [1958] (1983a), 'Diversity and Depth', in *Diversity and Depth in Fiction: Selected Critical Writings of Angus Wilson*, ed. Kerry McSweeney, London: Secker & Warburg, pp. 130–4.
Wilson, Angus [1967] (1983b), 'The Dilemma of the Contemporary Novelist', in *Diversity and Depth in Fiction: Selected Critical Writings of Angus Wilson*, ed. Kerry McSweeney. London: Secker & Warburg, pp. 238–51.
Wolmark, Jenny (1981), 'Problems of Tone in *A Scots Quair*', *Red Letters*, 11: 15–23.

Woolf, Virginia [1931] (1975), 'Introductory Letter to Margaret Llewelyn Davies', in Margaret Llewelyn Davies (ed.), *Life as We Have Known It*, New York: W. W. Norton, pp. xv–xxxix.
Woolf, Virginia [1937] (1977), *The Years*, Hammersmith: Grafton.
Woolf, Virginia (1978a), *The Pargiters*, ed. Mitchell A. Leaska, London: The Hogarth Press.
Woolf, Virginia [1941] (1978b), *Between the Acts*, Hammersmith: Grafton.
Woolf, Virginia [1925] (2000a), *Mrs Dalloway*, ed. David Bradshaw, Oxford: Oxford University Press.
Woolf, Virginia [1929/1938] (2000b), *A Room of One's Own/Three Guineas*, Harmondsworth: Penguin Classics.
Worpole, Ken (1983), *Dockers and Detectives*, London: Verso.
Young, Douglas F. (1973), *Beyond the Sunset: A Study of James Leslie Mitchell (Lewis Grassic Gibbon)*, Aberdeen: Impulse Books.
Žižek, Slavoj (2002), *Welcome to the Desert of the Real*, London: Verso.
Žižek, Slavoj (2006), *The Parallax View*, Cambridge, MA: The MIT Press.

Index

Adelphi, 62, 178, 179
Aldiss, Brian, 53
Amis, Kingsley, 175
Ardizzone, Edward, 190
autobiografiction, 18, 19, 20, 43, 46, 47, 48, 49, 102, 131, 138, 139, 143, 144, 155, 161, 178; *see also* Saunders, Max
'autogynephilia', 139

Baker, Zita, 17
Ballard, J. G., 53
Barke, James, 25, 27, 29, 30, 110–11, 113, 116, 130, 136
  Major Operation, 25, 110–11, 118
Barrett, Michèle, 27
Barstow, Stan, 22
Bell, Ian A., 114
Benjamin, Walter, 125, 127
Bennett, Arnold, 68, 157
Benton, Jill, 17
Beveridge, William, 195
Bluemel, Kristin, 50, 51
  Intermodernism, 50
Blumenfeld, Simon, 28, 29, 40
  Jew Boy, 40
bourgeoisie, 2, 11, 34, 41, 46, 48, 80, 118, 119
  bourgeois individualism, 15, 28, 33, 36, 42, 45, 64, 120, 147, 162, 179
  bourgeois patriarchal order, 80, 119, 171
  bourgeois public sphere, 58
  bourgeois society, 19, 36
  bourgeois values, 19, 25, 34–5, 119, 129, 147, 171, 176
  see also patriarchal order; symbolic order
Bowlby, Rachel, 82–3
Braine, John, 22
Brierley, Walter, 2, 6, 23, 24, 28, 29, 47, 91, 93, 105, 181
  Means-Test Man, 2, 22, 24, 28, 33, 40, 54, 104–6, 107, 134
  Sandwichman, 24, 91
Britain, 53
British Empire, 52

Britton, Lionel, 27
  Hunger and Love, 27
Burgess, Anthony, 53
  A Clockwork Orange, 53
Burton, Deirdre, 29, 114, 115, 134, 135, 136, 137
  'A Feminist Reading of Lewis Grassic Gibbon's *A Scots Quair*', 29, 114

Cabell, James Branch, 157
Calder, Jenni, 17
Campbell, Ian, 128
Carnie Holdsworth, Ethel, 29, 33, 40, 47, 103–4
  This Slavery, 40, 103–4
CCCS English Studies Group, 26, 50
  'Thinking the Thirties', 26
Cixous, Hélène, 16, 20
Clarke, Ben, 176, 181
Clute, John, 101, 130
  four stages of fantasy, 101, 130
Cold War, 22, 27, 36
Cole, G. D. H., 17, 195
comic primness *see* Empson, William
Common, Jack, 178, 179, 180, 182, 183
communism, 13, 14, 16, 18, 20, 31, 34, 38, 48, 49, 127, 129, 131, 132, 155
Communist Party of Great Britain, 23, 49, 94, 127, 129, 132, 134, 143, 153, 162, 186, 190
Connolly, Cyril, 22, 182
Conrad, Joseph, 68, 69
  The Secret Agent, 69
Craig, Cairns, 133
Crenshaw, Kimberlé, 8
Croft, Andy, 5, 22, 24, 28, 31, 32, 40, 90, 113
  Red Letter Days: British Fiction in the 1930s, 31–2
Cunningham, Valentine, 6, 30, 52, 54, 110
  British Writers of the Thirties, 30, 52, 54

Daily Worker, 185, 186
Day Lewis, C., 190
  The Otterbury Incident, 190

documentary, 10, 25, 28, 52, 119, 162, 163, 168, 177, 182, 183, 184
Dos Passos, John, 25, 160
  The 42nd Parallel, 160
  Manhattan Transfer, 160

écriture feminine, 16, 138, 171
Eliot, George, 43
  The Impressions of Theophrastus Such, 43
Eliot, T. S., 1–2, 36, 51, 69, 119
  The Waste Land, 1, 69
Empson, William, 2, 5–7, 12, 14, 16–17, 31, 41, 42, 43, 45, 46, 47, 50, 51, 54, 60, 67, 84–5, 102, 103, 106, 121, 133, 166, 175, 176, 181, 188, 189
  comic primness, 121–2, 132, 161, 180, 181, 189
  'Mrs Dalloway as a Political Satire', 84
  myth of the 'Worker', 108–9, 167, 176, 188, 191
  'Proletarian Literature', 5–7, 42, 189
  Seven Types of Ambiguity, 45
  Some Versions of Pastoral, 5, 121, 189
  'Virginia Woolf', 85
  see also pastoral; proletarian literature
Engels, Friedrich, 2
English Review, 54, 56, 64, 65, 68, 70, 71, 73
Englishness, 53, 59, 119
Essex 'Sociology of Literature' conferences, 26, 33
Esty, Jed, 51, 52, 54, 173
  A Shrinking Island: Modernism and National Culture in England, 51

fantasy, 17, 80, 101, 134
  male fantasy, 126
  'traversing the phantasy', 79
  utopian fantasy, 61, 117, 63
  see also Clute, John; Ford, Ford Madox; Gibbon, Lewis Grassic; imaginary identifications; Lawrence, D. H.; Mansfield, Katherine; Mitchison, Naomi; Woolf, Virginia
fascism, 4, 31, 34, 48, 49, 125, 129, 188
Felski, Rita, 139
feminism, 10, 15, 29, 33, 83, 104, 114, 115, 119, 134, 135, 154, 165; see also gender; patriarchal order; symbolic order
Ferrall, Charles, 90, 93, 95, 96, 108, 127, 130
  Writing the 1926 General Strike, 90
First World War, 1, 2, 67, 103, 126, 127, 179, 181
Ford, Ford Madox, 52, 54, 56–8, 59–68, 70–3, 74, 79–80, 81, 189, 197
  A Call: The Tale of Two Passions, 61–4, 66, 72
  England and the English, 57, 59, 61
  The Good Soldier, 60–1, 62, 63, 65, 68

imitative identification, 57, 59, 61, 66–7, 80, 81
  The New Humpty-Dumpty, 64–5, 73
  Parade's End, 63, 65, 67–8
  Portraits of Life, 56
  the promise of the 'Future', 57, 59–60, 66–7, 80
  The Soul of London, 57, 70
  The Spirit of the People, 61
  see also *English Review*; fantasy; future, the; imaginary identifications; modernism
Forster, E. M., 52
Fox, Pamela, 32, 136, 146
  Class Fictions, 32
Freud, Sigmund, 11, 79
  Freudian ideas, 20, 49, 159
future, the, 14, 19, 21, 28, 36, 39, 42, 48–9, 50, 51, 53, 54, 57, 60, 66, 67, 71, 80, 87–8, 89, 92, 93, 94, 99, 103, 104, 117, 118, 128, 131, 146, 152, 168, 171, 172, 176, 188, 191, 195, 200, 201; see also Ford, Ford Madox; Gibbon, Lewis Grassic, Jameson, Fredric; Lawrence, D. H.; Mitchison, Naomi; Orwell, George; Sommerfield, John; Wells, H. G.; Woolf, Virginia

Galsworthy, John, 68, 91–2, 93
  The Forsyte Saga, 91
  Swan Song, 91–2
Garnett, Eve, 190
  The Family from One End Street, 190
gender, 2, 7, 8, 9, 26, 29, 36, 37, 39, 50, 52, 88, 92, 95, 104, 107, 108, 110, 118, 125, 126, 133, 134, 135, 138, 141, 142, 145, 146, 151, 152, 157, 159, 164, 184, 185, 187, 188, 191, 198, 200
  gender binary, 139
  gender difference, 32, 142
  gender equality, 13, 18
  gender expression, 35
  gender relations, 33, 40, 54, 83, 87, 93, 94, 103, 105, 106, 137, 158, 181, 182, 184, 185
  see also feminism; imaginary identifications; mirror scenes, patriarchal order; symbolic order
General Strike (1926), 8, 54, 88, 91–4, 107, 127, 130, 131, 141, 142, 149, 164, 181
Geyer-Ryan, Helga, 48
Gibbon, Lewis Grassic, 6, 23, 26, 29, 30, 38, 47, 101, 107, 111, 112–40, 141, 142, 154, 169, 170, 171, 197
  Cloud Howe, 113, 122, 127, 130
  Gay Hunter, 127
  gendered critique of male behaviour, 114, 125–6, 129–30
  Grey Granite, 107, 112–40, 141, 142, 143
  Hanno, or The Future of Exploration, 127, 128

imaginary identification with the feminine, 134–9
Nine Against the Unknown, 128
A Scots Quair, 23, 27, 33, 41, 47, 54, 113, 114, 117, 126, 130, 134, 135, 136, 138, 154, 170, 195
Sunset Song, 113, 120, 122, 130
Three Go Back, 127
see also imaginary identifications; mirror scenes; modernism; proletarian literature; proletarian modernism
Gibbons, Stella, 26, 50
Cold Comfort Farm, 26
Gollancz, Victor, 22
Gorki, Maxim, 5, 6
Greenwood, Walter, 2, 23, 24, 28, 29, 93, 106–7, 141, 185
Love on the Dole, 2, 8, 22, 23, 27, 28, 29, 32, 33, 106–7, 109, 129, 141, 184, 185, 191, 197, 198
Grierson, John, 119, 162, 163
Drifters, 119
Gross, John, 176
Gurney, Peter, 151

Habermas, Jürgen, 58
The Structural Transformation of the Public Sphere, 58
Hall, Stuart, 190
'The Social Eye of *Picture Post*', 190
Hanley, James, 28, 29
Harding, Jason, 69
Harrison, Tom, 189, 192, 194
Hawthorn, Jeremy, 28, 29, 134
The British Working-Class Novel in the Twentieth Century, 28, 29, 134
Haywood, Ian, 6, 29, 33, 107
Working-Class Fiction, 29, 33
Hegelian dialectic, 118
Heslop, Harold, 2, 29, 30, 47, 50, 93, 108, 115
Last Cage Down, 2, 28, 108
Highmore, Ben, 54, 188
Hinton, James, 54, 151, 174, 197
Nine Wartime Lives, 54
Hobsbawm, Eric, 3, 41
'The Forward March of Labour Halted', 3
Hoggart, Richard, 175, 189
The Uses of Literacy, 175
Holtby, Winifred, 26, 50
Horizon, 22
Hunt, Violet, 63
Hynes, Samuel, 23, 24, 30, 33
The Auden Generation, 23, 33

imaginary identifications, 16, 17, 80, 133, 138, 139, 159, 188, 194
imaginary portraits and correspondences, 44, 47, 85, 176

landscape of the imaginary, 101, 182, 192, 195
see also fantasy; gender; intersubjectivity; mirror scenes; patriarchal order; symbolic order
intermodernism, 50–1, 80, 81, 82, 149
intersectionality, 8, 9, 13, 21, 24, 27, 30, 36, 40, 95, 101, 103, 115, 134, 142, 151, 152, 153, 198, 199
intersubjectivity, 2, 7, 25, 40, 42, 45, 47, 49, 50, 52, 62, 63, 64, 65, 66, 67, 73, 102, 110, 118, 120, 132, 145, 162, 163, 167, 169, 171, 172, 173, 189, 195, 199, 200
intersubjective selfhood, 15, 16, 133
self/portraiture, 43–5
see also imaginary identifications

James, Henry, 68
Jameson, Fredric, 14–15, 117
Johnson, Roy, 23
Jones, Lewis, 23, 24, 29
Cwmardy, 33
We Live, 24, 33
Joyce, James, 1–2, 36, 41, 42, 43, 44, 45–7, 48, 52, 109, 115, 116, 119, 127, 156, 176
Finnegans Wake, 116
A Portrait of the Artist as a Young Man, 43, 44–5, 46–7, 48
Ulysses, 1, 45–7, 48, 49, 116, 118, 163
'Work in Progress', 116

Kelman, James, 120
Klaus, H. Gustav, 24–5, 27
'Socialist Novels of 1936', 24–5
Kristeva, Julia, 27

Labour Party, 3, 15, 21, 127, 129, 174, 192
Laing, Stuart, 141, 163
Latham, Sean, 37, 199
Lawrence, D. H., 6, 11, 26, 29, 41, 42, 47, 52, 54, 56, 59, 68, 87–9, 90, 91, 92, 93, 94–103, 115, 119, 127, 134, 136, 139, 141, 159, 170, 171, 176, 181, 197
A Collier's Friday Night, 56
The First Lady Chatterley, 94–100, 101, 141
John Thomas and Lady Jane, 94, 98–100
Lady Chatterley's Lover, 41, 54, 87–9, 90, 91, 94–103, 110, 120, 130, 134, 170, 195, 197
'Odour of Chrysanthemums', 56
possibility of a future, 87–8, 89, 99, 103
The Rainbow, 120, 170
'Return to Bestwood', 88, 94, 96, 98, 99
Women in Love, 120
see also fantasy; future, the; imaginary identifications; mirror scenes; modernism; proletarian literature; proletarian modernism

Lee, Hermione, 74, 82, 83, 171
Left Review, 4, 112, 186
Lehmann, John, 22, 112–13
Lessing, Doris, 53
Lewis, Wyndham, 11, 51, 59, 68
Love on the Dole (film), 21
Lukács, Georg, 27
Lumsden, Alison, 138
Lynd, Helen Merrell, 19–20, 32, 41, 42, 45, 47, 137, 172
   England in the Eighteen-Eighties, 172
   On Shame and the Search for Identity, 19–20, 42

McCulloch, Margery Palmer, 115, 116, 117, 120, 124, 127
   'Modernism and Marxism in *A Scots Quair*', 115
   Scottish Modernism and its Contexts 1918–1959, 117
MacDiarmid, Hugh, 114, 116, 127, 130
McFarlane, Anna, 20
McIlvanney, William, 23
MacKay, Marina, 52
McKenna, Brian, 143, 146
McNeil, Dougal, 90, 93, 95, 96, 108, 127, 130
   Writing the 1926 General Strike, 90
Made in Dagenham, 192
Madge, Charles, 188, 192, 193, 194
Malcolm, William K., 131
Mansfield, Katherine, 54, 74–82, 83, 153
   'Bliss', 75
   'A Cup of Tea', 74–6, 77, 81
   'The Tiredness of Rosabel', 76–82
March-Russell, Paul, 53
Marcus, Laura, 173
Marwood, Arthur, 61–2, 63, 64, 65, 68
Marx, Karl, 2–3, 39, 55
Mason, Paul, 3, 38–9, 40, 87, 198
Mass-Observation, 7, 9, 49, 52, 54, 118, 119, 173, 174, 182, 183, 192–5, 197
   Britain by Mass-Observation, 188
   May the Twelfth, 118
   The Pub and the People, 182, 184
metropolitan perception *see* Williams, Raymond
middlebrow, 27
Miller, Tyrus, 50–1
   Late Modernism, 50–1
mirror scenes, 101, 135–7, 138, 139, 158–9; *see also* gender; imaginary identifications; patriarchal order; symbolic order
Mitchison, Dick, 195
Mitchison, Naomi, 6, 9–21, 30, 38, 41, 46, 47, 49, 53, 55, 95, 101, 117, 131, 133, 134, 137, 141, 142, 154, 167, 168, 171, 174, 192–5, 197, 200
   Among You Taking Notes, 194–5
   The Bull Calves, 17
   The Corn King and the Spring Queen, 10, 17
   Memoirs of a Spacewoman, 53
   Mitchison and Mass-Observation, 54, 174, 192–5
   The Moral Basis of Politics, 193–4
   Scotland's future, 14, 20–1, 194–5
   Travel Light, 17
   We Have Been Warned, 9–21, 30, 41, 46, 48, 49, 55, 95, 101, 117, 133, 134, 137, 142, 154, 167, 171, 192, 194, 195, 197
   You May Well Ask, 18
   see also fantasy; imaginary identifications; Mass-Observation; proletarian literature; proletarian modernism
modernism, 1–2, 6, 25, 26, 27, 33–8, 48–54, 68, 69, 73, 76, 81–2, 115–16, 154, 176, 197, 199–200
   English modernism, 26, 27, 68, 119
   high modernism, 1, 33, 50, 53
   modernism as autobiografiction, 43–5, 161
   music-hall modernism, 68, 73–4, 181, 197
   see also autobiografiction; intermodernism; proletarian literature; proletarian modernism
Modernism/Modernity, 37, 38
'modernist answer', 26; *see also* proletarian modernism
Modernist Cultures, 38
'modernist question', 1, 19, 25, 40–1, 44, 53, 60, 80, 116, 139, 169, 197, 199
   'pre-modernist question', 44
   see also 'proletarian answer'
Modernist Studies Association (MSA), 37, 38, 199
modernity, 36, 38. 50, 52, 59, 78, 80, 81, 99, 139, 161, 199, 200
Moorcock, Michael, 53
Murray, Isobel, 9, 136

Naughton, Bill, 23
New Modernist Studies, 36, 38, 50, 199–200
New Writing, 22
Nicholls, Peter, 37
   Modernisms: A Literary Guide, 37
Nietzsche, Friedrich, 35, 129
Norquay, Glenda, 138, 139, 170

Orwell, George, 2, 7, 21, 26, 31, 47, 48, 50, 52, 54, 55, 56, 62, 86n, 109, 119, 164, 174, 175, 176
   Animal Farm, 175
   Coming Up for Air, 119, 175
   Down and Out in Paris and London, 48
   Homage to Catalonia, 177, 179, 182
   Keep the Aspidistra Flying, 175
   The Lion and the Unicorn, 7, 164, 197
   Nineteen Eighty-Four, 174, 175, 179

'The Proletarian Writer', 2, 7, 54, 56, 86n, 164
The Road to Wigan Pier, 48, 176, 179, 180, 181, 182, 183, 185, 188, 191, 197
Our Time, 114

pastoral, 2, 5–7, 10, 12, 14, 16–17, 20, 41, 42, 43, 46, 47, 80, 84, 85, 95, 100, 102, 103, 106, 119, 121, 166, 175, 176, 181, 182, 189, 190, 197
  Edwardian pastoral, 54, 56–68, 91, 197
  mock pastoral, 43
  old pastoral, 14, 181, 189, 197
  postwar social-realist pastoral, 191, 192
  urban pastoral, 190
  see also Empson, William; proletarian literature
patriarchal order, 16, 36, 66, 68, 80, 100, 119, 120, 133, 136, 138, 139, 159, 171
  patriarchal binary thought, 20, 101, 192, 195, 197
  patriarchal society, 10, 35, 36. 40, 100, 101, 130, 135, 136, 139, 172
  see also bourgeoisie; gender; imaginary identifications; mirror scenes; symbolic order
Paul, Ronald, 8–9, 142–3, 145, 151, 152
Penguin paperbacks, 22, 38, 88, 186, 188, 197
Phelan, Jim, 28
Pinkney, Tony, 33, 34, 102
Plain, Gill, 194
Popular Front, 4, 26, 49, 92, 133, 142, 173, 177, 188
postmodernism, 36, 37, 50
post-scarcity emotional economy, 20, 47, 48–9, 101, 127–8, 133, 192
  post-scarcity economics, 49
  see also Gibbon, Lewis Grassic; Lynd, Helen Merrell; Mitchison, Naomi; shame
Pound, Ezra, 36, 68
'proletarian answer', 1–2, 41–2, 53, 80, 197–201; see also fantasy; future, the; imaginary identifications; intersectionality; intersubjectivity; post-scarcity emotional economy; proletarian literature; proletarian modernism; shame
proletarian literature, 1–9, 38, 40–1, 47, 48–9, 50, 52, 53–5, 56, 61, 80, 85, 90, 103, 106, 107, 112–13, 116, 139, 141, 142, 167, 168, 174, 176, 181, 191–2, 194, 195, 197, 201
  narrow sense of proletarian literature, 4–5, 41, 47, 91, 113–14, 134
  proletarian literature as pastoral, 2, 5–7, 14, 41, 47, 80, 103, 119, 166, 176, 181, 190
  reception history, 21–33
  see also Empson, William; Orwell, George; pastoral; proletarian modernism; Proletcult; socialist realism
proletarian modernism, 11, 28, 48–9, 53–4, 115, 116–17, 175, 180, 190, 197, 199–200
'proletarian question', 25–6, 139; see also 'modernist answer'
proletariat, 2–3, 20, 39, 113, 118, 174–5, 176, 200
Proletcult, 4–5, 41, 47, 91, 110, 113, 133

Queer Studies, 137

Radek, Karl, 5
Radford, Jean, 27
Red Letters, 23, 134
Richardson, Dorothy, 27
Rogers, Gayle, 37, 199
Russian Revolution, 1, 4, 127, 130
Ruttman, Walter, 28, 163

Saunders, Max, 18, 43, 56, 61, 62, 63, 68, 119, 155, 177
  Self-Impression: Life-Writing, Autobiografiction, and the Forms of Modern Literature, 43
Sayers, Dorothy L., 26, 50
Schachtel, Ernest, 47
science fiction, 17, 53
Second World War, 50, 53, 92, 149, 182
shame, 13, 19, 20, 42, 47, 88, 136, 137, 145, 168
Sillietoe, Alan, 22
  Saturday Night and Sunday Morning, 22
Smith, Agnes, 168
Smith, David, 27, 131, 146, 151
  Socialist Propaganda in the Twentieth-Century British Novel, 27, 131
Smyth, Adam, 54
Snaith, Anna, 165, 168
Snee, Carole, 23–4, 29, 105, 134
  'Working-Class Literature or Proletarian Writing', 23
social realism, 50, 81
socialist realism, 4, 5, 6, 24, 113, 114, 117, 130, 135, 136
Sommerfield, John, 6, 7, 9, 21, 25, 27, 38, 47, 49, 53, 54, 55, 117, 139, 141–64, 169, 171, 173, 182–8, 189, 190, 191
  The Imprinted, 49
  The Inheritance, 146
  May Day, 7, 8, 9, 25, 28, 40, 41, 49, 54, 55, 117, 141–56, 162–4, 169, 173, 184, 187, 190, 198
  North West Five, 53
  They Die Young, 155, 156–62, 163, 190
  Trouble in Porter Street, 146, 183–8, 190, 191, 197
  Volunteer in Spain, 182

Sommerfield, John (*cont.*)
  Waverley Steps, 163
  see also imaginary identifications; intersectionality; Mass-Observation; mirror scenes; modernism; pastoral; proletarian literature; proletarian modernism
Soviet Union, 6, 10, 13, 14, 16, 20, 112
Spender, Stephen, 6, 22, 182
Steedman, Carolyn, 32
Strindberg, August, 35
Sunday Worker, 4, 90–1
symbolic order, 16, 17, 44, 93, 94, 101, 133, 139, 159; *see also* gender; imaginary identifications; mirror scenes; patriarchal order

Taylor, Elinor, 146, 155
telephony, 62, 66, 172, 173
Tennyson, Alfred, 128
  Ulysses, 128
Todd, Selina, 7, 149, 150
  The People: the Rise and Fall of the Working Class, 1910–2010, 7, 149
Transatlantic Review, 116
transition, 116, 158
Tratner, Michael, *Modernism and Mass Politics: Joyce, Woolf, Eliot, Yeats*, 154
Tressell, Robert, 23, 27, 54n
  The Ragged Trousered Philanthropists, 23, 27, 54n
Trotsky, Leon, 4
  Literature and Revolution, 4
Trotter, David, 59, 75–6, 82, 173
  The English Novel in History 1895–1920, 59
  Literature in the First Media Age, 173
  Paranoid Modernism, 59

Upward, Edward, 26

Wain, John, 175
Waterhouse, Keith, 22
Webster, Roger, 28, 29, 32, 33
welfare state, 21, 39, 49, 52, 54, 89, 93, 174, 191, 192, 193, 195, 195, 197, 198
Wells, H. G., 64, 68–74, 92–3, 94, 176, 189, 197
  The Bulpington of Blup, 71–3
  The History of Mr Polly, 73
  Kipps, 73
  Meanwhile, 92–3
  Tono-Bungay, 68–71
  see also modernism: music-hall modernism

West, Alick, 1, 41, 45–7, 60, 109, 115, 142
  Crisis and Criticism, 1, 109, 115
West, Rebecca, 52
Wilkinson, Ellen, 29, 33, 47, 90, 93, 103–4, 141, 181
  Clash, 33, 40, 54, 90, 103–4, 191, 198
Williams, Keith, 162
Williams, Raymond, 33, 34–6, 45, 46, 48, 49, 52, 117, 118, 139, 159, 175, 176
  metropolitan perception, 35, 36, 37, 45, 52, 117, 120, 125
  The Politics of Modernism, 33–6, 176
Wilson, Angus, 53, 175
  The Old Men at the Zoo, 53
Wolmark, Jenny, 134–5
  'Problems of Tone in *A Scots Quair*', 134–5
Woolf, Virginia, 11, 26, 27, 36, 42, 48, 50, 51, 52, 53, 54, 73, 74, 75, 76, 82–6, 93–4, 116, 119, 127, 148, 157, 163, 165, 167, 175, 192, 195, 197, 198, 200
  Between the Acts, 195
  The Common Reader, 197
  'Introductory Letter to Margaret Llewelyn Davies', 165–8
  'Kew Gardens', 85
  Mrs Dalloway, 25, 82–6, 118, 148, 163
  Night and Day, 75
  Orlando, 197
  The Pargiters, 170, 171, 172
  'Professions for Women', 170, 171
  A Room of One's Own, 93–4, 169, 171, 172, 197
  Three Guineas, 165, 168, 170, 172, 174, 192, 195
  To the Lighthouse, 93
  The Years, 170, 171–2, 173, 174, 192, 193
  see also fantasy; imaginary identifications; modernism; proletarian literature; proletarian modernism
Woolworths, 38, 192
working class, 2, 3, 6, 7, 39, 47, 56, 88, 89, 101, 104, 113, 114, 124, 135, 147, 149, 166, 181, 185
  respectable working-class values, 89, 96, 97, 98, 99, 107, 152, 179
working-class writing, 5, 22, 23, 24, 28, 30, 32, 33, 36, 39, 40, 47, 90, 91, 95, 175, 198
Worpole, Ken, 6, 22, 28
  Dockers and Detectives, 28
Worthen, John, 56

Young, Douglas F., 131

Žižek, Slavoj, 78, 81

EU representative:
Easy Access System Europe
Mustamäe tee 50, 10621 Tallinn, Estonia
Gpsr.requests@easproject.com